For a Parliament Freely Chosen

The Rebellion of Sir George Booth, 1659

Andrew Abram

'This is the Century of the Soldier', Fulvio Testi, Poet, 1641

Helion & Company

Helion & Company Limited
Unit 8 Amherst Business Centre
Budbrooke Road
Warwick
CV34 5WE
England
Tel. 01926 499 619
Email: info@helion.co.uk
Website: www.helion.co.uk
Twitter: @helionbooks
Visit our blog http://blog.helion.co.uk/

Published by Helion & Company 2021
Designed and typeset by Mach 3 Solutions Ltd (www.mach3solutions.co.uk)
Cover designed by Paul Hewitt, Battlefield Design (www.battlefield-design.co.uk)

ISBN 978-1-914059-32-2

British Library Cataloguing-in-Publication Data.
A catalogue record for this book is available from the British Library.

For details of other military history titles published by Helion & Company Limited contact the above address or visit our website: http://www.helion.co.uk.

We always welcome receiving book proposals from prospective authors.

Contents

List of Abbreviations iv
Acknowledgements vi
Explanatory Notes and Conventions vii
Introduction viii

1 Recovery and Conflict in Cheshire, 1646–50 15
2 Cromwell and the Protectorate, 1651–59 26
3 Discontent, Plots and the Exiled Stuart Court 49
4 Rebellion: Strategy, Leadership and Cohesion 68
5 '... like Mahomet's angelical cocks, made up of fire and snow' 93
6 The Council of State and its Response 109
7 Winnington Bridge: the Battle and its Outcome 137
8 Aftermath 163

Appendices
I Documents of Sir George Booth 180
II Documents of Major General John Lambert 186
III List of prisoners taken at Winnington Bridge, Chester and elsewhere by government forces during the Booth rebellion. *Mercurius Politicus*, 18–25 August 1659; Ormerod, *History*, I, p.lxvi; *CWTC*, pp.174–5. 194

Bibliography 196

List of Abbreviations

A&O	Firth, C. H. and Rait, R. S.(eds), *Acts and Ordinances of the Interregnum, 1642-1660*, 3 vols (London: HMSO, 1911).
BCA	Birmingham, City Archives.
BJRL	*Bulletin of the John Rylands Library.*
BL	The British Library, London.
BLB	Dore, R. N. (ed.), *The Letter Books of Sir William Brereton*, 2 vols, RSLC, 123, 128 (1984, 1990).
Bod. Lib.	Bodleian Library, Oxford.
CCAM	*Calendar of the Proceedings of the Committee for Advance of Money.*
CCSP	*Calendar of the Clarendon State Papers.*
CH	*Cheshire History.*
CHJ	*Cambridge Historical Journal*
CJ	Journals of the House of Commons.
CL	Chetham's Library, Manchester.
CPCC	*Calendar of the Proceedings of the Committee for Compounding.*
CRO	Cheshire Archives (Record Office), Chester.
CS	*Cheshire Sheaf.*
CS	Chetham Society.
CSPD	*Calendar of State Papers Domestic.*
CSPI	*Calendar of the State Papers Relating to Ireland.*
CSPV	*Calendar of State Papers Relating to English Affairs in the Archives of Venice.*
CWTC	Atkinson, James,*Tracts Relating to the Civil War in Cheshire, 1641-1659* (Manchester: Chetham Society, 1909).
CWTL	Ormerod, George (ed.), *Tracts Relating to Military Proceedings in Lancashire during the Great Civil War* (Manchester: CS, 1844).
DRO	Derbyshire Record Office, Matlock.
DWB	*Dictionary of Welsh Biography.*
DWL	Dr Williams's Library, London.
EHR	*English Historical Review.*
FHSP	*Flintshire Historical Society Publications.*
FRO	Flintshire Record Office, Hawarden.
HJ	*Historical Journal.*
HMC	Historical Manuscripts Commission.

HR	*Historical Research.*
JCAS	*Journal of the Chester Archaeological Society.*
JFHS	*Journal of the Flintshire Historical Society.*
JFHistS	*Journal of the Friends' Historical Society.*
JNLW	*Journal of the National Library of Wales.*
JRL	John Rylands Library (The University of Manchester Library), Manchester.
LCRS	*Lancashire and Cheshire Record Society.*
LJ	Journals of the House of Lords.
LM	Coate, Mary, *The Letter-Book of John Viscount Mordaunt 1658-1660* (London: RHS, 1940).
LRO	Lancashire Record Office, Preston.
MS	Manuscript.
MSS	Manuscripts.
MS Add.	Manuscript Additional in the BL.
NH	Northern History.
NLW	National Library of Wales, Aberystwyth.
ODNB	*Oxford Dictionary of National Biography.*
P&P	*Past and Present.*
RSLC	Record Society of Lancashire and Cheshire.
TAPS	Transactions of the American Philosophical Society.
TCHS	*Transactions of the Caernarvonshire Historical Society.*
TDHS	*Transactions of the Denbighshire Historical Society.*
THSLC	*Transactions of the Historic Society of Lancashire and Cheshire.*
TLCAS	*Transactions of the Lancashire and Cheshire Antiquarian Society.*
TSANHS	*Transactions of the Shropshire Archaeological and Natural History Society.*
WHR	*Welsh History Review.*

Acknowledgements

In producing this book, I would like to thank the archivists and librarians ofvarious institutions, none more so than the Cheshire Archives, British Library, The National Archives, Bodleian Library, The National Library of Wales, Flintshire Record Office, Derbyshire Record Office, Chetham's Library and John Rylands Library.I am also indebted to Charles Singleton of Helion & Co. for his help and advice. My wife and fellow historian Dr Kathryn Hurlock – although seemingly disinclined to most forms of military history – has kept me going with encouragement, coffee and baked goods, for which I am eternally grateful. This book is dedicated, with love, to our children, Ada and George.

Explanatory Notes and Conventions

Although dates prior to 1752 are recorded with the year beginning 25 March, modern dating is used throughout, with the New Year being taken to start on 1 January. Spellings incontemporary manuscripts and printed sources (which varied considerably during the seventeenth century) have been modernised, while where appropriate, current forms of punctuation have been added to period accounts.

According to the Imperial system, contemporary monetary values have been quoted throughout. Hence, 12 pennies (12d.) = 1 shilling (1s.); 20 shillings = one pound sterling (£1); £1 = 240d. Moreover, lengths and distances are given in inches, feet, yards, ells and miles; weights in pounds (lb), 112lb = a hundredweight (cwt), 20 cwt = 1 ton.

In this book Cheshire corresponds with the historical boundaries that were lost to the new metropolitan authorities of Merseyside and Greater Manchester in 1974.

Introduction

On Monday 1 August 1659 Sir George Booth launched an armed rebellion at Warrington against the Rump Parliament. The following day, having been let into Chester by an agreeable mayor and aldermen, and accompanied by his fellow insurrectionist Sir Thomas Myddelton, Booth assembled the main body of his troops on Rowton Heath, two miles south-east of the city. According to the Royalist exile, Edward Hyde, the future Earl of Clarendon, 'all men's spirits were raised by the action of these two gentlemen'.[1] Booth thenceforth delivered his manifesto or *Declaration*, the preamble of which related:

> they accordingly met, being above 3,000 horse and foot, well mounted and armed, with drums beating, colours flying and trumpets sounding. After they were all drawn up in the heath, Colonel Brooke and Colonel Ireland divided the horse and foot into several bodies, placing them in sundry warlike figures and postures. After which, they were united and brought into one entire body, where Sir George made a speech to them, showing the grounds and reasons of their present engagement and undertakings, and withal (by several specious pretences) declared for a free parliament; publishing a declaration for the same end and purpose, and several invitations for all those that way affected to join with them, they holding a correspondence with those of the same party in the city of Chester, who it is said, and frequently discoursed, set upon the city gates, and gave them admittance.[2]

Sir George's *Declaration* made no mention of the King, but focused on the unrepresentative nature of Parliament, and its insincerity in blaming Oliver Cromwell for what they were doing themselves – governing through army intrusion – and cried for a free parliament. Booth proclaimed further that destabilised by the usurpation of the Rump and the ambition of the senior

1 W. Dunn Macray (ed.), Hyde, Edward, Earl of Clarendon, *The History of the Rebellion and Civil Wars in England* (Oxford: Clarendon Press, 1888), VII, p.322.

2 *A Declaration of Sir George Booth, at the General Rendezvous on Tuesday last, near the City of Chester, with the number other Horse & Foot, their advance to the City, & the joyning of Col. Ireland with their Army. Also, the securing of the Castle, the Governor's Resolution, and the mounting of the strong Walls, Bulworks & Towers, etc.* (London: G. Horton, 1659); *CWTC*, pp.164–7.

officers, without this freedom there could never be any settled foundation for religion, liberty and property. Although the rebellion in Cheshire was intended originally as but one of many planned throughout England and Wales, it soon became the most significant, for within days of proclaiming his manifesto Sir George Booth had around 4,000 men in arms. But the Council of State, after some hesitancy, dispatched John Lambert as commander-in-chief of an expeditionary force of veteran, regular soldiers from London, with a temporary commission as major general. They were to be joined by cavalry and dragoons from the north, as well as a brigade of troops sent from Ireland. During a particularly short, yet sharp campaign, Booth's army was defeated in detail at Winnington Bridge and removed had its grip on Chester removed, and on 24 August final resistance ended with the surrender of Chirk Castle to Lambert. By then, Sir George – who had escaped Chester four days earlier – had been discovered at the *Red Lion* in Newport Pagnell, disguised as 'Mrs Dorothy', and was taken into custody.

This book has been researched primarily from contemporary manuscript and published sources. As such, it aims to deliver a balanced interpretation of events by providing a full and fresh assessment of the rebellion, or armed uprising, aimed at overthrowing the recalled Rump Parliament, led by Sir George Booth during the summer of 1659. The episode has been variously referred to as the 'Booth rebellion', the 'Cheshire uprising', and 'the Chester expedition' by contemporaries and modern historians. Although it was nominally part of a wider 'revolt' against the Cromwellian State, following the resignation of Richard Cromwell and the ending of the Protectorate, by members of the Presbyterian gentry and some disaffected Royalists, the insurgency led by Booth has been habitually regarded as a localised 'Royalist' uprising aimed at restoring the Stuart monarchy. As such, the reasons for the armed rebellion in terms of the political, religious and military objectives of its leaders, supporters and participants have to some extent been misunderstood or misrepresented. Besides, modern accounts of the brief, yet dynamic military campaign involving Booth's soldiers, as well as New Model (or the standing) army regiments led by Major General Lambert (predominantly from London), as well as troops from Ireland have been largely reconstructed from the partisan accounts of the victors, who – except for Lambert and his officers, who fought in the campaign – attempted not only to discredit the rebels but to show that they were easily overcome by the armed forces of the State.

For a Parliament Freely Chosen offers a timely reconsideration of the generally perceived view of the insurrection, that it was essentially a local phenomenon which was poorly led, organised and executed. As such, the book explores the wealth of available primary source material – part of which remains obscure and unpublished in a variety of archives – in a much broader sense than has hitherto been attempted before. Whilst recognising the interpretations of scholars such as Godfrey Davies, R.N. Dore, J.S. Morrill, Henry Reece and others, much stress is placed on identifying and reconstructing the background, contacts and actions of Booth and his officers, and the forces under their command. It is also possible, by considering in more detail the surviving primary source material – albeit sometimes ambiguous and partisan in nature – to more precisely reconstruct the military forces of both sides, as well as the tactical aspects of the campaigns in Cheshire and its adjacent counties. This not only adds significantly to our knowledge of the causes, development and perceptions of the Booth uprising, but locates the event more firmly within the history of the Protectorate that followed the Wars of the Three Kingdoms. It also enhances more recent assessments of the circumstances that contributed to the restoration of Charles II in 1660.

Geographically small and of modest wealth, the county of Cheshire during the first half of the seventeenth century witnessed a considerable change to its agricultural landscape, through the enclosure of woodland, heath and waste, although cattle farming (above all, the production of cheese, but also leather goods) and salt remained historically important industries. Although a seaboard county, a relative lack of internal water communication restricted Cheshire and Lancashire to its north. The River Dee was not navigable above Chester, whereas little of the Weaver and Mersey could be used for transporting goods. In a national context, Chester was the only town in the north-west of England considered important in terms of its size and nearness to Ireland. However, with the silting up of the Dee, by the 1640s the port of Liverpool had begun to obtain much of the trade with Ireland, although it was yet to rival Chester in importance. In addition to this, the early modern period witnessed a development of population and industry in the north-east of the county, with a flourishing textile industry based around Stockport, which possessed important links to Manchester. The market towns of Knutsford, Congleton, Middlewich and Northwich added to the mercantile prosperity of the region. A marked level of religious and educational distinction developed, whilst Puritanism, which reached many commercial hubs, was encouraged as a counterpoise to papist west Lancashire.[3]

During the late 1640s and 1650s Cheshire and the North West was still recovering from the destruction and financial exactions of the First Civil War. The establishment of the Commonwealth of England in 1649 witnessed both recovery and conflict on a national scale, wherein disunity between Independents and Presbyterians, and attempts by the Commons to disband the New Model Army created significant tensions. In Cheshire war-weary Royalists remained largely immobile, but splits among the victorious Parliamentarians were beginning to reveal deeper roots in terms of political outlook and religious orientation. Moreover, the events of the Second Civil War and the Worcester campaign of 1648 and 1651 respectively, impacted directly on the county, both in terms of military operations and the increasing discontent of the Presbyterian gentry towards the government. Though peace was restored and authority successfully upheld in Cheshire via the commissioners of militia and the county trained band – raised and maintained by township quotas and the terms of tenants' leases – the remaining threat to the security of the region was Chester, whose early royalism and strategic

3 Dorothy Sylvester and Geoffrey Nulty, *The Historical Atlas of Cheshire* (Chester: Cheshire Community Council, 1958), pp.36–8; Norman Lowe, *The Lancashire Textile Industry in the Sixteenth Century*, CS, 20, Third Series (Manchester, 1972), pp.1–3.

position meant that there had always been the possibility of an attempt to recover the city for the Royalist cause.

It was not until October 1646 that Parliament deemed itself to be sufficiently in control of affairs in Chester to issue an ordinance for the purging of its Assembly.[4] At the time of the Second Civil War, in June 1648, a plan was discovered to betray the garrison of Chester into the hands of the Royalists, but this proved unsuccessful.[5] The stratagem provided Sir William Brereton (1604–61) as MP for the county and longtime adversary of the city, with a strong case for reducing the independence of Chester by joining its militia companies with that of the county, and thus bringing it under the control of the county palatine of Chester. Thus, the Parliamentary governor of the castle, Colonel Robert Duckenfield's commission was renewed, while he, Brereton and three others were added to the commissioners for the city's militia.[6]

In terms of the general aspects of the 1659 rising, and the political and military events preceding it, the Booth rebellion is well-served by published primary sources. The *Calendar of State Papers Domestic*, *Calendar of Clarendon State Papers*, *Thurloe State Papers* and several volumes of the journals of the House of Commons, for instance, include a range of documentation regarding the course of the rebellion from both official governmental sources and the exiled royal court. Although the survival of correspondence, contemporary accounts and other material belonging to Sir George Booth and his commanders is negligible, the various collected and published letters, memoirs and biographies of key observers, in the shape of the *Clarke Papers*, *Letter Book of John, Viscount Mordaunt*, *Memoirs of Edmund Ludlow* and *Life of Adam Martindale* are of enormous value. Similarly, documents relating Lambert's military response and his own reports of the brief campaign are reproduced in James Atkinson's *Civil War Tracts of Cheshire*. However abundant and fruitful such material appears to be, each source presents its own difficulties in terms of accuracy and balance, and in some cases, obvious inaccuracies.

As for the (mainly unpublished) manuscript material, the notebook of Colonel Roger Whitley (Bodl. Lib. MS Eng. hist. e. 309), produced in 1658, affords a blueprint for a Royalist rising, possibilities for foreign and internal aid, and an outline of organisation, and lists of men that might serve as officers. Although this highly significant document has been referred to by some modern historians, it deserves further scrutiny, as it has remained largely unnoticed since its discovery over four decades ago. Similarly, the almost entirely overlooked commission from Charles II appointing George Booth commander of the local Royalist forces in Cheshire, Lancashire and North Wales – attached to a later indemnity for all actions undertaken by him in accordance with the warrant – survives among the Dunham

4 *A&O*, I, pp.876–9. The ordinance was copied into the city's Second Assembly Book (CRO, ZA/B/2, fols 76r.–8v.).

5 James Hall (ed.), *Memorials of the Civil War in Cheshire and the adjacent counties by Thomas Malbon, of Nantwich, Gent., and Providence improved by Edward Burghall*, LCRS, 19 (1889), pp.214–6; HMC, *Thirteenth Report, App. I*, p.463.

6 *CJ*, V, p.622; CRO, ML/2/320 (4 July 1648).

Massey papers (JRL, EGR3/4/1/2), and is of great importance in assessing the expectations of his role by the exiled Stuart court. Similarly, collections of correspondence in the Cheshire Archives and the National Library of Wales shed considerable light on contacts between Booth and Royalist agents in London prior to the uprising, as well as the activities of Royalist officers in North Wales and the role of Sir Thomas Myddelton in declaring for Charles II.

Of considerable importance to any understanding of events in Cheshire during the weeks leading up to the insurrection are the petitions from township constables, inhabitants and trained band soldiers in the county quarter sessions files (CRO, QJF/88/3–4). Although necessarily limited in scope and produced in some cases over a year after the event, they also provide evidence of the mechanics of the issue and receipt of warrants from commissioned officers and local justices serving under Sir George Booth, as well as details of wounds, pay, and the names, ages and social origins of some of the rank and file who enlisted in his cause. Such material informs the hitherto largely overlooked records of the governmental investigation into the Cheshire rising as it affected not only the county, but North Wales and the city of Chester (TNA, SP23/263; SP28/25/29). Relevant to the latter are the Chester Assembly Books, 1624–1684 (CRO, ZA/B2), which not only include details of events within the city and maintenance of its militia companies against the Rump in August 1659, but also provide an indication of the motivations of the mayor and aldermen during this period.

Direct evidence for the raising, equipping and composition of Booth's estimated 3,000–4,000-strong force is limited due to the nature, and in some cases absence of sources. To a greater extent this aspect of the uprising has been either surmised or ignored by the majority of modern commentators. However, research indicates that to a degree the insurgents utilised more traditional localised methods of recruitment, akin to those previously employed by Brereton, the deputy lieutenants and Parliamentarian army officers during the First Civil War in Cheshire. More is currently of the survival and composition of the trained bands during the late 1640s, as well as the county forces raised for the Second Civil War and the Worcester campaign. Furthermore, it is possible to accurately reconstruct the composition and service of the Booth's regular army opponents, including Lambert's regiments and the brigade transported over from Ireland to support them.

Sir George Booth's rebellion has come under the spotlight of a modest number of twentieth-century historians, both in a national and local context. However, there remains a certain lacuna in any focused approaches to the topic over the past 40 years or more. The first attempt to reconstruct and explain the uprising was made in 1939 by Reginald Petty, who provided a well-researched overview of events.[7] Godfrey Davies produced a more thorough account from a more national perspective some 16 years later, which also identified the broad range of primary sources available to researchers.[8] Corresponding with the tercentenary of the rising, J.R. Jones again adopted a

7 Reginald Petty, 'The Rebellion of Sir George Booth, August, 1659', *JCAS*, 33 (1939), pp.119–37.

8 Godfrey Davies, *The Restoration of Charles II* (Oxford: Oxford University Press, 1955), chap. 8.

national viewpoint, although his work particularly benefitted from a valuable analysis of the recently unearthed manuscript of Colonel Whitely.[9] In the same year the Cheshire scholar, R.N. Dore, identified more localised reasons for the mutiny, whilst John Morrill devoted a chapter to it in his study of the county's community government and society (which posed various questions surrounding Booth's motivations, as well as differing interpretations of the impact of his rebellion).[10] Although some aspects of the events of August–September 1659 have been covered in later works on the Cromwellian Protectorate and the Restoration of Charles II, key explanations of the revolt continue unchallenged and therefore warrant reassessment.[11]

9 J.R. Jones, 'Booth's Rising of 1659', *BJRL*, 39 (1957), pp.416–43.

10 R.N. Dore, 'The Cheshire Rising of 1659: A Study of Local Origins', *JLCAS*,69 (1959), pp.43–69; J.S. Morrill, *Cheshire 1630–1660: County Government and Society during the 'English Revolution'* (Oxford: Oxford University Press, 1974), chapter 8.

11 For example, David Underdown, *Royalist Conspiracy in England 1649–60* (New Haven: Yale University Press, 1960); Ruth Mayers, *The Crisis of the Commonwealth* (Woodbridge: Boydell, 2004); Henry Reece, *The Army in Cromwellian England 1649–1660* (Oxford: Oxford University Press, 2013); Tim Harris, *Restoration: Charles II and his Kingdoms* (London: Penguin, 2005).

1

Recovery and Conflict in Cheshire, 1646–50

The period between the end of the First Civil War in 1646, and the establishment of the Commonwealth of England three years later, was one of both recovery and conflict on a national scale. Disunion between Independents and Presbyterians, with attempts by the Commons to disband the New Model Army were offset in Cheshire, where war-weary Royalists remained largely immobile. The split among the victorious Parliamentarians (evident from as early as 1644) was beginning to reveal deeper roots, however. Once Chester – known also by contemporaries as West Chester, given the city's prominent position in north-west England – surrendered to Parliamentarian forces on 3 February 1646, the last Royalist resistance ended, and Cheshire returned to a state of relative peace. With Royalist forces remaining active in the Midlands, Sir William Brereton led a force (which included a significant number of troops from his Cheshire army) into Staffordshire, where several garrisons, such as Lichfield Close, were still held for the King. During the spring Brereton's military subordinate, Sergeant Major Jerome Zankey, led 400 Cheshire horse in North Wales under Colonel Mytton, and on 4 June he acted as a commissioner at the surrender of Caernarfon.[1] In Cheshire the burden of supporting opposing forces and the destructive effects of the marches of major field armies ceased. Nevertheless, the full cost of the war had yet to be counted. The previous summer George Manley, head constable of Eddisbury Hundred, had described to his brother:

> a poor and miserable country we live in, and if these Leaguers continue, it is like to be worse, if there be a possibility of being worse, for the taxes are so many, and the payments laid upon us, is more than our land is worth, our stocks all wasted and we are put into a way of ruin, not easily to be recovered but by great providence and length of time, the lord look down in a mercy upon his poor distressed people. It is a great grief to men to be reduced to so low an ebb, that I cannot relieve your wants with your own for your land and tithe for this year

1 BCA, MS 595611, pp.24, 26, 67–8.

> will not yeald you about £20 your tenants are so oppressed it will hardly be gotten from them. And so with a troubled and grieved heart, he bids you fare well that will ever be your loving brother.[2]

During the early months of 1646 the remaining arrears of pay owing to Brereton's soldiers were substantial. This was aggravated by the slow imbursement of the promised payment of a bounty (consisting of an extra month's wages) for participating in the capture of Chester. These troops had already shown, by desertion and mutiny, the level of their bitterness at insubstantial promises of payment. Pay arrears among the Cheshire army had reached near epidemic proportions in 1645 and 1646. On 18 December 1645 the Cheshire horse was some four months behind, while portions of the foot suffered considerably.[3] Probably the hardest hit was Colonel Robert Duckenfield's regiment. He was exceedingly devoted to his soldiers, who were amongst the earliest recruited for Parliament in the county and from the farthest parts of Cheshire. On 5 April 1645 Robert reported to Sir Samuel Luke:

> My regiment hath passed upon very hard duty for this twelvemonth, especially last winter at the siege of Beeston Castle, and in Wirral where many of my men were lost and maimed, for all which service they have received but a month's pay and now they begin to mutiny and will break presently, unless some competent means be allowed them'.[4]

In the summer of 1646 some of the men took direct action by threatening and seizing local officials, from whom they attempted to extract money. The constable of Over Peover, for instance, related, 'when Colonel Booth's soldiers came for the first time for moneys to Mobberley and took me with them to Bowden, and kept me there two days a prisoner'.[5] In June 1646 garrison troops revolted in Chester. Parliamentary sequestrators and tax collectors were assaulted, and the disturbances were only calmed by hurried loans on the part of the deputy lieutenants and the promise of £2,000 from London.[6] More severe was the mutiny by five companies of the Nantwich garrison a month later. According to the lawyer and writer Thomas Malbon:

> [they] did by violence draw some of the committee of sequestrations for Nantwich hundred (being in peaceable manner executing their office for the state) forth of the office where all their books and records were, and fetched some of them (and one of the collectors) forth of several houses, wherein they were at dinner, and put them all in the common prison in Nantwich amongst cavaliers, common thieves and horse stealers (which were then there) having been the common prison from

2 TNA, SP23/197/39.

3 BL, MS Add. 11333, fols 30r.-v.; *BLB*, II, 1040.

4 H.G. Tibbut (ed.), *The Letter Books of Sir Samuel Luke* (London: HMSO, 1963), p.505; T.W. Barlow (ed.), *The Cheshire and Lancashire Historical Collector* (Manchester, 1853), pp.95–6.

5 BL, MS Harley 2126, fol. 103r.

6 *Perfect Occurrences*, 27 June–3 July 1646; *Kingdome's Weekly Intelligencer*, 28 July–4 August 1646.

> the first making the town a garrison … Neither would they allow them to have either meat or drink, or quarter in any other house or place, although it desired both by the high sheriff [Henry Brooke], and many of the deputy lieutenants and justices of the peace being then in town … neither would they suffer them to go further for doing of their needs during the whole space of 54 hours (laying nothing to their charge) but alleged that their wages were presently paid. Although they knew that the same committee never paid them, nor no other soldiers any, neither had they any warrant to pay them any, for they received their pay always from the treasurer, by warrant of the deputy lieutenants. But as some of them said, they would beat Jack for Jill, yet they would not deliver them further until Colonel Lothian and some other gentlemen had undertaken for their pay.[7]

Acting independently of their officers, the soldiers forwarded representatives to the county committee, backing their demands with veiled threats of further action. These men had showed themselves capable of conducting processes in defiance of their officers, and had reasoned their case some eight months before the election of agitators in the New Model Army. Disorder on the part of the Cheshire soldiers finally abated in mid 1647, although not before the provision of £12,000 from Parliament and the disbanding of the Nantwich garrison, as well as a further mutiny in Chester during which Colonel William Massey, the Parliamentary governor and others had been arrested.[8] However, the disquiet among the troops during the subsequent years served to show that similar flare-ups could be repeated. Consequently, Lieutenant Colonel Henry Bradshaw warned the mayor of Macclesfield in November 1650, to 'send out your warrants with all expedition. If you be herein neglect, expect that the soldiers who complain they are much in arrears will visit you for it'.[9] The diminution of Cheshire's financial responsibilities was offset by a drastic decline in the source of revenue that had been most steady in 1644 and 1645. From early 1646 onwards the sequestered Royalists paid composition fines and were gradually restored to their estates. The leading Parliamentarian gentry, whilst anxious to censure them, also attempted to reconcile old friends who had fought for the losing side. Afraid of estranging them permanently, they sought to return former Royalists to the social, though not administrative, leadership of the county. Their achievement can be discerned in the almost total inertness of Cheshire during the Second Civil War, during which Cheshire soldiers had provided support to Parliament against what was perceived to be a common foe. On a more national scale, the Parliamentarian gentry faced less of a peril from their former adversaries. The Royalists had not only wearied themselves by 1646, but had also, in some instances, become disillusioned with the King. When Parliament offered them the chance to regain their properties, many of them took advantage of it.[10]

7 Malbon, *Memorials*, pp.208–10.

8 J.S. Morrill, 'Mutiny and Discontent in English Provincial Armies 1645–1647', *P&P*, 56 (1972), pp.49–74, (p.61).

9 Bod. Lib., MS Top. Cheshire e. 3, fol. 9v.

10 Morrill, *Cheshire*, pp.180–1, 203–4.

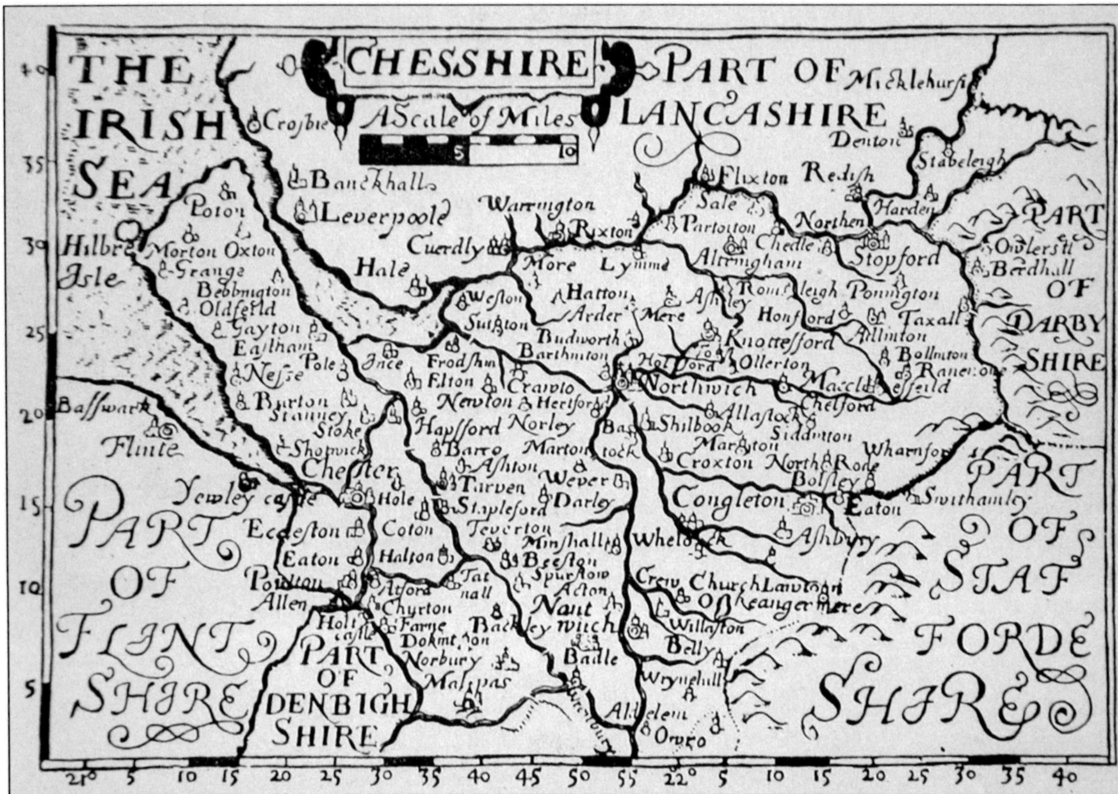

Contemporary map of seventeenth-century Cheshire. John Bill, *The Abridgement of Camden's Britannia* (1626). (Author's collection)

The struggle for control over local government presented distinct problems during this period. As Underdown suggests, in some counties the religious and political moderates were pushed aside 'by energetic young men lower down the social scale, lesser gentry and townsmen, often of radical Puritan inclinations, aiming at power as well as Reformation'.[11] However, in Cheshire, where the radicals had long possessed a significant portion of authority, the trend was in the other direction. The breach among the victorious Parliamentarians in the county – control of which had been held by Sir William Brereton as commander-in-chief of its armed forces from 1642 to 1646 – started mainly by opposition to his personality and power. Possibly the greatest stumbling block in establishing Brereton's authority in Cheshire was the Booth family of Dunham Massey, led by Sir George Booth the elder (1566–1652). Sir George was much respected in the county and, until 1642, regarded as particularly trustworthy by the government. As a young man he had participated in the Earl of Leicester's expedition in the Netherlands, was knighted by Elizabeth I and given a baronetcy by King James. As the chief link between the central government and the county, in 1628 Booth and other Cheshire gentlemen (relying they asserted, entirely upon his recommendation as trustworthy men) were given permission to arm and

11 David Underdown, *Pride's Purge: Politics in the Puritan Revolution* (Oxford: Clarendon Press, 1971), p.34.

train their servants and tenants. He led the movement which brought about the Cheshire Remonstrance against Presbytery in the summer of 1642.

Like many of his brother justices Booth refused to submit to Charles I when he came to Chester in September 1642, and after the collapse of the Peace of Bunbury the following January, he joined the Parliamentarian cause, acting as a leading deputy lieutenant and commissioner for assessments. Sir George Booth senior was in his religious outlook a Presbyterian.[12] From late 1642 his advanced age, however, and the youth of his grandson and heir, George junior, meant that the military leadership of the Parliamentarians in the county fell to Sir William Brereton, the only one of the local MPs for the area who was not a Royalist. This was a considerable rise in power for a relatively minor gentleman of an estate of some 3,000 acres, and thus rather galling to the pride of the far more socially and economically superior lords of Dunham Massey. Sir William's marriage at the age of 19 to the elder George's daughter Susanna, had been followed rapidly by a baronetcy and a seat in parliament, and the new MP made full use of his father-in-law's prestige and influence in lawsuits. From 1644 onwards the Booths led an anti-Brereton faction in Cheshire, which sought to undermine and halt Sir William's authority as commander-in-chief. In this they recruited like-minded Presbyterian deputy lieutenants and officers under Colonel George's command.

Another opponent, who shared a level mutual of dislike and jealously with Brereton, was Colonel Henry Mainwaring of Kermincham, who had overall commanded of Parliamentarian troops in Cheshire before Brereton's arrival from London in January 1643. This, however, ended when on 7 May 1644 Mainwaring was removed from all military commands and his role as deputy lieutenant at the prompting of his adversary.[13] In addition to this, Captains Witney and Massey were cashiered for 'disservice to Parliament' in mid 1645, while in the November, Sergeant Major John Marbury was removed on the recommendation of the Commons Committee for Examinations.[14] Colonel George Booth, who had been 22 at the outbreak of war, was a proficient officer, but his increasing opposition to Brereton eroded his military and administrative effectiveness, and he resigned his commission in April or May 1645. Several of Sir William's former officers and agents – men of homegrown ability, such as Robert Duckenfield, Gilbert Gerard, Robert Venables, Henry Bradshaw and his lawyer brother John – held immoderate religious and political views. Duckenfield's family chapel housed possibly the first independent or 'gathered' congregation in Britain. It was here that Samuel Eaton was preacher. As a radical congregationalist Eaton had been suspended from West Kirkby in 1631, spending periods of

12 For an overview of the Booth family, see Thomas Helsby, (ed.), George Ormerod, *History of the County Palatine and City of Chester*, 3 (London: Routledge, 2nd edn, 1874), pp.523–3; John Swarbrick, 'Dunham Massey Hall', *TLCS*, 42 (1925), pp.53–79; Ernest Axon, 'The family of Bothe (Booth) and the church in the 15th and 16th centuries', *TLCAS*, 53 (1938), pp.32–82; Dore, *Civil War in Cheshire*, pp.15, 21; Morrill, *Cheshire*, p.224.

13 *CJ*, III, p.484. For a more comprehensive analysis of the issues between Brereton and the Booth party, see Morrill, *Cheshire*, pp.83–6; *BLB*, I, pp.12–13.

14 BL, MS Add. 11333, fol. 96v.; *BLB*, II, 837.

time in Holland and New England before returning to Cheshire in 1640. He was patronised by Brereton and especially Robert Duckenfield, who had installed him at Duckenfield Hall and appointed him as chaplain to the Chester garrison in 1647. Samuel had also succeeded Nathaniel Lancaster as chaplain to Brereton's regiment of horse and preached at the Leaguer of Chester in 1645.[15]

Eaton's commentaries infuriated the Presbyterian clergy, who were particularly strong in Cheshire. Nearly 40 parishes had been 'purged' of their Royalist ministers during and after the war, and although Sir William Brereton had been instrumental in making most of the early changes, his influence was replaced by the Booths and their Presbyterian allies. To Adam Martindale, the young Lancashire puritan vicar of Rostherne, the year 1647 represented not so much a time of the last futile negotiations between Charles I and his opponents, but 'that bustling year wherein the Presbyterial and Congregational governments were like Jacob and Esau struggling in the womb'.[16] Between 1646 and 1648 the majority of the Cheshire parliamentary gentlemen adhered to the more moderate standpoint of the Booths and their friends. Thus, in 1648 when Charles I thought the discord among his enemies was bitter enough for him to make a bid to regain the throne, it was no more certain in the county than in the rest of the country how the various groups that had supported Parliament between 1642 and 1646 would respond. The King brokered a treaty known as the 'Engagement' with some of the Scottish Covenanters, who agreed to support him against their mutual enemy the English Independents, in return for the acceptance of Presbyterianism throughout the Three Kingdoms. But although there were serious risings in South Wales and the south-east of England, in Cheshire and the North West most Royalists were unprepared to take new risks, and besides, they were not reconciled to the recent conversion of the Scots to the King's cause.[17] John Aston, brother of the Anglican Royalist Sir Thomas, remarked that 'The Scots have eternally lost their honour with us, therefore we heed not their invasion'.[18]

Hopes that the Presbyterians might join the Scots were dashed by old Sir George Booth's emphatic rejection of Royalist overtures, having received an obscure appeal from 'Your loving friends in the city though nameless'.[19] It spoke of risings around London and 'the gathering of our disbanded soldiers', but their desire to him 'to interrupt publicly by force or otherwise the proceedings of Duckenfield and his confederates' met with disapproval. However, Cheshire was reluctant to rearm itself to meet the threat. Lieutenant Colonel Henry Bradshaw, who had served under Duckenfield during the first civil war, complained that his attempts to recruit in Macclesfield hundred – formerly the hotbed of Parliament and puritanism in the county – recounted

15 BL, MS Add. 11333, fol. 118v.; *BLB*, II, 1237 note 6; J S. Morrill, 'Sir William Brereton and England's Wars of Religion', *JBS*, 24 (1985), pp.311–32, (p.319); Anne Laurence, *Parliamentary Army Chaplains, 1642–51* (Woodbridge: RHS, 1990), pp.122–3.

16 R. Parkinson (ed.), *Life of Adam Martindale* (Manchester: CS, Old Series, 4, 1845), p. 61.

17 Dore, *Civil Wars in Cheshire*, pp.71–2; J.M. Gratton, *The Parliamentarian and Royalist War Effort in Lancashire 1642–1651* (Manchester: CS, 2010), pp.150–2.

18 BL, MS Add. 36914, fol. 237r.

19 HMC, *Thirteenth Report, App. I*, p.462.

that 'there came not forty soldiers in all, and most of those without arms, some townships wholly absent'.[20] In neighbouring Lancashire the deputy lieutenants reported on 25 July 1648 that 'the soldiery in the garrison at Liverpool' had not been paid for three and a half months, while in November the governor of Chester pressed the Committee of the Lords and Commons for the Army to provide £200 from the assessments from the county for the sending of 100 horse to quarter there, 'and the extreme need for payment of the garrisons of Liverpool and Lancaster'.[21] On 1 August 1648 the government had ordered the raising of three infantry regiments in Cheshire, consisting of 600 men each, under the command of Colonels James Lothian, Thomas Croxton and William Massey. Moreover, William Carter – a former cavalry officer under Brereton – was commissioned captain of a troop of horse, and it was directed that 'ammunition may be speedily provided and sent to the garrison of Chester'.[22]

These forces would be placed under the overall charge of Colonel Duckenfield, now military governor of the city. Lothian, the veteran Scots professional, who had previously been adjutant general to Sir William Brereton's army of Parliament, was appointed colonel of the 'standing regiment of this county', which mustered on 19 August and 2 September. A contemporary pay warrant identifies him as having employed his officers and soldiers to collect taxations levied upon Wirral and Broxton hundreds.[23] The sum of £625 0s. 10d. was disbursed by the county treasurer to 'Colonel James Lothian, and to the officers and soldiers of a regiment of foot raised in the county under his command in 1648', with a further £14 3s. 6d. paid out for colours.[24] Although raised in Chester, Lothian's regiment was diverted to assist Major General Mytton at Ruthin in combating the Royalist uprising in North Wales, and led the assault on Beaumaris town and castle on 1 October, losing three of its officers in the process.[25] In the colonel's company Benjamin Croxton was commissioned as captain-lieutenant, the other junior officers being Lieutenant James Smallwood and Ensign William Salmon. Colonel Lothian and the sheriff of Cheshire, Roger Wilbraham, accepted the surrender of the remnants of the Scottish army at Warrington, which had been defeated by Cromwell and Lambert at Preston and Winwick in late August. On 7 October 1648 the Commons granted Lothian £1,000 out of the sequestrations of rebels in North Wales, who had taken up arms.[26] Moreover,

20 Bod. Lib., MS Top. Cheshire e.3, fols 1r.–4v.

21 CL, CPP/2/65, 74. A letter from Robert Scawen, chairman of the committee to Humphrey Chetham, high sheriff of the county, dated 7 February 1649 refers to 'the payment of £250 to persons appointed by the commissioners in Lancashire for the payment of officers and soldiers in Lancaster Castle on their disbanding'. On the reverse is a note concerning the disbursement of £60 to Lieutenant Robert Collie, governor of Lancaster, for payment of the officers and soldiers of the garrison (CPP/1/49).

22 *CSPD 1648–9*, p.227.

23 TNA, SP28/224/2, fols 308v., 310r., 316v.

24 TNA, SP28/128/13, fol. 23r.

25 Malbon, *Memorials*, p.220; Edward Parry, *Royal Visits and Progresses to Wales, and the Border Counties* (Chester, 1850), pp.388–9.

26 TNA, SP28/224/2, fols 267v., 308v., 317v.–318r.; *CJ*, IV, pp.139, 621; V, pp.688–9; VI, pp.43–4, 46; VII, p.539; *LJ*, VI, pp.715, 609; X, p.533.

the Army Council authorised the payment of £800 to 'persons appointed by the Commissioners in North Wales for the payment of the horse under the command of Major General Mytton in North Wales on their disbanding'.[27]

Hence, Royalist and Presbyterian assistance for the Scots in Cheshire and the North West failed to materialise, while Colonel John Booth, the former Parliamentarian officer was arrested for assisting the rising. The remaining threat to the security of the region was Chester, whose early royalism and strategic position meant that there had always been the possibility of an attempt to recover the city for the Royalist cause. It was not until October 1646 that Parliament deemed itself to be sufficiently in control of affairs in Chester to issue an ordinance for the purging of its Assembly.[28] Both during and after the First Civil War the government of the city was divided between civil and military authorities, although relations between the two were never harmonious. The shake-up presented Parliament with an opportunity to reduce the composition of the Assembly, and make it easier for the parliamentary aldermen to control its members by insisting on the strict interpretation of the city's constitution as laid down in the governing charter of 1506, which had established Chester as a 'county of itself'.[29] At the time of the Second Civil War, in June 1648, a plot was discovered to betray the garrison of Chester into the hands of the Royalists, but this proved unsuccessful. The Cheshire lawyer and writer, Thomas Malbon, presented a detailed account of events:

> On Tuesday 20 June 1648, the city of Chester had like to have been betrayed and surprised by some cavaliers lurking in the city after the same was reduced, and the throats of the governor, captains and officers practised to have been cut. But it pleased God that the same was disclosed by one Thomas Swyndall … his conscience accusing him, he voluntarily made Colonel Duckenfield acquainted therewith, whereupon Major Houghton, being one which was accused, was immediately apprehended and sent to prison. And being searched there was found in his pocket a letter from Colonel Edward Moldsworth, who was also apprehended and imprisoned … [These and their confederates duly confessed] that they had conclude to have surprised the said city and castle upon Tuesday the 20th of June; and upon the surprisal notice should have been given unto the said Moldsworth, and others were appointed to lie in the house near the castle, by shooting the great guns, and Lieutenant Oldham should have been governor of the castle. For which offence they were some of them tried by council of war, and had judgement to die. Lieutenant Oldham and William Ashton were shot against the wall in Northgate Street for their offence.[30]

27 CL, CPP/1/39, 43–4.

28 *A&O*, I, pp.876–9. The ordinance was copied into the city's Second Assembly Book (CRO, ZA/B/2, fols 76r.–8v.).

29 A.M. Johnson, 'Politics in Chester during the Civil Wars and the Interregnum', Clark, Peter and Slack, Paul (eds), *Crisis and Order in English Towns 1500–1700: Essays in Urban History* (London: Routledge, 1972), pp.204–36 (p.218).

30 Malbon, *Memorials*, pp.214–6.

The deputy-governor, Colonel William Daniell – who would later be given command of a regiment of Cheshire and Lancashire foot, which was initially intended for Irish service, but instead marched to Scotland – reported to the Speaker:

> The governor being absent in taking steps for the payment of the assessments of some neighbouring counties allotted for the supply of this garrison was prevented from giving this first speedy relation. On Friday last, the 16th, there was some discovery of a most deep and desperate plot to have betrayed this garrison into the hands of the malignant party of the kingdom. This present Tuesday there hath been some further knowledge thereof, and yet are there so many examinations of engaged persons behind, that the bottom of the plot cannot for the present be presented to your Honour, only this much in general, that some of the greatest in this city and county that have served with and against the Parliament since the beginning of the late war are accused to be prime actors in the business, and that God Almighty hath frustrated their expectations and preserved this place in safety, and these parts of the kingdom from an open and desperate war, and the lives of many godly persons from the malice of unreasonable men.[31]

This stratagem provided Sir William Brereton as MP for the county and long-time adversary of the city, with a strong case for reducing the independence of Chester by joining its militia companies with that of the county, and thus bringing it under the control of the county palatine of Chester. Brereton also urged that the city should be under the command of the governor, and if not, the governor's power might be negated. His proposal was agreed to by the Commons, who ordered that 'Colonel Duckenfield the governor of Chester, Sir William Brereton knight, Colonel Booth, Peter Warburton, Thomas Stanley, esquires, be added to the commissioners for the militia in the city of Chester'.[32] The pre-war Chester trained band appears to have consisted of one company of around 100 men. In 1613 the part-time members included one carpenter, three maltsters, seven tanners, seven bakers, six hat-makers, six butchers, three drapers, 13 shoemakers, five glovers and seven tailors. Their officers in 1639 were Captain Dutton, Lieutenant William Maxey and Ensign Jacob, all professional soldiers, who were paid £5 10s.[33] When Charles I paid a fleeting visit to Chester on 23 September 1642 he was escorted by musketeers of the city militia,

Sir William Brereton (1601–64). John Vicars, *England's Worthies, Under Whom all the Civill and Bloody Warres since Anno 1642, to Anno 1647, are related* (London, 1647).

31 HMC, *Thirteenth Report, App. I*, I, p.463.

32 *CJ*, V, p. 622; CRO, ZML/2/320 (4 July 1648).

33 CRO, ZML/2/325, 465.

and met at Boughton by the sheriffs and their officers, dressed in scarlet. Chester was eventually secured for the King on 21 October, when the assembly ordered 'that for the defence of the city 300 men, inhabitants of the city, should be raised [in addition to the trained band] and that they should be armed with muskets and their appurtenances'.[34] This order formed the origin of the regiment of volunteer townsmen commanded by Sir Francis Gamull during the siege of Chester.

The execution of Charles I in January 1649 and the establishment of the Commonwealth heralded a general dismay among a large part of the population of Britain, but reactions to it in Cheshire, as elsewhere, were subdued by the power of the Army. Edward Burghall, the fanatical puritan minister of Acton, wrote in bewilderment of 'a strange act and the like never seen or known before', whereas Henry Newcome, curate of Gawsworth, recorded, 'A general sadness is put upon us all. It dejected me much I remember, the horridness of the fact and much indisposed me for the service of the Sabbath next after the news came'.[35] Although the relatively settled nature of national politics during the following decade ensured a degree of stability in local politics, from the beginning of the Commonwealth a number of Chester aldermen continued to oppose oaths of allegiance to the new regime. Ralph Davenport, clerk to the Pentice – the centre of city government, housed in a timber building attached to St Peter's Church near the Town Cross, where the trained band's arms and equipment were also stored – recalled later that from the outset, and on many occasions afterwards, when he came to administer the oaths he received express instructions to the contrary, 'with a variation from a kingly to Commonwealth government notwithstanding'.[36] When the mayor and Assembly were required by the Council of State to take the Engagement early in 1650 they were conspicuously sluggish in subscribing to it. In May the Assembly was ordered to replace the mayor, William Crompton, and to hold an election to choose his successor.[37]

When no notice was taken, the Council wrote again before the mayoral election of October 1650, reminding Crompton that in the elections of city officials for the coming year the Assembly must respect the rules as laid down by Acts of Parliament. He was further instructed to return a list of any in the city who held office contrary to the Act of Engagement. Thus, when the city authorities attempted to hold an election, the governor of the Chester garrison was ordered to intervene. According to Randle Holme III, 'some companies [were] drawn to St Werburgh's churchyard to oppose the choice of this election [led by the governor], some draw to circumround the hall and lane ends, and stairs with lit matches, their muskets loaded in front, and threat to the civil government and ancient privileges of the city in choice of their mayor'.[38] Of the event *Mercurius Politicus* for 14 October 1650 reported:

34 CRO, ZML/2/565.

35 Malbon, *Memorials*, p.226; *Autobiography of Henry Newcome*, p.13.

36 TNA, SP23/263, fol. 119r.

37 *CSPD 1650*, p.31.

38 BL, MS Harley 2125, fol. 73r.

From Chester of the tenth instant, we are informed of a great hurly burly about the election of their new mayor, whereby you may perceive what spirit reigns there still among them. The malignants were very confident to have made one Alderman Owen Hughes their mayor, one that had formerly been a sequestered man, and shows himself still to be of their own complexion; whereupon the faithful governor, Colonel Duckenfield, knowing him to be uncapable of bearing office, by the Ordinances and Acts of Parliament, resolved to oppose them in any such election; and for that end, commanded 200 men and upwards to the market place, where they were drawn up just as the bell tolled for the town Assembly. Two captains [John Whitworth and William Smith] went in to tell them plainly what end they came for; being resolved to have no cavalier mayor, and if they did proceed to any such election, both sword and mace should be taken from them. Notwithstanding this, the rude multitude seemed not to fear; but when it came to voices, they voted generally for Hughes. Whereupon, the drums beat, and the soldiers began to bestir themselves, and drew up in the very face of them, every man in a posture for service, with his match lighted, etc. At this, the gentlemen began to cool, and in the end they changed their notes, and voted Master Leycester mayor, which gave good content. After this, the soldiers pulled down those badges of our slavery, called the king's arms, and some other baubles in the hall, and then marched away.[39]

39 *Mercurius Politicus*, 10–14 October 1650.

2

Cromwell and the Protectorate, 1651–59

The end of hostilities in 1648 enabled a return to the search for a peaceful settlement, a search that ultimately ended in the death of Charles I and the creation of the Republic. This quest necessarily entailed replacing many of the country's local military governors with new and less experienced men, and as in the case of Cheshire, Lancashire and others, a dramatic remodelling of county militias. The militia, important both for the security and peace of the state, and as an alternative source of power to the regular army, had been a key issue in the lead up to Pride's Purge – when in December 1648 troops of under the command of Colonel Thomas Pride forcibly removed from the Long Parliament all those who were not supporters of the grandees in the Army and the Independents. All parties had scrambled to ensure that authority was in the hands of their allies in the provinces. The new Militia Ordinance, passed on 2 December, would have removed power away from the new men who had come to prominence during the wars, and returned it to the traditional elite. Pride's Purge followed four days later, and the Ordinance was repealed later that month, before it could be implemented.[1] The Rump's *Act for Settling of the Militia of the Commonwealth of England*, passed on 11 July 1650, demonstrated that the militia was intended as an adjunct to the Army, under the power of the Council of State, which would ensure national security.

At a local level, control was in the hands of commissioners, who were given statutory authority to undertake measures such as disarming or detaining suspected malcontents, administering finance and military activities. The militia (known as the 'general militia') was to be supported by assessment on all those with an annual income of over £100 or £200 worth of property.[2] The reshaping of the militia in 1649 and 1650 was a vital stage in the formation of the new regime. To Blair Worden, the 'zealous' creation of the new militia by the Commonwealth indicated 'the regime's determination to bring the localities under control', although Underdown asserts that it represented

1 *A&O*, I, pp1238–9; *CJ*, VI, pp.97–9.

2 *A&O*, II, pp.397–402.

Colonel Robert Duckenfield (1619–89). Chetham's Library, Bridgewater Scrapbook 248. (Copyright of Chetham's Library)

'one more stage in the undermining of the county communities in favour of Whitehall'.[3] Having been due to terminate in January 1651, the Rump's measures were extended until May and then revived in order to help combat the Scottish invasion of England in support of Charles Stuart, which terminated with the Battle of Worcester and the rout of the King's supporters on their way back through the north-west of England. The services of the local trained bands lapsed after the threats posed by this campaign, however, and the legislation expired in December 1651. Ironically, the militia had performed particularly well and comprised one third of Cromwell's army, in what has been described as the Interregnum militia's 'crowning achievement'.[4] Other county forces were kept in arms as garrisons in key locations, such as Chester, Shrewsbury and Hull.

The names of officers returned from Cheshire to act as commissioners for the militia was approved by Parliament on 2 April 1650. Subsequently, the Council of State issued colonel's commissions to Henry Brooke, Robert Duckenfield, Thomas Croxton and Henry Bradshaw on 8 July, to raise and command regiments of militia foot in the county. Each of these men had been loyal and able senior officers in the army of Parliament under Sir William Brereton during the First Civil War, and thus were highly experienced. Moreover, Duckenfield and Croxton had remained in service, the former as governor of Chester and the latter in charge of a locally recruited infantry regiment which opposed the Scottish-Royalist invasions of 1648. Parliament further issued commissions for the remaining regimental officers of foot, as well as those of a troop of horse, commanded by Duckenfield as captain.[5] At Middlewich on 2 April 1650, the Cheshire militia committee agreed that four regiments of foot should be raised, consisting of 700 men each, to be commanded by three field officers and five captains in each regiment.[6] Most of the field officers and company commanders, like their colonels (and likely many of their men), were veterans of Brereton's army and thus practiced in warfare. Except for Duckenfield's regiment, each of the others were disbanded immediately after the Worcester campaign.

During the New Model Army's invasion of Scotland, begun in July 1650, a regiment of 10 companies had been raised from Cheshire and Lancashire,

---

3 Blair Worden, *The Rump Parliament 1648–53* (Cambridge: Cambridge University Press, rev. edn, 2008), pp.223–4; Underdown, *Pride's Purge*, p.303.

4 J.G.A. Ive, 'The Local Dimensions of Defence: The Standing Army and Militia in Norfolk, Sussex and Essex, 1649–1660', PhD thesis (Cambridge, 1986), p.341.

5 *CSPD 1650*, pp.76, 507, 509–10; Ormerod, *History*, I, p.lxiv.

6 *Mercurius Politicus*, 3–9 September 1651; *Weekly Intelligencer*, 3–9 September 1651; Ormerod, *History*, II, pp.xxxix, xl; III, pp.60–1.

under the command of Colonel Daniell.[7] Commissioned on 16 May, he was a highly competent and trusted officer, who had been a captain in Colonel Henry Brooke's regiment in Cheshire between 1643 and 1646, and served as governor of Chester in 1648.[8] The senior officers of the regiment were equally experienced and known to Daniell, something which would have aided their selection with the assistance of Colonel Robert Duckenfield, the current governor of Chester. Thus, Lieutenant Colonel Richard Smith had formerly been in Colonel Mackworth's regiment of foot in Shropshire; Sergeant Major John Jolly had served as lieutenant under Duckenfield in the Cheshire forces from 1643 onwards; Captains Richard Heath and Joseph Witter had been lieutenant and ensign respectively to Daniell between 1643 and 1647; Captain Edward Barker was lieutenant to Lieutenant Colonel Gilbert Gerard in Brereton's army and to Captain Watson in Duckenfield's 1650 militia regiment; Captain Hugh Birtles had been captain lieutenant to Colonel John Leigh in Cheshire.[9] Colonel William Daniell's regiment participated in the Battle of Dunbar on 3 September 1650, and remained at Leith when Cromwell and the Army marched to Glasgow. Moreover, in July 1651 Daniell's command led the army's march into Fife, which brought about the overwhelming defeat of Sir John Browne's Scots at Inverkeithing on 20 July, fighting alongside Lambert's regiment in the action.[10]

Cheshire Militia Units Raised in 1650–1

Colonel Henry Brooke's Regiment of Foot
(raised from Eddisbury hundred, and parts of Bucklow and Northwich hundreds)
Lieutenant Colonel John Brooke
Sergeant Major John Bramhall
Captain Ralph Pownell
Captain John Lownes
Captain Edward Stelfox
Captain Thomas Lathom
Captain Cheney Bostock

Colonel Thomas Croxton's Regiment of Foot
(from Nantwich and part of Northwich hundreds)
Lieutenant Colonel Gilbert Gerard

7 *CSPD 1650*, pp.141, 174, 184, 210; Firth and Davies, *Regimental History*, II, pp.489; Wanklyn, *Reconstructing the New Model Army*, II, pp.58–9.

8 BL, MS Harley 1999, fol. 75v.; MS Harley 2128, fol. 48v.; MS Add. 11333, fols 45v., 69r., 109v., 117v., 101v.–2r.; *BLB*, II, 1063, 1113, 1200–1, 1212, 1247.

9 TNA, SP28/78, fol. 2r. (Smith); SP28/128/10, fols 4r., 8r.; SP28/152/4, fol. 10; SP28/208, fols 20v.–1r. (Jolly); SP28/124/1, fol. 13r.; SP28/30/7, fol. 684r.; SP16/513/1, fols 91v., 72v., 74v.; *CJ*, VII, pp.762–3 (Heath); TNA, E121/5/7/95, fols 61r.–5r.; SP28/124/1, fol. 13r. (Witter); SP28/152/4, fol. 15v.; SP28/123/2, fols 190v., 196r.; SP28/123/1, fols 38r., 50r. (Barker); TNA, SP28/513/1, fol. 91r.; BL, MS Harley 2144, fol. 56v. (Birtles).

10 Whitelocke, *Memorials*, III, pp.321–3.

Sergeant major George Malbon
Captain John Delves
Captain Hugh Whitney
Captain Thomas Malbon
Captain Thomas Whalley
Captain John Holford

Colonel Henry Bradshaw's Regiment of Foot
(from Macclesfield, and part of Bucklow hundreds, namely the parishes of Bowden and Mobberley, and part of Rostherne)
Lieutenant Colonel Lawrence Downes
Sergeant Major Alexander Newton
Captain William Fitton
Captain William Fallowes
Captain William Watson
Captain Edward Alcocke
Captain Richard Grantham

Colonel Robert Duckenfield's Regiment of Foot
(drawn from Wirral and Broxton hundreds)
Lieutenant Colonel Henry Birkenhead
Sergeant Major Simon Finch
Captain John Stockport
Captain Thomas Partington
Captain John Corbet
Captain Henry Green
Captain Jonathan Ridge

Although most county forces were ordered to disband after Worcester, local expediencies meant that some were retained in key strategic locations.[11] Colonel Duckenfield's regiment employed in the expedition to the Isle of Man, with two other foot regiments, against the forces under the Earl of Derby. Following the Royalist capitulation on 31 October 1651, five of Duckenfield's (those of Lieutenant Colonel Finch, Sergeant Major Duckenfield, and Captains Stockport, Birtles and Massey) were placed under the command of Finch, and the following Spring went to Ireland with the intention of completing Colonel Waller's regiment.[12] However, when they got there they discovered that Waller had already raised his command to full strength from units already in Ireland, and so the Cheshire companies remained unregimented.

In October 1651 the company commanders of Duckenfield's regiment were:[13]

11 *CJ*, VII, p.24.
12 TNA, SP28/87, fol. 178r.; SP28/88, fol. 148r.; Ludlow, *Memoirs*, I, p.323; *CSPD, 1651–52*, pp.78–9, 110, 117, 184.
13 TNA, SP28/96, fols 35v., 169r.

Colonel Robert Duckenfield
Lieutenant Colonel Simon Finch
Sergeant Major William Duckenfield
Captain Godfrey Gimbert
Captain William Watson
Captain James Stockport
Captain Edward Birtles
Lieutenant Colonel Gilbert Gerard (serving as captain)
Captain Thomas Massey
Captain Philip Egerton acted as marshal to the regiment from 1651 to 1653.[14]

The Cheshire Troop of Horse[15]
Colonel Robert Duckenfield (as captain)
Lieutenant William Shepley
Cornet John Griffith
Quartermaster Gardner

Rather than standing down after the Worcester campaign, the 100-strong troop was employed in guarding prisoners from Chester to London. It went then to the Isle of Man for the duration of three weeks 'beyond the time they were ordered to be disbanded', and on 25 December 1651 the Army Committee was instructed to pay the unit for its extra service, from the cornet downwards.[16]

On 1 August 1651, four days before a Scottish army of 14,000 men, commanded by Lieutenant General Leslie, crossed the border into England, the Council of State instructed the militia commissioners for Salop, Chester, Lancaster and others to mobilise their respective forces:

> That there might be forces ready against all emergencies, we have given order to Colonel Walton to raise a proportion out of the late militia of your county, to be taken into pay for three months; they should be armed with the arms belonging to the said militia, which were to be secured by our late instructions sent to you. Give Colonel Walton your best assistance in arming those forces with all expedition.[17]

Additionally, the governor of Chester was ordered to:

> Confer with Colonel Birch and Colonel Mackworth, and raise ten new companies of 100 each, out of the late militia forces of cos. Lancaster, Chester, and Salop, for three months; six of the old companies, viz., four out of Chester, one out of Liverpool, and one out of Shrewsbury, to be forthwith drawn into the field, and six of the new companies put in their place in the garrisons; such six old companies and four of the new, under a lieutenant and a major, to march forthwith for Scotland.

14 *CSPD, 1651–52*, pp.39, 70, 185, 320, 330.
15 *Mercurius Politicus*, 3–9 September 1651; *Weekly Intelligencer*, 3–9 September 1651; Ormerod, *History*, II, pp.xxxix, xl; III, pp.60–1.
16 *CSPD, 1651–52*, p.79.
17 *CSPD 1651*, p.302.

During the subsequent Worcester campaign, the Cheshire forces served under Major Generals Harrison and Lambert, as part of the delaying operations against the progress of the Scots army through Lancashire and Cheshire. On 14 August Harrison reported that 'Cheshire hath been very forward in levies, most of the before mentioned foot being from thence'.[18] Moreover, one unidentified company doggedly defended Warrington Bridge for an hour and a half, while the Parliamentarian commanders drew off other troops to Knutsford Heath, in order to deploy their cavalry. The Scots broke contact, however, and hastened south, yet the Cheshire foot brigade joined the pursuit by Cromwell's army towards the eventual conflict at Worcester.[19] During the battle on 3 September, militia regiments from Cheshire, Essex, Norfolk and Suffolk were instrumental in breaking into the city, and routing Charles Stuart's troops. Colonel Bradshaw's regiment, leading the Cheshire contingent, sustained seven soldiers killed, and one ensign and 12 soldiers wounded. Bradshaw himself was slightly injured. Furthermore, Sergeant Major Simon Finch of Colonel Duckenfield's regiment – a former captain in Ireland, who defected to Brereton's Cheshire forces in 1644 and served actively as a dragoon officer – distinguished himself during the action.[20]

In their absence, the garrison of Chester dispatched 200 foot (two companies) to reinforce Colonel Robert Lilburne's regiment of horse, which had marched into Lancashire to counter the Earl of Derby's attempt to raise Royalist forces in the county. Derby attacked them at Wigan Lane on 25 August, wherein in the absence of the Lord General's regiment of foot under Lieutenant Colonel Charles Worsley, which had hastily arrived at Manchester from Nottinghamshire, the Cheshire foot stood fast, as Lilburne later explained, 'our horse not being able to do any service but in lanes'.[21] The Royalist defeat was total, Derby escaped wounded, while over 400 of his officers and soldiers were taken prisoner. Undoubtedly the militia forces raised from Cheshire contributed effectively to the military operations brought about by the appearance of Charles Stuart and invasion of England by Scottish troops. As Dore noted, 'When, therefore, Cromwell's 'crowning mercy' at Worcester on 3 September 1651 at last brought peace, Cheshire soldiers had done far more than give negative support to the regime'.[22] Yet with the crisis safely over, the first parliament of the Protectorate resumed previous attempts to reduce the standing army of some 50,000 men and take back control of the militia from the localities. Hence, on 28 October 1651the Council of State informed the Cheshire militia commissioners that:

---

18 *Mercurius Politicus*, 18–25 August 1659.

19 *Perfect Diurnall*, 18–25 August 1659; *Mercurius Politicus*, 18–25 August 1659; *A True and Full Relation of the late Skirmishes at Warrington, etc., with the present condition and station of our own and the enemies forces, drawn out of severall expresses from Knotsford, Congerton, etc., on the 17th and 18th instant* (London, 1659).

20 Ludlow, *Memoirs*, I, p.323; Charles Firth and Godfrey Davies, *The Regimental History of Cromwell's Army* (Oxford: Clarendon Press, 1991 edn), I, p.358.

21 *A Great Victory by the Blessing of God obtained by the Parliament's forces against the Scots forces, commanded by the Earl of Derby, on the 25 of August 1651, near Wiggon in Lancashire, certified by a letter from Col. Lilburne and two letters from Chester, also a letter from Col. Birche to Mr Speaker* (London, 29 August 1651); *Two Letters from Colonel Robert Lilburne*.

22 Dore, *Civil Wars in Cheshire*, p.77.

> Captain Griffith's troop still continues together, notwithstanding orders for their despite orders for their disbanding, to the great oppression of the county, for which disobedience no pretence can be given, there being no service to which they are appointed. Second your orders to them for disbanding, and require them, all excuses set aside, to give obedience thereto; the restoring of horses of the troop to the proprietors who raised them Council leaves to your judgement, not doubting but you will have respect to such of the soldiers as have deserved well for courage and good affection to the service. Council likewise to examine the oppressions acted upon the county by this troops to such of the country as have suffered from them. For the affronts offered you in discharge of your trust, the authority by which you act has empowered you to do yourselves right, and we hope that neither this nor the murmurings of any malignant spirits against you, for your forwardness and zeal expressed to the service – by sending such considerable forces, so much beyond your proportion, against the enemy in the late invasion – will discourage you from acting still with the same cheerfulness, but will rather excite you to a continuance, especially when you consider how the blessing of God went along with your endeavours, to the finishing of a most happy work in the destruction of the enemy, maugre the devices of malignant and discontented spirits. The great faithfulness of your country is generally taken notice of to your honour, and Parliament and Council will, on all fitting occasions, be sensible thereof to your just encouragement.[23]

Captain Griffith is probably the same John Griffith who served as clerk to Sir William Brereton's troop of horse in the Cheshire army of parliament. If Gough is to be believed, he came from Myddle in Shropshire, and was an apothecary and relative of his.[24] In 1647 Griffith acted as quartermaster to the reformed troop, then under Sergeant Major Jerome Zankey (Brereton's former captain lieutenant). His continued service as a cavalry officer is confirmed by a report to Secretary Thurloe in March 1655, in which he recommending reliable men to serve as officers, adding, 'I must confess my ignorance, and every way my incapacity as to foot service, my whole time in all the late wars being spent in horse service, till after Worcester fight'.[25] Although Griffith was commissioned cornet in Duckenfield's Cheshire militia troop of horse on 22 August 1650, he was promoted to captain soon afterwards and continued to act as a valued agent to Thurloe until the Restoration.

In the autumn and winter of 1654–5 the internal situation in the British Isles provided would-be plotters against the Cromwellian regime with fertile soil in which to propagate conspiracy and rebellion. The dismissal in 1653 of the Barebones Parliament had particularly alienated the Fifth Monarchists, men like Major General Thomas Harrison, whom Cromwell had hitherto shown most sympathy. Equally, when the first Protectorate Parliament, which sat from 3 September 1654 until 22 January 1655, failed, petitions

23 *CSPD 1650*, p.509; *CSPD 1651*, pp.500–1.

24 TNA: SP28/152/7, fol. 17r.; SP28/225/4, fol. 764r.; BL, MS Add. 11332, fols 38v.–40r.; *BLB*, II, 796 n.9, 838, n.1; P.E. Razzell (ed.), Richard Gough, *The History of Myddle* (Pittsburgh, PA: Caliban Books, new edn, 1979), p.167.

25 *Thurloe*, III, p.217.

from Army colonels and the fleet indicated that several republican-minded officers were anxious of the increasingly severe nature of Cromwell's rule. Moreover, with MPs ready to reduce the financial burden on their constituents, the Lord Protector was forced to agree to a reduction to the level of both the monthly assessment and the army establishment. In his closing speech to the Parliament the profoundly downhearted Cromwell warned that the imminent prospect of a Royalist revolt made it inadvisable to reduce the size of the army, angrily declaring that 'instead of peace and settlement, instead of mercy and truth being brought together … weeds and nettles, briars and thorns have thriven under you, shadows, dissettlement and division, discontent and dissatisfaction, together with real dangers to the whole have been more multiplied within these five months of your sitting that in some years before'.[26] Yet for all his apprehensions at the way his Commonwealth was being undermined, the first unconcealed Royalist attempt to upset its structure, which followed closely on Parliament's dismissal, only served to prove the steely power of Cromwellian control.

Oliver Cromwell, Lord Protector (1599–1658). John Vicars, *England's Worthies* (London, 1647).

Accurate information on the Sealed Knot, the dissident Royalist organisation formed in 1653 to coordinate plans from the exiled Court, was fed to Secretary Thurloe through a web of spies. This allowed thorough countermeasures to be taken; troops were recalled to England from Ireland and Scotland in anticipation of an uprising, while on 15 February 1655 a warrant was issued ordering the raising in London of three new regiments of foot. The story of the insubstantial yet bold rising led by Colonel John Penruddock in the West Country was one of chaotic preparation, cohesion and direction, and one that set the model for all Royalist conspiracies of the Interregnum. Although there were meetings of small groups of conspirators in Northumberland, Yorkshire and Nottinghamshire, which were quickly dispersed, so little a threat had the Penruddock rebellion ever constituted, that Cromwell felt himself able to deal with the insurgents mercifully by the standards of the day. Penruddock himself was hanged with others, and thus spared the dreadful indignities of being drawn and quartered.[27] Throughout

26 Walter Cortez Abbott, (ed.), *The Writings and Speeches of Oliver Cromwell* (Oxford: Oxford University Press, 1988)), III, pp.511, 582, 588.

27 For details of the planning and suppression of Penruddock's Rebellion, see David Underdown, *Royalist Conspiracy in England 1649–60* (New Haven: Yale University Press, 1960), pp.149–57; A.H. Woolrych, *Penruddock's Rising, 1655* (London: The Historical Association, 1955); Andrea E. Button, 'Penruddock's Rising, 1655', *Southern History*, 19 (1997), pp.99–111; J.M. Gratton, and P.H.W. Booth, 'Sir George Middleton of Leighton, a Lancashire Penruddock?: documents on preparations for a failed Royalist rising in north Lancashire, 1655', *TLCAS*, 91 (1995), pp.17–33.

the country commissioners were ordered to raise and train new militia forces, and to recruit men 'fit for war', to put down insurrections, disarm papists and other measures. In anticipation of further revolts, Cromwell's officers in North Wales and the Welsh borders had remained watchful. Their reports, as well as the intercepted letters of plotters, reveal the extent to which local leaders, such as the former Parliamentarian commander Sir Thomas Myddelton of Chirk (who had sided with the cavaliers in August–September 1651) were involved in the organisation of a rebellion in various parts of the region.[28] On 8 March 1655 Colonel Humphrey Mackworth junior, the ever-vigilant governor of Shrewsbury, reported:

> Since the receipt of your highness's letter, I received from four several parts in this county this ensuing intelligence, that there is a sudden insurrection intended all over England and Wales. One Sir [Edward] Blaney is commander-in-chief over Montgomery forces, and keeps his rendezvous this evening with hopes to be possessed of Chirk Castle this very night; and that Sir Thomas Harries (the gentleman your highness mentioned) keeps rendezvous about the same time in his own park five miles off this place, with intention to surprise this town and castle about eight or nine of the clock this night, and likewise that one Ralph Kynaston of this county hath privately listed a troop of horse, in order to the prevention hereof I sent one this morning to give Sir Thomas Myddelton notice of the designs in his parts, and against this castle.[29]

However, by the end of the month all attempts at insurrection had been eliminated, prompting John Griffith, then sheriff of Chester and captain of militia horse to tell Thurloe on 24 March:

> The storm seems to be over in these parts, we being at present in quiet, and putting ourselves into a posture to preserve us so; but Captain Ridge being discontent, that he hath not command himself, I have some cause to suspect, that he may endeavour to asperse our proceedings, or the persons entrusted; of which nature if anything come to your hands, I earnestly began account thereof. Upon Monday next our commissioners all meet for the county, of whose proceedings you shall have an exact accompt; and then also you may expect a more satisfactory answer from Colonel Duckenfield. Colonel Croxton expects a particular order to the present government of the castle for the reduction thereof, &c. Be pleased to signify your pleasure concerning Sir Richard Mauleverer and Mr Walters. There are some of our countrymen yet at liberty, whom I hope the commissioners at their meeting will take care to secure.[30]

Although Griffith's reports were full of detail and the notion of energetic action on his part, comparatively little Royalist activity occurred in Cheshire during this period. Throughout the 1650s a minority of malcontents had

---

28 *CSPD 1651*, pp.200, 204, 226, 337, 340.

29 *Thurloe*, III, p.209.

30 *Ibid.*, p.300. For examples of similar intelligence reports see pp.207, 209, 216–17, 304, 337, 344, 682.

attempted to create difficulties, but their identity was well known to the authorities and they were detained whenever their plotting had been regarded as particularly dangerous. Consequently, Colonel John Booth was arrested four times between 1648 and 1656, while Robert Werden, a former Royalist colonel, was also kept under close surveillance. During the latter's compounding in July 1646 the county committee had declared him 'a most violent enemy, administering general astonishment and terror to the whole country'.[31] In 1655 Werden planned to surprise Chester Castle, but the handful of men who gathered beneath its walls were so discouraged at the appearance of fresh sentries on the walls that they scattered without attempting anything.[32] As with the Booth uprising four years later, the complicity of the city authorities in the actions of the insurgents was noticeable. Some months later, on 24 July, Captain Griffith wrote to Thurloe of 'one Mathew Cowes, who had bought up many muskets, pistols, and other arms (which I then seized and brought up to the town hall), and as it then appeared furnished, this same Mr Ravenscroft, about twenty days before the breaking out of the said plot, with a case of pistols'. He added that they and others were 'so high in their expressions and actions, that frequently at their meetings they drink their pretended king's health, at which they burn their hats, and some other of their garments, and have offered violence unto and abused several persons, that have refused the same, and still continue their practice, and threatening the well-affected with a change of government'.[33]

Werden was captured by Captain Spillman's troop in Flintshire and interrogated at Chester Castle by the Cheshire commissioners for the militia. Also detained were various gentlemen in the county who were undoubted Royalists – George Warburton of Arley, Peter Leycester of Tabley and John Booth.[34] Leycester and Booth were specifically accused of receiving two Royalist spies (Halsall and Lisson) at the time of the rising at Tabley Hall. According to Leycester's account, he admitted that two strangers had come to his house, spoken to his uncle and stayed to dinner. Booth also said that he did not know the identity of the men, but they had made suggestions to him about the revolt, to which he 'could not safely hear or keep any council of theirs'.[35] This rather implausible testimony failed to convince the newly appointed Charles Worsley of Platt Hall, Manchester – the most rigorous of the Cromwellian major generals – when he arrived in Cheshire in early November 1655. Fully convinced that Griffiths had been correct in his suspicions, Worsley informed Thurloe on 17 December, 'I leave it to your consideration, when your leisure will permit, to let me have the examinations about Booth, Warburton, Leycester, and Werden. I am afraid I shall find some more of that gang'. Moreover, in complaining that the power of local officials to pursue such men was limited, he added four days later:

31 *CJ*, IV, pp.611, 721; *LJ*, IX, pp.5, 7.

32 *CSPD 1655*, pp.216, 220; *CCAM*, p.103.

33 *Thurloe*, III, pp.676–8, 722.

34 *Ibid.*, IV, pp.337–8.

35 CRO, DLT/B3, unfol.

Major General Charles Worsley (1622–56). (Copyright of the Royal Armouries)

> The commissioners are not free to meddle with the estates of Booth, Warburton, Leycester and Werden, till they see what you have against them, and the orders require what is to be done in that case to be three at the least. We now find, that many in these countries, that have been very active against the parliament, and were looked upon to be men of good estates, will hardly be brought within the compass.[36]

But despite all Worsley's efforts to convict them (and the later capture of the spy Halsall), they were ultimately released on payment of substantial sums for indemnities. Ironically, the Protectorate government was more eager to fine than to execute suspects, 'lest it should stir up a blood-feud and alienate the passive support which, apart from its army, was its main support'.[37]

The question of the actions of Sir George Booth the younger during the period of Penruddock's Rising and the subsequent 'rule' of the major generals is an important one, especially as it relates to his leading of the Cheshire uprising later. Despite the portrayal by the Royalist agent Captain Titus of him as 'one the most considerable of our party', and that his uncle was again suspected of Royalist strategising, no hint of distrust appears to have been directed towards him. Although modern observers have claimed that Booth's military experience was limited, during the First Civil War he served in the Cheshire army of parliament with some ability as colonel of a regiment of foot, captain of his own cavalry troop and deputy lieutenant of the county. He was described by Sir John Meldrum in September 1644 as 'a young gentleman of great expectation'.[38] However, his increasing opposition to Sir William Brereton eroded his military and administrative effectiveness, and he resigned his commission in mid 1645. If by the 1650s the conflicts had removed possible Royalist rivals, they had also marked out the Booths, as Dore puts it, as 'upholders of a middle-of-the-road conservatism standing between a Royalist autocracy on the one hand the breakdown of the national Church, republicanism and the possible overthrow of the social order on the other'.[39] Thus, in March 1652 a number of horses were provided for the Cheshire militia troop, being part of 'the Parliament's forces under Colonel George Booth'.[40] Much of the quarrelling among the triumphant Cheshire Parliamentarians was due to jealousy and local faction, but it did reflect in some measure on the smaller local stage the great national conflict between

36 *Thurloe*, IV, pp.322–3.
37 Dore, 'Cheshire Rising', p.54.
38 *CSPD 1644*, p. 543.
39 Dore, 'Cheshire Rising', p.47.
40 BL, MS Harley 2127, fol. 45r.

Presbyterians and Independents, with all the manifold constitutional, social and religious cleavages which this covered. But some evidence marks out features reflecting a more national rift.

Accusations that Brereton employed low-born men to further his military aims is noteworthy – particularly in conjunction with his determination to end the war with a clear-cut victory. Oliver Cromwell, of comparable background and devotional sensibilities to Brereton, faced similar attacks.[41] The admiration for the Dutch system of religious toleration which runs through Sir William's journals, mark him out to have held Independent tendencies, whereas in 1645 old Sir George suppressed Mr Bate, a sectarian minister in the neighbouring parish of Mobberley.[42] Notions of religious toleration would come to the fore again during the rebellion of 1659. The Lancashire Presbyterian minister Adam Martindale complained that the *Declaration* of Sir George Booth 'promised universal toleration, either to everyone without exception, or at least all who joined with them, which must be a perfect cheat, that being promised which they never intended to perform, or else a serious promise of that which I utterly abhorred'.[43] Moreover, in giving evidence against Dr Peter Harrison, minister of Cheadle (who played an important role in support of the insurrection) on 28 October 1659, before the Cheshire commissioners for sequestrations, a tenant of Brereton's in Handforth stated that he:

> having that evening [31 July] some private conference with the said Mr Harrison, and telling him that he heard that the late rising was intended to obstruct Sir William Brereton, who was then expected to come to Cheshire to settle the militia, he, the said Mr Harrison, then said that about a year before, he, the said Mr Harrison, had some discourse with Sir William Brereton, who declared his dislike about toleration of religion, but that now the Parliament had confirmed it, he, this examinate replied that he well-knew that what the Parliament did was by majority of voices, and that Sir William Brereton would not prevent the allowance of toleration, to which Mr Harrison in a passionate manner answered that he marvelled why Sir William Brereton did not then run away and leave them, meaning the Parliament, which he with great earnestness spoke several times over.[44]

The events of 1646–51 widened the breach. Brereton was not a regicide – although he was nominated to, but did not sit on, the commission that condemned Charles I – but he arguably condoned the offence by resuming his seat in Parliament and accepted a place on the Rump's Council of State.[45] By

41 Christopher Hill, *God's Englishman: Oliver Cromwell and the English Revolution* (London: Penguin, new edn, 1990), pp.74–5, 116–7; J.S. Morrill, *Oliver Cromwell and the English Revolution* (London: Longman, 1990), p.95.

42 BL, MS Add. 11331, fols 10v.–11r.; *BLB*, I, 302–3; R.N. Dore, 'The Early Life of Sir William Brereton', *TLCAS*, 63 (1953), pp.1–8; Edward Hawkins (ed.), Sir William Brereton, *Travels in Holland, the United Provinces, England, Scotland, and Ireland* (Manchester: CS, 1844), p.70.

43 *Life of Adam Martindale*, p.139.

44 TNA, SP23/263, fol. 81r.; *East Cheshire*, I, p.226.

45 *CSPD 1651*, p. 44; *CJ*, VI, pp.532–3.

comparison, young Colonel George Booth was associated with the moderate Presbyterian group in Parliament, and was among the MPs excluded by Pride's Purge in December 1648.[46] His uncle, Colonel John Booth, went much further. Between 1648 and 1651 he was three times caught on the point of going over to the Royalists. On one occasion the King's commission was found on him and he was sent to the Tower. Each time a considerable deposit as security money was paid and the influence of his father helped to secure his release.[47] The Rump continued to treat old Sir George with the greatest esteem, although his sectarian neighbour, Robert Duckenfield, was instructed 'to keep arms and ammunition requisite for the defence of his house, and that the residence be left to his disposal, he engaging to secure them in some safe place, that they may not be surprised by any enemy [that is, Charles II's army on its march to Worcester]'. Despite certain misgivings about the trustworthiness of Sir George Booth's son, five days later the Council of State offered a bountiful apology to him:

> When we, in tenderness to you, occasioned through the sense we had of your merits to the public, lately permitted your son John to put in bail, and that before yourself, notwithstanding our then informations and strong apprehensions of his guilt, we could not imagine he should still have resolved to precipitate himself into further destructive courses, as we now find he has done, whereof you will hear more particulars ere long. Touching the seizure of your arms and ammunition, no direction has gone from hence, but we suppose that some command is given from Scotland, in respect of a dangerous conspiracy touching your parts lately happily discovered, wherein your son John has had too great a share, to secure your warlike provisions, lest ill use should be made thereof by your son and his party, so as we well approve of Colonel Duckenfield's care in that behalf. Yet to show our confidence in you, and willingness to comply with your desires so far as may consist with safety, we have given him order touching your arms, as you will perceive by the enclosed. Our only aim as to you is to prevent that surprise of those provisions which was and is designed by the enemies, and not to give you the least disturbance upon any other than the public account; with this declaration we conceive you will remain well satisfied.[48]

Yet however well Sir George stood in the estimation of the new government, it is obvious that even before this that he and his family were already identified by some as the link which in Cheshire might unite all opponents of the 'upstart and blasphemous regime' that had ended the monarchy, truncated the Parliament and seemed about to destroy the national Church. On 13 June 1648 a letter to Booth from 'Your loving friends in the City though nameless' informed him:

46 C.H. Firth (ed.), *The Clarke Papers: Selections from the papers of William Clarke, secretary to the Council of the Army, 1647–1649, and to General Monck and the commanders of the army in Scotland, 1651–1660*, 4 vols (London: Longmans, Green & Co., 1891–1901), II, pp.137–8; Underdown, *Pride's Purge*, pp.176, 350.

47 *CCSP*, I, p.439; *CSPD 1648–9*, pp.197–8, 215; *1649–50*, pp.174, 376–7; *1651*, p.99.

48 *CSPD 1651*, pp.99, 101.

> The prevailing party in the two Houses last voted the disarming of the kingdom, and intended to rule us by an arbitrary power and their army if they can. The Kentish trained bands are dispersed by force and craft, but Sussex, Hampshire and the adjacent counties are rising. We have a considerable army of resolved men now in Suffolk, and as it moves our disbanded soldiers and the cavaliers gather to it. We doubt not but a little will lay Independent flat. Our city stands neuter. We desire you to interrupt publicly by force or otherwise the proceedings of Duckenfield and his confederates. You and Colonel Mainwaring may do much.[49]

Sir George Booth the younger (1622–84). (Copyright of the National Portrait Gallery)

Crucially, this combination against Independency and its possible consequences might be interpreted as the key to the 1659 rising, for behind the Booths and the cause young Sir George eventually represented, ranged not only the dispossessed and disheartened Royalists, but also the still powerful Presbyterians and their spokesmen, the parish clergy. Their actions further widened the breach between themselves and the Independents in Cheshire and Lancashire, and 'rendered all former endeavours fruitless and an engagement almost hopeless'.[50] When in the summer of 1658 Colonel Roger Whitley, described as 'a gentleman at the court of the king of England at Brussels', constructed a blueprint for a rebellion in England and Wales, he put his finger on the importance of the relative freedoms enjoyed by the Presbyterians.[51] Whereas the Royalists were disarmed, dispersed, without good horses, their movements watched, riven with faction and the prey of turncoats and informers, the Presbyterians – who had not been broken by force but rather supplanted – kept their arms, their mounts, their freedom of correspondence and contact. They were not watched, and cohesion and morale were kept up among them by the influence of their ministers, who would use church meetings for the dissemination of propaganda. It was Whitley who added that the Presbyterians were particularly strong in Cheshire and Lancashire, and many of them kept their arms:

> The Presbyterians have been in power both in the Parliament and arms since the Royalists were defeated, and consequently have had a latter influence on the nation; they were not broken by force (as the Royalists) but rather supplanted

---

49 HMC, *Thirteenth Report, App. I*, p.462.

50 J. Turner Horsfall (ed.), *The Rev. Oliver Heywood, BA 1630–1702; His Autobiography, Diaries, Anecdote and Event Books* (Brighouse: A.B. Bayes, 1882), I, p.174. See also *Life of Adam Martindale*, pp.131–3.

51 *CSPD 1658–59*, p.376. For further details of Whitley's career as a Royalist soldier and agent, see Norman Tucker, 'Colonel Roger Whitley', *JFHS*, 22 (1966), pp.9–24; Jones, 'Booth's Rising' of 1659', pp.416–43.

> consequently not so many of them destroyed in their persons nor their estates sequestrated, neither are they totally disarmed.[52]

As a Welshman with estates in Flintshire and Cheshire, Whitely possessed connections throughout North Wales and the north-west of England, in addition to those forged during his previous military service. As Sarah Clavier Ward asserts, the motivations of both he and his fellow Welsh gentry should be considered within the context of the impact that their Welshness. She states, 'The distinctiveness of north-east Wales in this period is as a united and unwavering bastion of Anglicanism and royalism that was largely unaffected by the apparent permanence of the godly governments. The Puritanism espoused by the godly was alien to many aspects of Welsh culture in the seventeenth century'.[53]

Colonel Whitley's text consists of four parts: suggested heads for a royal declaration; a discussion of the possibility of foreign assistance; an evaluation of the problems and methods of organising a successful rebellion; and extensive lists of those whose services could be utilised. Many of the names are endorsed as being already active, and Whitely provided suggestions as to the commissions and duties with which they could be trusted. He identified (among other things) that a solitary uprising had no hope of realisation, and that concentrated action was made difficult by inadequate communication and lack of mutual confidence. It could not be ascertained in advance where Charles II, or an army from abroad, would be able to disembark; therefore, the plans must be malleable enough to provide for several outcomes. England and Wales would have to be split into associations of counties combined together for military purposes, whilst each association was to be led by a single officer, guided by a small council, and given powers to grant commissions and to treat with those who had formerly waged war against the King.

The officers should prepare for action in the closest detail, enlisting men, obtaining supplies, gathering intelligence and keeping enemy forces under constant surveillance; particular districts could be employed for the maintenance of horses without prior suspicion; if failure was to be avoided, local tactics must not be improvised at the last moment. Thus, Whitely argued, the standing army, faced by a series of semi-independent revolts, would be prevented from reacting decisively, for by the time it had secured London and the South East, and progressed outwards, the Royalists would have had time to regroup, train their troops, and muster an overwhelming field army which although lacking in experience would be of a considerable size.[54] The plan rejected the possibility of employing 'foreign force and aids', instead placing emphasis on the possibility of obtaining the formal assistance

---

52 Bodl. Lib., MS Eng. hist. e.309, pp.75–9, 67–9 (Notebook containing information for a Royalist rising, dated 'Bruges 1658', including list of Royalists in England and Wales, arranged by county) – formerly JRL, MS Mainwaring, Book 24.

53 Sarah Clavier Ward, "Horrid Rebellion and Holie Cheate': Royalist Gentry Responses to Interregnum Government in North East Wales, 1646–1660', *WHR*, 29 (2018), pp.51–72, (p. 71); '"Round-head Knaves": The Ballad of Wrexham and the subversive political culture of Interregnum North-East Wales', *HR*, 91:251 (2017), pp.39–60, (p. 41).

54 *Ibid.*, pp78–85.

of France and Spain. Although he did not say so explicitly, Roger suggested that given the unreliability of promises from foreign rulers and because of the hostility which the presence of foreign troops would provoke in England, it would be better for Charles to owe his restoration to his own subjects.

The parish clergy in Cheshire, as elsewhere, was chiefly Presbyterian and seemingly abhorred both the killing of Charles I in January 1649 and the Rump's views on the national Church. Edward Burghall, the puritan vicar of Acton-near-Nantwich, called the execution 'A strange act and like never seen or known before', whilst Henry Newcome, minister at Gawsworth, said 'a general sadness it put upon us all. It dejected me much, I remember, the horridness of the fact and much indisposed me for the service of the Sabbath next after news came'.[55] Even stronger was their view of the Rump's religious policy. Harrison later claimed to have berated Sir William Brereton to his face because of his support of toleration. When the Rump was replaced with the Barebones Parliament on 4 July 1653 Newcome expressed a general anxiety among the clergy that 'they were about to vote down the national Church' and suggested forebodingly that a 'Munsterian anarchy' might ensue.[56] That a number of Presbyterian ministers propagated the rebellion led by Sir George Booth in Cheshire, Lancashire and further afield in 1659, there is little doubt. As attempts were being made by the exiled royal court during the summer to win over other former Parliamentarians who were dissatisfied with the government, Colonel Silius Titus, an ardent devotee of Charles II, made an unavailing attempt to influence Major General Browne who had great influence in Presbyterian London. However, 'the wary soldier at first refused to make any move unless there was evidence that there would be a force capable of opposing the army'.[57]

Henry Newcombe (1627–85). (Copyright of the National Portrait Gallery)

In broad terms the Royalists were careful to give their Presbyterian collaborators prominence, and indeed the rising was to be made, not in the King's name, but against the Rump and for a 'free parliament', although Charles sent a declaration promising parliamentary rule and liberty of conscience. In the Midlands, Obadiah Grew approved the revolt of the 'new Royalists' in August 1659, and though threatened by Lambert's soldiers, who were marching through Coventry *en route* to Cheshire, refused to read the proclamation of treason against Sir

55 Malbon, *Memorials*, p.226; Newcome, *Autobiography*, pp.13; Catherine Nunn, 'Henry Newcome and his circle: Presbyterianism in South-East Cheshire in the 1650s', *THSLC*, 150 (2003), pp.7–31.

56 Newcome, *Autobiography*, pp.46, 119.

57 Baker, *Chronicle*, p.667.

George Booth, as required by authority.[58] But in Cheshire the Irish nonconformist divine Zachary Crofton and other ministers, including Harrison, Martindale and the Lancastrian Joshua Stockport, preached rebellion from their pulpits, and several others – Newcombe, Robert Eaton of Walton and Booth's personal chaplain, Mr Finch – directly participated in the uprising.[59] Under interrogation by the committee of sequestrations Harrison denied accusations of his direct involvement in the rebellion, despite much evidence to the contrary. Amongst other things, the committee stated that at:

> diverse times in and before the late rebellion did, in his public preaching, speak against the then present government, and did use many encouraging expressions to his then hearers to take up arms in the late insurrection, saying that they must not only pray for the peace of Jerusalem, but pay for it, and if there were occasion, fight for it, though to the loss of life and blood, and said it was a time to rise when the gentry were up and the Church in such danger; and further said that the heretics, schismatics, separates and the rest of the sectaries were the disturbers of the Church's peace.[60]

Especially damning were the depositions of local witnesses who testified against Harrison's conduct. John Ardern of Cheadle, for example, reported:

> he was present and heard Mr Peter Harrison, minister of Cheadle, the Lord's day before the fight at Winnington Bridge, preach at Cheadle upon this text, pray for the peace of Jerusalem and so forth, and amongst many other things to use these expressions to this or like effect, that we were not only to pray for the peace of Jerusalem, but likewise pay for the peace of Jerusalem, and if necessary require it, to fight for it, with many other expressions, and … the said Mr Harrison by his said preach did endeavour to stir up the people to take up arms, and join with Sir George Booth and his party.[61]

Perhaps unsurprisingly, when such Presbyterians encountered Lambert's junior officers and soldiers during the military campaign in the north-west, some of them were blamed for stoking the fires of rebellion. Martindale reported that soon after the parley the day before the Battle of Winnington Bridge on 19 August:

> I being accidently in the company of an officer of the army, he boldly charged all the ministers of Cheshire as having a hand in this design of our gentlemen. I told him it was false, for I had none, and I questioned not but there were many others as innocent as I. He replied, that for as much as we had not declared against it, we could not expect but that the parliament might justly take it for granted and proceed against us in general.[62]

---

58 *Nicholas Papers*, IV, pp.180–1.

59 *CCSP*, IV, pp.280–1; Whitelocke, *Memorials*, IV, p.682.

60 TNA, SP23/263, fol. 80r.; Earwaker, *East Cheshire*, I, p.226.

61 TNA, SP23/263, fol. 82r.; Earwaker, *East Cheshire*, I, p.228.

62 *Life of Adam Martindale* p.140. See also Newcome's comment that at Manchester on 21 September 1659 'The rage of the Anabaptist soldiers was now very high. That Captain Turner, that quartered at Mr Hartley's, one Lord's day when they came from church, said, in a great deal

If the parish clergy thought in this fashion during the 1650s, the moderate Presbyterian gentry – except for few separatists, such as Duckenfield and the Anabaptist Gilbert Gerard – were unlikely to differ markedly. During the years 1653–8 when the first Rump was expelled and then the experiment of a nominated Parliament of sectarian 'saints' was abandoned by Cromwell for a less visionary and more conservative reform. Yet even Duckenfield remained distant from Cromwell after the dissolution of the Parliament. In response to his offer of a colonelcy of a regiment of horse, he wrote on 23 March 1655, suggesting that the Protector raise about 2,000 cavalry equally out of all the counties on the north side of the River Trent, and 'to impose the charge of maintaining and finding them only upon such as are convicted or suspected notoriously for malignancy'.[63] Robert's letter announcing his refusal of the commission tendered by Cromwell offers valuable insights into the local situation. It appears that he was being pressured by his fellow gentry, for he wrote that his former military activities on behalf of the Parliament 'have been taken in ill part', but he also refused the offer because Cheshire was 'so wonderfully impoverished, as without destroying of it, not many soldiers can be raised therein in the way you intend'. He further contended that the attitude of the militia commissioners in the county had been 'so corrupted of late, by the subtilties of the jesuited party', so much so that those entrusted with arms would not prove faithful and he refused to work with them. Robert Duckenfield was doubtless one of the few who possessed the forwardness to inform Oliver that 'Charles Stewart hath 500 friends in these adjacent counties, for everyone friend to you amongst them, and he doubts not of finding you work enough, whilst he lives'.

Cromwell's government, conscious of its unpopularity and keen to make itself acceptable to the moderate opinion throughout England, regarded the young Sir George Booth – who was returned as MP in each parliament – as 'an important prop in local law and order'.[64] That he stood throughout and was accompanied at different times during this period by men of similar religious and political complexion, indicates the prevailing attitude among the county's gentry. Moreover, barely a month after the dissolution of the institution of the monarchy and the House of Lords in April 1653, a new list of JPs was drawn up for Cheshire, and all but two of the 33 men nominated were politically conservative and unlikely to advocate radical social change. But even though the appointment of the major generals, primarily to prevent recurrences of the Royalist rising of 1655, was disliked because it supplanted the traditional leaders of the counties with low-born military men, the commission acting under Charles Worsley in Cheshire 'possessed a distinctly and godly flavour, it also contained a reasonable representation of the traditional ruling families of the county'.[65]

---

of passion, "Oh, when will the Lord put an end to these delusions of the priests?"' (Newcome, *Autobiography*, pp.149–50).

63 *Thurloe*, III, p.294.

64 Dore, 'Cheshire Rising', p.51.

65 P.J. Pinkney, 'The Cheshire Election of 1656', *BJRL*, 49 (1967), pp.391–2, 399–402; Durston, *Major Generals*, pp.60–1.

Yet whilst the Booths of Dunham Massey and the majority of their gentry colleagues were broadly against the Interregnum regimes, a few, such as the Brookes of Norton, occupied more of a 'middle' ground, rather as they had done during the First Civil War, when Parliamentarian control of Cheshire had been split between Sir William Brereton and the 'war party', and their Presbyterian opponents. On 27 February 1655 Lieutenant Colonel John Brooke, a serving soldier and county commissioner, reported to Cromwell:

> Fear of being tedious to your highness' patience prohibits me to speak of anything that concerns my native country, Cheshire, where my relations as to the public service, interest in and alliance to most of the principal gentry therein, enables me to manifest upon your highness' command, who are most zealously affected to the present government, and for piety and prudence in the magisterial function are of singular note amongst us. I have presumed too far, and shall add no more; but blessed be the Lord, who for the love he had to these nations, hath set you over them; and grant you more and more all enlargement of heart, with spiritual graces and wisdom to go in and out before so great a people committed to your charge and government.[66]

In the meantime, however, Sir George Booth enjoyed a high reputation among both his contemporaries in Cheshire and farther afield. Even after Penruddock's rising of 1655, when his uncle, Colonel John, was again implicated, one of the principal local agents of the government, Captain John Griffith, informed Secretary Thurloe, 'Although some of those, as Sir Thomas Myddelton, Sir George Booth, etc., in some things possibly were unsatisfied, yet against the cavaliers' interest you may as safely trust them as ever, and it will not be convenient to sleight persons of eminency and interest in their country, being assured of their fidelity'.[67] That Cromwell was only too ready to accept this assurance of Booth's reliability is obvious from the latter's appointment to Major General Worsley's commission, despite its nature and the suspicion that still surrounded his uncle. Even so, Sir George commented in January 1655 that 'the major generals were Cromwell's hangmen', resulting in Colonel Charles Howard's 'sharp reply', the altercation nearly ending in a swordfight.[68] Yet if the government was still anxious to secure Booth's support, those who opposed it had already marked him down as a man whose help would be valuable, perhaps on a wider scale. On 22 September 1654 he received a missive from 'W. Adams' [Charles II], congratulating him on his election to the first Protectorate Parliament, and hoping that 'while he is obliged to attend the public service, he give his uncle and his other friends charge to have a care of the writer's concernments'.[69] What is clear from this is that Colonel John Booth was now regarded as an accredited Royalist, and that Sir George, whose broad estates gave him local power which his landless uncle lacked, was held as one whose allegiance, if it must remain secret for the time being, was much desired in the future.

---

66 *Thurloe*, III, p.179.

67 *Ibid.*, p.216.

68 Bod. Lib., MS Clarendon 53, fol. 244r.; *CCSP*, III, p.242; Durston, *Major Generals*, p.214.

69 *CCSP*, II, p.392.

In neighbouring Lancashire, the majority of the 62 Lancastrians who acted as magistrates and committeemen during the Interregnum appear to have been moderate. They were practical men, who were prepared to cooperate with the Republic. The reasons for this, however, are unclear. Although some of the county gentry may have merely sought any type of permanent political settlement, B.G. Blackwood suggests that 'Other moderates may have supported the Commonwealth and Protectorate for religious reasons, because the new regime gave them, as magistrates, the opportunity to reform the religion and morals of the people'.[70] Yet perhaps the main reason why so many Lancashire gentlemen supported the Republic was a strong fear of royalism. The county had been engrossed by a fear of papist activity both before and during the First Civil War, during which the Earl of Derby, and a significant proportion of army officers and their soldiers were Catholics.[71] The prospect of Royalist resurgences in 1648 and 1651, and the perceived menace of Quakerism in the late 1650s further added to the concerns of the Protestant gentry in particular. But in Lancashire not a single Parliamentarian gentleman appears to have joined the King's forces as they marched through the county in 1648. On 19 May the 'officers and soldiers' of the county declared, 'As for papists, popish persons, malignant abettors of former innovations, usurpations or oppressions, or any other disaffected persons which were or shall be in arms to disturb religion, righteousness and peace, we from the bottom of our hearts do detest them, and with our lives and fortunes will endeavour to oppose them'.[72]

Critically, as much as they disliked the sectaries, the Parliamentarians hated the Royalists, papists and their Scottish allies even more. To counter the invasion the Lancashire committee mobilised various 'Presbyterian' regiments of horse and foot, who under the direction of Major General Ralph Assheton fought alongside Cromwell's troops at Preston and the mopping up operations in the county afterwards.[73] During the Third Civil War, when in the name of the Commonwealth, the Army fought the two very dissimilar groups that had proclaimed Charles II – the confederate forces of the Catholic Irish and the Covenanting army of the Scots – the Presbyterian gentry of Lancashire and Cheshire were regarded with suspicion by the government because the clergy, many of whom they had appointed, were so open in their disapproval. As Charles was marching southwards through the two counties with a Covenanting army in the summer of 1651, he sent for Major General Edward Massey, the well-known Presbyterian defender of Gloucester in the 1640s and himself a Cheshire man, to go ahead of his main forces to rouse them and left the Earl of Derby in his rear to arrange an understanding between them and the Lancashire Royalists. As part of

70 B.G. Blackwood, *The Lancashire Gentry and the Great Rebellion* (Manchester: Manchester University Press, 1986), p.74.

71 J.M. Gratton, 'The Earl of Derby's Catholic Army', *THSLC*, 137 (1988), pp.25–54, (pp.30–1).

72 *Declaration of the Officers and Soldiers of the County Palatine of Lancaster* (London: 19 May 1648).

73 Ernest Broxap (ed.), *The Great Civil War in Lancashire, 1642–1651* (Manchester: Manchester University Press, 1910), pp.164–70; Stephen Bull and Mike Seed, *Bloody Preston: Battle of Preston, 1648* (Lancaster: Carnegie, 1997), pp.60–1.

the preventative measures taken by local authorities, several Presbyterian ministers were detained in Liverpool, while the erstwhile disloyal Colonel John Booth was placed under arrest with a royal commission concealed about his person, and later sent to the Tower.[74]

During their march through Cheshire towards eventual defeat at Worcester, the Scottish soldiers received little assistance from the countryside, other than some supplies of provisions. In an attempt to gain the support of the Cheshire Presbyterians, Charles issued a commission and pardon to the four leading justices – Thomas Marbury, Henry Brooke, Edward Hyde and John Crewe – who 'were allegedly ready to return to their allegiance', but in the event appeared openly in defence of the Rump.[75] Brooke, in fact, commanded one of the militia regiments from the county that participated in the subsequent Worcester campaign. According to John Secombe, in his somewhat patchy history of the Stanley family, the Earl of Derby was assured by Charles II that 'not only his own party, but that the Presbytery also would join him, in order to his Majesty's restoration in England'.[76] Derby made a passionate appeal to the gentleman of Lancashire to 'join with me in the present work where in the Glory of God His [Majesty's] personal safety and rights, the laws of our nation, our own liberties and estates are also nearly concerned'. He also called on all 'to be far from reflecting upon differences which heretofore have past betwixt us', and hoped that 'all impediments may be removed, which might in any kind hinder our unanimous and cheerful conjunction'.[77]

Despite the concerns that many in the county might rally to the royal standard, when Derby and Massey met certain Presbyterian leaders in Warrington on 16 August, three days after Charles had left Cheshire, they rebuffed them, chiefly because they would not serve with papists and their stipulation that the Earl should take the Covenant was refused. As Dore notes, 'This was to be a stumbling block in all Presbyterian-Royalist alliances until the eve of the Restoration'.[78] However, the spectre of a combined threat to the Commonwealth government remained. Following the routing of Royalist forces at Wigan Lane on 25 August 1651, the Parliamentarian victor, Colonel Robert Lilburne, warned the Speaker that the Earl of Derby:

> began to beat the drum, and raise men in all places where he came, and would have been very strong in a short time, not only through the access of many malignants, papists, and disaffected persons, but that assistance the ministers and those that are called Presbyterians afforded, and would more abundantly appeared, for they are them who are grown here more bitter and envious against you than others of the old cavalier stamp.[79]

---

74 *CSPD 1651*, pp.99, 171–2; Underdown, *Royalist Conspiracy*, p.134.

75 CRO, ZCR/63/1/30, unfol.; Dore, *Civil Wars*, p.75.

76 John Secombe, *Memoirs containing a genealogical and historical account of the ancient and honourable house of Stanley* (Liverpool: Sadler, 1741), pp.294–5.

77 Bod. Lib., MS Tanner, fol. 17r.–v.; Broxap (ed), *Lancashire*, pp.177–204.

78 Dore, *Civil Wars in Cheshire*, p.75.

79 *Two Letters from Colonel Robert Lilburne, the one to the Honourable William Lenthall, Esq., Speaker of the Parliament, the other to his Excellency the Lord General, containing the*

Perhaps as equally conspicuous as the scale of Derby's overthrow was the more general lack of support for Charles, especially from former Royalists from Lancashire and Cheshire. On 20 April 1652 the habitually suspicious sequestration commissioners for Cheshire reported:

> We cannot hear of any in this county who appeared for Charles Stuart. Most of the county declared for Parliament, and four regiments of foot and one large troop of horse, raised at the county's charge, marched to Worcester and were at the battle. The old delinquents that had compounded aided the said troops, and kept aloof from Charles Stuart.[80]

By 1655, following the Cromwellian government's defeat of further attempted Royalist rebellions, the nature of the problems encountered by the advisors, agents and supporters of the exiled Charles II had become clear. Yet such failure did not deter all Royalists, and though the Sealed Knot showed itself to be ineffective, some younger men were eager for another attempt to overthrow the Cromwellian regime. In the spring of 1658, the situation seemed to be encouraging. The prospect of military assistance from abroad, as Charles now possessed several regiments under his control in the Netherlands, had begun to emerge. For over 12 months, the Royalists' activities had been observed by Thurloe's agents, most of whom were highly critical of their appearance and conduct. On 5 May 1657 the well-informed John Somers told Thurloe from Ghent:

> The country is full of Charles Stuart's soldiers who are better versed in begging than fighting, being all ragged miserable creatures; within town they are the most importunate beggars and without, on the highway sturdy. A month ago they mustered 4,000, the Duke of York's Regiment, near 800, and the Duke of Gloucester near 600, are quartered at Berges, near Dunkirk, Ormonde's Irish Regiment, 900 is at Carri, by Bruges; the English under Lord Wilmot; at Sier between Brussels and Antwerp; the Scots 800, under Lord Newburgh at Bintzi, ten miles above Brussels. Since winter, many of Lord Cranston's Scots have come from the Swedish army, one Captain Hamilton landed at Ostend with 64 officers. And a new army is to be raised under Lord Bristol, beginning with 300 ragged Irish, who came over from St Ghislain.[81]

In the event, nothing happened. Preventative arrests broke up the Royalist organisation in England before anyone could take the field. The King had

---

particulars of the total Rout and Overthrow of the Earl of Derby, and the Forces under his command, in Lancashire, on the 25th August, 1651. By Parliament's forces under the said Colonel Robert Lilburne (London, [30 August 1651]); George Ormerod (ed.), *Tracts Relating to Military Proceedings in Lancashire during the Great Civil War* (Manchester: CS, 1844), p.301; Broxap, *Civil War in Lancashire*, pp.186–7.

80 *CCAM*, p.103.

81 *Thurloe*, V, pp.521, 533, 493. For further details of these forces, see C.H. Firth, 'Royalist and Cromwellian Armies in Flanders, 1657–1662', *TRHS*, New Sers, 17 (1903), pp.67–119; John Barratt, *'Better Begging than Fighting': The Royalist Army in Exile in the War against Cromwell 1656–1660* (Solihull: Helion & Co., 2016), pp.29–32.

been assured that the chances of success were good, but when at great risk the Duke of Ormonde crossed from Ireland to investigate he discovered that these positive reports had little grounding in reality.[82] The shortcomings of the would-be leaders of any insurrection were acute, and their plans incomplete. Ormonde discovered further difficulties when he attempted to negotiate with the Presbyterians, yet found that the Royalists had reached no accord with them, and so he had no alternative but to recommend caution and delay. Moreover, as the Cromwellian navy commanded the seas, including a blockade of Ostend, any invasion at that time by exiled Royalist forces was unviable.

82 Carte, *Letters*, II, pp.176–9; Clarendon, *Rebellion*, VI, pp.54–5.

3

Discontent, Plots and the Exiled Stuart Court

During the summer of 1659 the political and military situation in Britain much altered with the overthrow by army grandees of Richard Cromwell, Lord Protector of the Commonwealth of England, Scotland and Ireland, and the dominions thereunto belonging. With dwindling support, he had little choice but to agree to the army's demands and dissolve Parliament on 22 April. A fortnight later, under severe pressure from republican colonels and junior officers, the grandees abandoned Richard and recalled the same Rump that they had dispensed with so ignominiously six years before. To Clarendon, the fall of the Protectorate and the recall of the Rump had seemed to Royalists, 'to be the most dismal change that could happen, and to pull up all the hopes of the king by the roots'.[1] The troubled history of Richard Cromwell's seven-month rule is well known and requires no further retelling here.[2] However, with the death of his 'dear and tender father' on 3 September 1658 the army stood exposed and insecure. Days later, Lieutenant General Charles Fleetwood, who was initially supportive of his brother-in-law, wrote to Henry Cromwell, lord deputy of Ireland, 'The Lord keeps the army in a quiet condition, and have expressed a readiness to what is done, by their attendance and affection in what was required or expected from them, though I think with the saddest hearts reflecting upon what they lost, as ever army did, who have not lost a general and protector only, but a dear and tender father to them and all the Lord's people'.[3] Richard Cromwell's limited political tendencies were towards the civilian grouping of moderate

1 Clarendon, *Rebellion*, VI, p.105.

2 A.H. Woolrych, 'The Good Old Cause and the Fall of the Protectorate', *CHJ*, 13 (1957), pp.133–161; Ivan Roots, 'The tactics of the Commonwealths men in Richard Cromwell's Parliament', Donald Pennington and Keith Thomas (eds), *Puritans and Revolutionaries: Essays in Seventeenth-Century History Presented to Christopher Hill* (Oxford: Clarendon Press, 1978), pp.283–309; Barry Coward, *The Cromwellian Protectorate* (Manchester: Manchester University Press, 2002), pp.94–112; Jason Peacey, 'The Protector Humbled: Richard Cromwell and the Constitution', Patrick Little (ed.), *The Cromwellian Protectorate* (Woodbridge: Boydell, 2007), pp.32–52.

3 *Thurloe*, VII, p. 375.

Parliamentarians and former Royalists, that had supported the offer of the crown to his father in 1657.

General George Monck had previously counselled the new Protector to take an active role in the management of the Army. On 20 October 1658 Henry Cromwell wrote that the Army should be 'so governed, so that world may never hear of them, unless there be occasion to fight'.[4] In this context it is not surprising that there was much agitation within the Army. In their address to the Protector on 21 September 1658 the commanders requested that the regiments be retained under the command of godly and honest officers, while the following month further pleas were made that no officer should be removed unless convicted by court marshal, and that Fleetwood be appointed commander-in-chief with authority to commission all junior officers.[5] Cromwell made two impressive speeches to the Army's officers in October and November 1658 in which he promised that there would be no arbitrary dismissals; that no appointments would be made without consultation with senior commanders; and that Fleetwood would be commander-in-chief under him. The Army had received the assurances it had been seeking, and from November 1658 to January 1659 'things looked fair again', and the country was politically at peace. But persuasive speeches could not solve the pay arrears of the armies of the three nations, which stood at £300,000 (the financial debt owed by the regime being an estimated £2 million).[6]

But despite the reduction in the size of some regiments to save on money, and the crushing of a mutiny among the Dunkirk garrison over lack of pay, discipline remained largely respectable and the army did not take further action. By the end of March 1659, the military forces of England, Scotland and Ireland were in excess of seven, four and 14 months in arrears of pay respectively, with three months' pay allotted to the regiments in England. The General Council of the Officers framed a forceful petition to the Protector, which he received on 6 April, but Parliament failed to act on the Army's suggestions, instead bringing articles of impeachment against Major General Boteler, who was accused of mistreating a Royalist prisoner in 1655. On 14 April over 500 officers attended a General Council, where it was agreed that every officer should testify that the execution of Charles I had been just and lawful. In response, four days later the Commons voted that no more meetings of Army officers should take place without the express permission of both Cromwell and Parliament, and that all officers should swear an oath that they would not disrupt the sitting of Parliament by force.[7]

For the next three days the army grandees attempted unsuccessfully to convince Richard to dissolve Parliament. But when the London regiments formed up at St James's Palace on 21 April the outcome became clear, and the Protector had no choice but to agree to dissolve Parliament. Within a fortnight Richard was sent 'into early retirement' by the Army grandees, whose hands had been forced by the overwhelming demands of the republican colonels and

4 *Ibid*., p.454.

5 *Ibid*., p.436; *Clarke papers*, III, p.165; Reece, *Army in Cromwellian England*, p.192.

6 *CSPD 1658–9*, p.80.

7 Woolrych, 'Good Old Cause', pp.159–61.

junior officers. According to Austin Woolrych the Protectorate fell because Richard Cromwell and Parliament 'proceeded too fast and too clumsily in reducing the political role that this always-political army felt to be its due'.[8] More recently Reece suggests that had Richard possessed his father's political acumen, he would have followed his example of the previous year and:

> dissolved parliament on sight of the army's petition because of the clear evidence it contained of the growing amount of republican support in the army. Equally, if the Presbyterian and former Royalist supporters of the Protectorate in parliament had been able to put aside their hostility to the army, and address pay and indemnity, they would probably have strengthened the army grandee's position sufficiently to withstand republican agitation from the junior officers in London.[9]

The Rump Parliament. *Knavery of the Rump* (1679). (Author's collection)

Yet when the Rump was reconstituted on 7 May there was little expectation that the improbable alliance between Parliament and the military would last. Members of the Rump believed that they could hope to retain power only by a definite assertion of the supremacy of the civilian over the military power. The appointment of the seven commissioners as a check to Lieutenant General Fleetwood's authority, and Parliament's insistence that every officer should receive his commission at the hand of the Speaker in the House made the Army's leaders furious. Even so, Colonels Hacker and Lawson appeared on 8 June, and Fleetwood and Ludlow came the following day, the former receiving commissions as colonel of foot, colonel of horse, and commander-in-chief.[10] Lambert arrived to accept his commissions as colonel of regiments of horse and foot on 11 June, professing his unswerving fidelity to Parliament. In all, between June and September 1659 some 1,400 new commissions were issued.[11] But the chief weapon which the Rump hoped to employ against the Army if necessary was the militia. Although its reorganisation was placed in the hands of the Committee of Safety as early as May 1659, the bill for settling the militia was introduced on 2 July and passed on the 26th.[12] However, as the emergencies of the following months would show, the militia proved less

8 A.H. Woolrych, 'The Cromwellian Protectorate: A Military Dictatorship?', *History*, 75 (1990), pp.207–31, (p.229).

9 Reece, *Army in Cromwellian England*, p.195.

10 *CJ*, VII, pp.675–6; Ludlow, *Memoirs*, II, p.91; Whitelocke, *Memorials*, p.680.

11 *CJ*, VII, p.680; Ludlow, *Memoirs*, II, p.98.

12 *CJ*, VII, pp.649, 663; *CSPD 1658–9*, pp.343–4; *CSPD 1659–60*, pp.42–3.

Richard Cromwell Lord Protector (1626–1712). Emmet Collection, from The New York Public Library. (Public Domain)

than adequate in suppressing armed rebellions, this task proving effectively the domain of the more professional and experienced regular forces.

In the meantime, the relationship between Parliament and Army was moving towards a deepening crisis. Purges of junior officers had reduced the military significance and morale of the troops.[13] Similarly, the pay of the common soldiers had fallen greatly into arrears, whilst the civilian population of London and the rest of the country showed themselves extremely restless under the burden of heavy taxation imposed for the maintenance of the army, worsened the plight of the rank and file. Yet given this, the warring factions were drawn together temporarily by the menace of the 'common enemy' in the shape of armed risings in various parts of England. On the death of Oliver Cromwell on 3 September 1658 and the acceptance of Richard as his father's successor, Royalist exiles had been plunged into despair. Many old cavaliers, who had given so much to the Stuart cause, began to consider that further activity was not only dangerous but futile. Moreover, according to Clarendon, the fall of the Protectorate and the recall of the Rump the following summer had appeared to Royalists, 'to be the most dismal change that could happen, and to pull up all the hopes of the King by the roots'.[14]

This viewpoint was reflected by their anguish when the Rump was restored with so little opposition. On 16 May 1659 Mordaunt wrote to Hyde, relating their disappointment 'that the king cannot assure them of forces to second their attempt', and that 'opportunities are lost and dangers increased by delay'.[15] Of the nobles of great authority only two were left. The Earl of Southampton contented himself by sending periodical messages and gifts to his exiled master from the privacy of his estates, while the Marquess of Hertford excused himself from correspondence on grounds of his old age and feebleness.[16] The leaders of the party and the King's immediate advisers alike urged a policy of caution.

Yet by the summer of 1659 significant numbers of the King's supporters in parts of England and Wales had received a fresh impetuous. Many Presbyterians, including most of the secluded members of parliament, had warred against their king and though hostile to Oliver Cromwell had been almost won over by Richard, but their abhorrence of the Rump drove them to join forces with their former enemies. They were warmly welcomed by letters from the exiled King. Between early May and July Charles

13 Reece, *Army in Cromwellian England*, p.225.

14 Clarendon, *Rebellion*, VII, p.13.

15 *CCSP*, IV, p.204.

16 *Ibid.*, pp.189, 202.

cajoled a group of ex-Parliamentarian commanders, including the Earl of Manchester, Denzil Holles and Major General Richard Browne (MP for the city of London in the Third Protectorate Parliament of 1659).[17] The Royalist clergyman John Barwick reported to the King of Sir Thomas Myddelton's eagerness to serve him. Charles II's reply, dated 2 June, from Brussels, is typical of many others: 'I have never been without thoughts of him, and of the use he would toe to me, and longed very much for an opportunity of sending to him'.[18] This correspondence led to the formation of a core group in North Wales, consisting of Myddelton, his relative Richard Wynne, Sir John Owen and Lord Herbert of Chirbury, who had served the Royalist cause during the 1650s, and were enthusiastically loyal and awaiting orders for action. Critically also, Royalists and Presbyterians were ready to cooperate in Cheshire under the leadership of the Booths. Here, it seems, timing was everything. As Dore asserts:

> If the standard of revolt had been raised in Cheshire in the autumn of 1658, it is doubtful whether any but inveterate adventurers like Colonel John would have followed it and virtually certain that Sir George would have led it. But by the time the summer of 1659 had come Richard [Cromwell] had revealed that he lacked not only the ability but desire to rule and had vanished from the political scene.[19]

In addition to this, according to the faintly anti-government reports of Francesco Giavarina, Venetian Resident in England, Cromwellian officers dissatisfied with republican rule, and others anxious to see a stable government, swelled the ranks of those demanding action.[20] They condemned the indolence of their leaders and urged them to adopt more forceful measures. An immediate danger, however, was a rising by 'young people whose zeal may lead to premature attempt'.[21] Although Charles placed confidence in men who had served his father, and especially to the shrewd and vigorous Edward Hyde, many Englishmen feared the influence of the Roman Catholic group among the exiles, whose leader was the queen mother, Henrietta Maria. Though James, Duke of York avowed to be an Anglican, the papists knew better and looked confidently to him as the Joshua who would one day lead them to an England dominated by their Church. The wiser Royalist leaders wanted to see a restoration enacted only by Englishmen and were distressed at the various projects for a return of the exiles backed by foreign troops. Crucially, they were reinforced by the knowledge that Hyde shared their opinions. He disliked both papists and Presbyterians, and did not desire Charles to be placed in the debt of either France or Spain. Consequently, he progressively opposed the plans for a French marriage alliance.[22]

---

17 *Ibid.*, pp.190, 196.

18 G.F. Barwick (abr. & ed.), *The Life of Dr John Barwick, Dean of St Paul's* (London: Robinson & Co., 1903), pp.96–7, 110.

19 Dore, 'Cheshire Rising', p.58.

20 *CSPV*, pp 29–30, 35.

21 *CCSP*, IV pp.209–10.

22 Carte, *Letters*, II, pp.189–92.

John Mordaunt, 1st Viscount Mordaunt (1626–75). (Copyright of the National Portrait Gallery)

In his opposition towards an agreement with either of the great powers, Hyde had the support of John, Viscount Mordaunt, younger brother to the Earl of Peterborough. Not old enough for the First Civil War, in 1648 he joined his brother, Henry, in leading a Royalist uprising, and escaped with him to the Continent when it failed. He had returned to England by 1652, again engaged in Royalist conspiracy. Mordaunt was arrested and charged with treason in 1658, although he was acquitted. This narrow escape did not deter his clandestine labours on behalf of Charles II, but though he was trusted by the King, Ormonde and Hyde, many Royalists (including the members of the Sealed Knot) disliked and distrusted him. Charles, who created him Viscount Mordaunt on 10 July 1659, considered him the leader of his cause in England. Mordaunt's colleagues were Sir John Grenville, William Legge, Sir Thomas Peyton (a Catholic) and the Presbyterian Arthur Annesley. Yet above all others, he was trusted by the King and was regarded as a point of contact by ex-Parliamentarians eager to rekindle their allegiance to the Crown. It was Mordaunt who gave Charles a sketch of the universal situation, based on his own knowledge, and on other reports of Royalist agents' activities, and articulated the belief that there were hopes of a successful rising. Colonel Roger Whitley came from Brussels to England in late June bearing instructions from Mordaunt and military commissions from the King in Flanders for those who were to lead the rebels, although in a letter to Hyde on 2 May 1659 Mordaunt reported that he had already 'spoken with the leading men of that party, [and] Lord Willoughby, Waller, Booth, Townsend and Howe have received commissions from [the] writer'.[23]

Mordaunt's arrival and leadership were crucial as they immediately transformed the situation. Despite their constant failures the Sealed Knot complained that they were being sidelined. His vigour and independence they described as rashness and impudence. They excused their own inactivity by claiming that a fitting opportunity for an uprising had not yet presented itself.[24] The increasing dissensions among the republicans encouraged them to recommend further delay, while they made no effort to conceal their misgivings about the Presbyterians, and their dislike of Mordaunt's intention to place so much reliance upon such former enemies. Frustrated by their postponements and refusal to cooperate, Mordaunt went even further than Whitley in his condemnation of the Royalists, whom he described as sluggish and irresolute. The mindset of the Knot made Presbyterian assistance even more vital, and by reason of his family connections – his puritan mother disapproved of his Royalist activities – Mordaunt was ideally placed to

23 *Ibid.*, p.184; *CCSP*, IV, pp.235–6, 194.
24 *CCSP*, IV, pp.193, 196.

negotiate for their support. From the start the signs were only partially encouraging, yet by 21 June plans seemed to be so far advanced and promises of support so forthcoming for Colonel Titus to promise action upon the receipt of 40 hours' notice from the King.[25] Later developments exposed such estimates as overly optimistic. In the South West, Massey started to suspect John Howe (who had been expected to raise 1,000 foot) when he discovered that persons reported by him had not even been contacted, and when the latter came under the spotlight of the Council of State and he was summoned to London, all his plans collapsed.[26] The Major General's report to Charles, dated 23 June 1659, reveals his highly despondent outlook for the chances of success, in striking contrast to the more buoyant account of Titus.[27]

The situation worsened when talks designed to bring the prominent Presbyterian Colonel Popham onboard broke down. Titus serious miscalculated by considering that this indispensable officer, who had promised to raise large forces if the King landed in the west, that the business was far advanced without him. Popham thus renounced undertakings which had been made in his name, and denied that he had provided Charles with encouragement on the capture of Bristol and Gloucester.[28] Hence, when Mordaunt made his situation report on 6 June, the King and his advisors promptly detected its shortcomings.[29] Preparations do not appear to have progressed much either by 16 July, when he described to Charles, 'regretfully slow preparations for the rising. Mr Popham disturbed. Henry Cromwell's base compliance checks Sir George Booth, who apprehends enemies from Ireland.'[30] Although Mordaunt was forced to delay the date on which it was to begin, the plan was for a simultaneous rising throughout England and Wales, and commanders were appointed to raise the standard in the several shires. In terms of the organisation and conception, it was analogous to what had been envisaged in 1655, but with certain differences and noticeably more prospect of success. The chief task of raising the country had necessarily been left to the Sealed Knot, but in association with Mordaunt. A particularly promising aspect of the situation – and one of especial importance to Cheshire – was the revulsion and unease with which the Presbyterian clergy had received the recall of the Rump and its coalition with the Army. There existed a better prospect of Presbyterian assistance than there was in 1655, and in many ways, Mordaunt was well-placed to harness it. Like Whitley, the King's main contact in Cheshire, he realised that if Charles II placed too much reliance on the puritans in the county, he might become obligated too closely towards them at a later point.

Nevertheless, Mordaunt recognised that their greater freedom and resources made their support indispensable at the beginning of the uprising. There was also the chance that several high-ranking army officers would at

25 *Ibid.*, pp.242–3.

26 *Nicholas Papers*, IV, pp.114–8, 158–9.

27 *Ibid.*, pp.158–9; HMC, *Tenth Report, App. VI*, p.200.

28 *CCSP*, IV, pp.209, 238, 249–51; *Nicholas Papers*, IV, pp.97–9, 158–9.

29 *LM*, pp.31–3; *CCSP*, IV, pp.215–6, 269.

30 HMC, *Tenth Report, App. VI*, p. 215; *LM*, p.27.

King Charles II (1630–85). Theodor van Merlen. (Public Domain)

least stop short of supporting the government, and thus assist in hindering its response. Although the rising of 1659 has come to be associated with Sir George Booth, in the original scheme it was a secondary part to other events in London, the South West and the Midlands. Thus, the veteran Sir Thomas Myddelton was to raise Flintshire, and was to be supported by Lord Newport and the Shropshire gentry. Sir John Carter was made responsible for Denbighshire. Similarly, Edmund Dunch and others were to lead in Berkshire, while Colonel Popham promised to secure Bristol and Taunton.[31] Massey, Howe and others were to lead in Gloucestershire. As early as May the government, with good reason, had suspected Howe of Royalist sympathies, but he had been able to satisfy the Council of State.[32] Other Parliamentarians, such as the Earl of Stamford, Lord Willoughby of Parham and Colonel Edward Rossiter received commands in Leicester, Suffolk, and Lincolnshire respectively, while Sir William Compton and his associates decided that Hertfordshire would provide its quota of horses and troops.

The Presbyterians were numerous in East Anglia, the stronghold of the old Parliamentarian cause, and a region ever more vital because of the ports through which an army could easily be brought from Ostend. Hence, the Royalists were hopeful of securing King's Lynn, a key port of enormous strategic importance. As Mordaunt expressed to the King on 19 May 1659, if the town was to be taken, the local MP, Sir Horatio Townshend, had great confidence that he could raise Norfolk in arms.[33] Surrey and the home counties were to be commanded by Sir Francis Vincent, Sir Adam Brown, and Mordaunt himself. Promises of assistance came from Major General Egerton in Staffordshire and Colonel Richard Arundel in Cornwall, expressly if Charles II would come to England in person, whilst other leaders were reported to the King as ready to appear for him.[34] The plan also called for the seizure of ports such as Bristol, Portsmouth, Sandwich and Dover, into which the King, his brother the Duke of York and foreign aid would come. Chester was considered an addition, both because of its distance from the south of England, and the lack of a leader who was a Royalist of any importance and influence.

In Cheshire, as elsewhere, success depended upon the participation of both Royalists and Presbyterians. Yet in one fundamental respect it differed

31 HMC, *Tenth Report, App. VI*, pp.203, 255.

32 Ludlow, *Memoirs*, II, p. 87; *Nicholas Papers*, IV, pp.115–6; *CCSP*, IV, pp.190, 195, 202.

33 *CCSP*, IV, p.205.

34 *Ibid.*, p. 295; Underdown, *Royalist Conspiracy*, pp.187, 191, 232, 243.

Detail of Dunham Massey by Jan Kip and Leonard Knyff, 1697. (Author's collection)

from other local rebellions in that the details were left largely to Booth himself. The Presbyterians accepted him as their natural leader, and he would act within the county, where he was to 'be joined by the Lancashire Royalists under the Earl of Derby'.[35] There is less evidence, however, as to how the Royalists themselves were contacted and organised. Whitley had arrived in London on the eve of the rising clutching royal commissions, and most of those Royalists who participated appear on the list he had compiled the previous year to serve as officers. There must have been more detailed organisation beforehand, and although there had been some cooperation between cavalier gentlemen and Presbyterians in 1651 and 1655, and some families of both persuasions were linked by marriage and business, it is not clear whether all of the Royalists had any local connection with Sir George Booth for any period of time before the uprising began.

Booth's original commission from Charles II, dated 22 July 1659, appointed him 'commander-in-chief of all Royalist forces in Cheshire, Lancashire and North Wales, with full power and authority to order, conduct and command the same in all things according to the laws and customs of war, and therewith to fight, kill and destroy all who are, or shall be, in arms against the King'. A duplicate, issued in Brussels on 9 August, is likely to have reached Sir George during his final, hectic week of operations as the government's troops were arriving in Cheshire. A letter of indemnity from the King, written on 21 March 1670, states:

> Sir George Booth was appointed commander of the Royalist forces by a commission dated 22 July 1659, a duplicate of which remains in the hands of Sir George, dated 9 August 1659, through the troubles and imprisonment wherewith the usurped powers of those times persecuted the said Lord Delamer for his loyalty to Us. We have thought fit as well in remembrance of the early and eminent endeavours of the said Lord Delamere for our Restoration, of which We

35 Clarendon, *Rebellion*, VII, p.323; *CCSP*, IV, p.235.

> will ever retain a very particular sense, as more especially in justification of him, for what he did and acted in Order to Our happy Restoration and return ... to declare that the same was done, acted and commanded by him in virtue of Our said commission. The same do serve not only for the justification and indemnity of the said Lord Delamer's actings and doings at that time, but also that it be and remain as a mark of the particular esteem We have of the merit of his service in that so important a conjuncture.[36]

Sir George clearly came highly recommended. Mordaunt assured Charles that he was 'although a Presbyterian in opinion, yet so moral a man, if ever any of that principle were to be relied on, I think your Majesty may safely on him and his promises, which are considerable and hearty'.[37] Early in May 1659 Sir George Booth had taken a step which indicated that he had not forgotten his constitutional dispute with the Rump, nor his belief that they were no true Parliament. With a group of others, who had been ejected by Pride's Purge, he attempted to take his seat and was once more turned away by the troops. As Dore notes, 'It was a well-calculated move that advertised once again his championship of the sovereignty of Parliament and freedom from military interference'.[38] The predominance of the Booth family in Cheshire, in terms of estates and wealth, second only to the Stanley earls of Derby, and the increasing autonomy enjoyed by Sir George in particular, allowed him to send his brother and uncle as couriers unhindered to London in July 1659 to work in tandem with Mordaunt, the King and his agents in exile.

General George Monck (1608-70) Thomas Skinner, *The Life of General Monk: Duke of Albemarle* (1720).

Something of the flavour of this relationship can be gleaned from correspondence from Sir George to Mordaunt during this period. On 13 July Booth advised him that:

> This gentleman, the bearer thereof (one that looks to my affairs in my own private fortune) [his brother Nathaniel] I have had experience of his fidelity and honesty, he has something considerable to acquaint you with from me. Pray give him credit, and fear not to say to him what you have to say to me. I am still the same you expect while my power continues, as befits, Sir, your most faithful servant [unsigned] the person you did chide for not leaving my agent in London.

Two days later he added that he was:

> proceeding with the business you pleased to entrust me with that concerned the lady [the King] in this country, I have been very faithful in. My uncle [John Booth] and my brother (who with his own hands

36 JRL, EGR3/4/1/2/1–2.

37 *CCSP*, IV, p.205.

38 Dore, 'Cheshire Rising', p.60.

> presents you this) have been very serviceable to you in it. You will therefore please to take notice of it to my brother (the bearer hereof) to whom you may as safely impart anything as to myself. You will also please to encourage both my uncle and my brother, by owing their care and endeavours: it will not be lost. I know it will not be unpleasing to you to know how my little family here does. I have therefore desired my brother to wait on you, from what you may receive a perfect account of whatsoever you shall please to ask him. And by him I hope to hear your sweet lady, yourself, and all yours are well.[39]

The situation had developed significantly enough by 18 July for Sir George Booth to write again to Mordaunt:

> I hope by this time my brother is with you, and has made some recompense for my not leaving a person in London to perfect the bargain with you. For my constancy you need not doubt it, nor your friend [the King] you were with lately, I hope the bargain on your part will be performed, that I both lose and be laughed at. With these lines you will receive some propositions most necessary to the business. As for leaving my agent in London, the time was so short I could not find one to my mind, and then I thought it was better to have none. And for your friend you lately visited, whether there be anything more concerning me, then the civility, *ex post facto*, yet I am still the same; and particularly Yours very humbly.[40]

As July progressed and Mordaunt remained at odds with the Sealed Knot – their leaders arguing for a postponement for the start of the insurrection – he advocated that they must act as soon as possible because although the Rump and the army remained at variance in most things, their military preparations were coalescing against them. In this respect, Booth also hesitated when on 15 June 1659 Henry Cromwell, Oliver's fourth son and lord deputy of Ireland, unexpectedly submitted to the government. There would be no prospect of winning his successor, the republican Lieutenant General Edmund Ludlow. However, by mid July Sir George appeared satisfied that any military intervention would not be sufficient enough to defeat him in the North West if the rest of England mustered. On 15 July he assured Mordaunt of his loyalty and determination to go ahead.[41] In the event, 15 days later the Council of State instructed Ludlow to send to England 1,000 foot and 500 horse, which participated in the suppression of North Wales.[42] Evidence from later personal accounts and quarter sessions petitions reveals that by then preparations in Cheshire were well progressed, and that Presbyterian ministers, who had been preaching to their congregations, and local gentry, who had been organising and equipping their tenants did not wish to stand by and let counties more distant from Ireland to strike the first blow.

39 HMC, *Tenth Report, App. VI*, pp.214–5; *LM*, pp.26–7.

40 *LM*, p.28. Mordaunt travelled to Brussels to see Charles after 23 June; he had returned to England before 6 July (*CCSP*, IV, p.244).

41 *Thurloe*, VII, p.684; HMC, *Tenth Report, App. VI*, p.214.

42 Ludlow, *Memoirs*, II, p.110.

Thomas Jenner, *The Military Discipline* (1642), showing musket postures. (Author's collection)

As 1 August 1659 was the day fixed for the rising, news was brought that Charles himself would come to England. Yet by the time that he had summoned the turncoat Sir Richard Willis abroad on 28 July, the discouragement spread by the Knot made any chance of success increasingly unlikely. The subsequent collapse of the rebellion, however, should not hide the fact that the position of the government was extremely precarious. It is therefore possible that had Mordaunt shown himself to be less hasty, and the rising been postponed for a barely fortnight, its chances of success might have been better. Once more the Royalists suffered because of the inadequate nature of their intelligence and the isolation of their agents from each other. On 6 July Charles was requested to make further tempting proposals to General Monck, but it was not until around 5 August that a royal emissary (Monck's brother Nicholas, a clergyman) left London to negotiate with him in Scotland.[43] Monck had spent more than a fortnight weighing up all the possibilities, remaining anxious over the powers being transferred to the Army leaders, and refused to send troops to assist his rival Major General Lambert.[44]

Another Royalist envoy was dispatched to Copenhagen to meet Edward Montagu, Earl of Sandwich, admiral and general-at-sea of the fleet on the Sound. They arrived on 23 August when the rebellion was almost over. Montagu had already been approached by Hyde and promised his support should circumstances be favourable.[45] Neither Monck nor Montagu had any affection for the new government, and in the next year both men were to be chiefly responsible for the Restoration. But although they gave assurances of being ready to aid the rising of August 1659, and Montagu brought a squadron to blockade the Thames, 'having heard of the party up in Cheshire', by the time that they were able to act it had ended in failure.[46]

The pessimism and delays perpetuated by the Sealed Knot acted as the final nail in the coffin of the general risings. On 30 July they sent messengers to announce that the whole kingdom had deserted the enterprise. As the few hundreds of cavaliers who assembled in the southern and Midland counties were shattered and disbursed by units of militia horse, largely without having to rely upon the assistance of the Army, this message was accepted, seemingly with relief, by many who had only days before assured Mordaunt

43 *CCSP*, IV, pp.293–4.

44 *CSPV*, p.57; Peter Reese, *The Life of General George Monck: For King and Cromwell* (Barnsley: Pen & Sword, 2008), pp.120–1.

45 Clarendon, *Rebellion*, VII, p.157; Carte, *Letters*, II, p.186; *CCSP*, IV, pp.296–7.

46 Carte, *Letters*, II, p.202.

of their readiness. The following day – that designated as the start point for the rising – Mordaunt's own efforts in Surrey were discovered, forcing him to go to ground, and no troops arrived at southern ports because none were even threatened, let alone taken by local revolutionaries. One of the final letters the Knot penned was to Sir George Booth. It arrived on 31 July as he was meeting his advisors. Mordaunt, who had his information from Colonel Roger Whitley, who was by now with Booth, reported to the King:

> what an effect an express sent from him [the bearer, Sir William Bruce] had on Sir George Booth, your Majesty will conclude when you hear Colonel Whitley's relation, which I have often persuaded him to repeat to me, that your Majesty may be fully and truly informed of that transaction by a person who acted his part in it. On the Sunday before the engagement, some advices which came to Sir George Booth changed his humour so visibly, that from a cheerful temper he was observed to be pensive and sad; and so as if he were indifferent whether to rise publicly next morning or no; but several persons of quality assuring him of their ruin in case he desisted, he frankly determined on the attempt, and from that time carried himself very worthily in it.[47]

Confirmation that Mordaunt was recycling Whitley's reports comes from a mention in the former's letter to Charles II from Calais on 12 October 1659 of being in possession of 'a full account from Colonel Whitley of the Cheshire engagement'.[48] What the 'persons of quality' told Sir George Booth was the actual truth, for it was too late for most of them to withdraw from the enterprise without discovery. The organisation for the rising in Cheshire was well advanced – weapons, horses and ammunition had been gathered, and the gentry prepared, it seems, with the authorities remaining completely in the dark about both them and the identity of its leaders. As Booth's *Declaration* stated, 'The gentry of Cheshire, as well as those in Lancashire, carried on this design with abundance of secrecy, as well as policy, and after a considerable time spent in private listings and buying of arms, the word was given for a general rendezvous'.[49] Such unawareness on the part of the government is difficult to explain, except that, it can be assumed, the informers who revealed so much of other plans had never heard of those of Booth and his associates. Distrustful of the Knot, the Presbyterian leaders had kept their strategies from it, and were probably equally careful with others. On 5 August one Royalist agent, Dr Moore, expressed some surprise that Sir George was 'a man we never dreamt of [and that] all Lancashire and Cheshire under Colonel Ireland are with him'.[50] Similarly Martindale, the minister of Gorton, later claimed not to have known about the launch of the rebellion until some time afterwards:

---

47 *Ibid.*, pp.194–200; *LM*, pp.70–1; *CCSP*, III, pp.552–3.

48 *CCSP*, IV, p.406.

49 *A Declaration of Sir George Booth, at the General Rendezvous on Tuesday last, near the City of Chester, with the number bother Horse & Foot, their advance to the City, & the joyning of Col. Ireland with their Army. Also, the securing of the Castle, the Governor's Resolution, and the mounting of the strong Walls, Bulworks & Towers, etc.* (London: G. Horton, 1659); *CWTC*, p.167.

50 *CCSP*, IV, p.312.

> All was on wheels in these two counties by the rising of Sir George Booth and his party in the beginning of August 1659; concerning which I was much misrepresented and transduced as an enemy to it, and devoted to the interest of the fag-end of the old Parliament, called the Rump, which, after the death of Oliver Cromwell, and the setting up and deposing of his son Richard was again sat in the saddle. But the truth is had I been so affected I could easily have spoiled all of the sport, for I knew of it (though not just when it would be) a good while before, as my revered brother, Mr Henry Newcome of Manchester very well knows, and could with a post-letter have easily prevented all … But I had, long before that, often showed my dissatisfaction with that protean vagrant government by a succession of usurpers; and went so far to say, from the bottom of my heart, that if I were to be sure that the usurpers would continue my liberty (as they had hitherto done), and that a king and a free parliament would throw me out … I had not any discovery made to me by any of my neighbours (though many were engaged in it), much less invitation to come to them, till they were actually in arms; and it is usually said, ''tis a bad dog that is not worth whistling'.[51]

Even so, it had been impossible during the final week of preparations to obscure everything. Lieutenant General Ludlow, on his was to Anglesey to take ship to Ireland had been informed by an officer out of Chester, who had named Sir George Booth as the leader, and had forwarded such information to London.[52]

The first local reports of the insurrection came from army officers in Lancashire. Colonel Thomas Birch, who lived just north of Manchester, had been tipped off on 31 July 1659, apparently by Quakers, who also implicated Booth. A veteran of the conflicts in Lancashire, Birch had served as sergeant major to Colonel Ralph Assheton senior's regiment of foot. He was promoted with a colonelcy of his own regiment by Lord Fairfax in 1644, and was an active and radical member of the Lancashire county committee. Appointed governor of Liverpool in 1649 Birch had also been given command of a regiment of foot in the Lancashire militia the following year, while in 1651 he led the force that occupied the Isle of Man.[53] His account provides an important insight into the genesis of the Booth rebellion in Lancashire and Cheshire. His letter to the Speaker of 2 August is reproduced below:

> I could not safely nor sooner give you an account hereof, but being escaped hither with wearied horses, I hope this may wait on you before I can reach London. Sir, I came into the next confines of Lancashire upon Thursday night last, where by a Quaker that followed and called after me I was informed obscurely of great preparation of arms, and that Sir George Booth and some other gentlemen of Lancashire and Cheshire, who live next bordering upon the confines of both counties, were endeavouring an insurrection. At home my wife told me that the same man and some others had been the day before at my house with the same relation, expecting to have found me at home. Upon the Friday I went to

51 *Life of Adam Martindale*, pp.132–4.

52 Ludlow, *Memoirs*, II, p.104.

53 Blackwood, *Lancashire Gentry*, pp.92–6; Reece, *Army in Cromwellian England*, p.148.

> Manchester, where I was much more confirmed in the truth of it; and that night I heard of some cart loads of arms carried from Manchester to Sir George Booth's house in Cheshire; whereupon forthwith I sent my man to our county troop and another troop of the army, that were about twenty miles off, to give them notice, and the better to avoid a surprise, that they would keep moving and quarter together for their safety. Understanding, also, that very many Cheshire gentlemen were in the plot, I sent to Colonel Bradshaw, my Lord Bradshaw's brother, to give notice of it to the sheriff of that county and to Colonel Croxton, the governor of Chester Castle, to look after the safety of that city, and to desire them immediately to give the Parliament and Council of State to know, for where I was at home, surrounded with them all about me, it was not possible for me to send to you either by letter or messenger. I sent, further, to our sheriff of Lancaster, and to such gentlemen as I best listed in other parts of the county, to let them know it; but all this while it was but intended. Upon the Saturday Sir George Booth came to Manchester, where met him Colonel Ireland, Colonel Assheton, Colonel Holland and diverse other Lancaster men; and then upon the Lord's day all broke out by public directions in parish churches to call the country into arms, and where Sir George Booth had tenants in either country they were the first sent unto to come to his house at Dunham; and then followed the [others] from several parts, but especially from … of Manchester; and upon the Monday they [assembled] up at a rendezvous, and so marched away. I heard they were put upon the subscription [of an] engagement, and that declarations were ready … to be read unto them of the grounds of their [taking] up arms, and themselves give it out they will have a king, a House of Lords and of Commons (meaning Charles Stuart, who some that I discoursed with said expressly was undoubtedly their lawful sovereign). Sir, I stayed at home the longer, and to the greater hazard then discretion allowed me, that so I might give you the more certain lie of their proceedings. When I came from home yesterday at two of the clock I heard they were like to be about … or 1,500, but within this week they … I believe, 3,000 or thereabouts, which will … number both of horse and foot when … most. They take in all cavaliers … Some of them give out that Charles [Stuart and] General King, but I rather believe Major General Massey, that is amongst [them]. They tell much of the expectation they [have] of other forces out of Wales and neighbour counties, but I hear of no stirring anywhere else.[54]

The first troops raised by Booth were probably the tenants from his own estates in Cheshire and Lancashire, who were (perhaps weeks beforehand) assembled, regimented and equipped at Dunham Massey, with the 'cart loads of arms carried from Manchester to Sir George Booth's house in Cheshire'.

It would follow that his leading supporters, Henry Brooke and Henry Mainwaring, mustered and equipped both the trained bands and volunteers under their command on their estates at Norton and Kermincham respectively, while various other officers recruited men on a lesser scale. In Brooke's case, during the First Civil War his home, Norton House, had been a Parliamentarian garrison, which had resisted Royalist attacks in 1643, and was

54 Bod. Lib., MS Tanner 51, fols 108r.–v.; *Clarke Papers*, IV, pp.287–9.

Colonel Robert Venables (c. 1613-87) Townshend, L. P., 'Some Account of General Robert Venables of Antrobus and Wincham, Cheshire (with an engraving from his portrait at Wincham); together with the autobiographical memoir, or diary, of his widow, Elizabeth Venables', *CS*, 83 (Manchester, 1871), pp. 1-28.

used for the assembling, training and provisioning of soldiers throughout the conflict. Moreover, following the defeat of the Scots at Winwick in August 1648 Sergeant Major Sanderson's troop of Lilburne's regiment quartered at Norton during Henry's absence.[55] Moreover, during the summer of 1659 the militia companies of Lancashire and Cheshire made no attempt to hinder the rising's inception, and on 1 and 2 August were withdrawing into scattered garrisons. Colonel Gilbert Ireland, the governor of Liverpool, went over to Booth with the county troop of horse, to be joined by different opponents of the republic, Ralph Assheton junior of Middleton, and the sheriff of Lancashire, Sir Richard Hoghton of Hoghton[56] On 8 August President Whitelocke notified Lambert during his march northwards that 'the lieutenant of Colonel Croxton's militia troop in Cheshire, having gone over to the enemy, the Council appoints Captain John Carter ... to his place, and has given him a commission; and to George Gleave, to be quartermaster, both being highly recommended, and their knowledge of Chester county may be of use'. Similarly, Richard Deane informed Colonel Lockhart of 'the treachery of two of our county troops whom they seduced to their party', thus indicating the defection of the Lancashire militia horse as well as around half of the Cheshire troop, which ordinarily numbered 100 men, besides and officers and non-commissioned officers.[57]

Colonel Croxton, whose garrison of 200 foot and 50 horse had retreated inside Chester Castle, later complained that the local militia largely failed to stir. But quite apart from these revelations it had become virtually impossible to stop the revolt in the North West because it had already begun. The preachers sounded the alarm, providentially on the Sunday before the national revolt. As Newcome describes, the tinderbox was sparked in the collegiate church of Manchester and other religious establishments in the locality. The alleged purpose for calling out the people was that the fabricated claim that Quakers were up in arms:

> Mr Heyricke [the warden] absenting himself from the church this day (though he knew of the business as well and as soon as I), I was unwilling to have had it begun as it was. He told me he was resolved to invite the people to arms upon the score of the Quakers being up. I did know that they were very insolent and troublesome, yet was unsatisfied that the thing was true that they were up in arms, and his grounds were not sufficient to persuade a belief in me of the certainty of it, and

55 P.R. Hill and J.M. Watkinson, *Major Sanderson's War: The Diary of a Parliamentary Cavalry Officer in the English Civil War* (London: Spellmount, 2008), p.121.

56 *CSPD 1659–60*, pp.24, 145, 171.

57 *Ibid.*, pp.86–8.

> so I told him. I was as cordial for the business as any man; but I resolved I would in the best cause, if I knew it, deal with nothing but truth, and further than that would go with me, I would trust God with it, who needed not my lie.

Another minister, Mr Stockport, who had preached a sermon in Cheadle on the same day, claimed that the rising 'broke out by a public direction to call the people to arms', but added:

> after I had done the afternoon sermon, he called out for arms to purpose, and told all and more about the Quakers, and in very unwary expressions, which after were retorted on us with no small reflection. Great was the confusion among the people upon it, and I was greatly affected therewith, and thought we might now have had our last peaceable Sabbath for some time. That night all was afloat. Sir George Booth came to the town in the night, and went in the morning to Warrington, where the rendezvous was appointed on 1 August. This day the gentlemen met; and the next the town engaged and mustered 500 men in arms.[58]

The manipulation of such rumours by the Presbyterians, and even some of the more moderate Lancashire Parliamentarians, played on popular notions of members of the group, whose sometimes rowdy behaviour and opposition to oath-taking, had given them the appearance of social and religious revolutionaries.[59] It has been suggested that Quakerism was strongest in the Furness district of Lancashire, and relatively weak in the Presbyterian south-east and Catholic south-west of the county. Of greater importance, perhaps, is the social status of the main occupational groups amongst the early Quakers. Apart from the scattered group in the north, the residual and largest body of Quaker weavers was found in the linen areas of the south-west, particularly in Warrington and the surrounding villages, and townships to the north-west.[60] In December 1655 the vigorous Major General Worsley complained that in Lancashire, Cheshire and Staffordshire, 'We are much troubled with them, that are called Quakers; they trouble the markets, and get into private houses up and down in every town, and draw people after them. I have and shall take what course I can, but I could wish to have some further power or direction from you in that case'.[61] A week before Sir George Booth's rebellion in July–August 1659 the militia committees throughout the country placed into the hands of those whom Clarendon called 'persons of no degree or quality', while in Lancashire most of the schismatics or sectaries were Quakers, whose support came mainly from the lower-middle classes.[62]

Significantly, however, some Cheshire gentlemen cautiously avoided involvement in the revolt. Among them were the sheriff, Colonel John Leigh

58 *Autobiography of Henry Newcome*, p.109; Earwaker, *East Cheshire*, I, p.228.

59 Christopher Hill, *The World Turned Upside Down: Radical Ideas During the English Revolution* (London: Penguin, new edn, 1991), chap. 10; Kate Peters, 'The Quakers and the Politics of the Army in the Crisis of 1659', *P&P*, 231 (2016), pp.97–128.

60 Alan Cole, 'The Social Origins of the Early Friends', *JOFHS*, 48 (1957), pp.99–117, (pp.102, 106).

61 *Thurloe*, IV, p.333.

62 Clarendon, *Rebellion*, VI, p.176; *A&O*, II, p.1326.

Southwest prospect of the city of Chester, Nathaniel and Samuel Buck, 1728. (Author's collection)

of Norbury Booths (an experienced Parliamentarian soldier and deputy lieutenant), Colonel Robert Duckenfield, and the magistrate Thomas Stanley of Alderley. The commissioner of the peace, diarist and former sheriff, Thomas Mainwaring of Over Peover, ostensibly went into hiding.[63] After the demise of the Rump Colonel Robert Venables – who had served in Cheshire during the First Civil War under Brereton, participated in the Cromwellian conquest of Ireland, and led the expedition to the West Indies in 1655–6 – appears to have been singled out as a possible sympathiser, but although some Royalist sources later claimed that in resentment at his later treatment by Cromwell he turned towards supporting a Restoration, there is little evidence of it.[64]

On 12 May 1659 Hyde wrote to Mordaunt, 'If Sir George Booth can be sure of Venables, Chester can easily be secured', and during the months following Sir George's uprising continued to enquire about his condition.[65] Robert seems not to have supported Booth's rebellion. Barwick later contended that he 'being not in the action, watching an opportunity … to perform his duty in another place, kept himself private, and perhaps not much suspected'.[66] How true this was is unknown, because sometime later (6 April 1660) Barwick recounted to Sir Edward Hyde:

63 *Autobiography of Henry Newcome*, p. 110; *Life of Adam Martindale*, p.139; *CSPD 1659–60*, pp.84, 87–8.

64 In his 2004 *ODNB* entry for him John Morrill suggested that '[Venables] was over-promoted and under-supported in a high-profile fiasco in the Caribbean that cost him his reputation. He had to live out his life as a disgraced man with a sharp-tongued wife who disapproved of all he stood for' ('Venables, Robert (1612/13–1687)').

65 *CCSP*, IV, pp.201, 240, 614.

66 *Life of Dr John Barwick*, pp.110, 116.

> a serious discourse with Venables who has been in town these two days; as for his not engaging at Chester, he says besides his sickness, he did not agree with the way things were carried on; he gave Sir George Booth the best advice he could for laying the design, and after they had taken Chester, for attacking the Castle; when they went into the field he gave instructions in writing, but with one exception nothing was observed. He speaks very [well] of Colonel Worden which makes writer believe that Sir Thomas Myddelton spoke partly out of passion. Venables complains that he only finds in Chester Castle about 2,000 arms and 26 barrels of ammunition, whereas he expected four times as much of each. Besides being governor, he is colonel of the militia.[67]

Yet when Monck marched south in January 1660 he appointed Venables governor of Chester. Hyde sounded out loyalist gentry in Cheshire about whether it was safe to retain him, once the King returned, writing to Barwick:

> I am very glad that Colonel Venables is governor of Chester, of whose affections the king hath not the least doubt; yet I have thought to ask you a question concerning him long, whether he be of the Independent party in point of religion; which I have heard constantly averred by some who have great kindness for him; and together with that a great opinion of his parts and understanding which methinks should hardly consist with the other.[68]

Even so, on the Restoration Colonel Venables was replaced and received no royal favour from Charles II.

67 *CCSP*, IV, p.640.
68 *Ibid.*, pp.143, 152.

4

Rebellion: Strategy, Leadership and Cohesion

If Sir George Booth's rebellion was intended as one of many throughout the country, it was only in the north-west of England that such action developed into a significant military and political threat. On Sunday 1 August 1659, the day appointed for the uprising to begin, the Royalist agent Cooper brought the news that Charles II himself would come to England. Mordaunt's emissary, Colonel Roger Whitley had also recently arrived in Cheshire from the Continent bearing blank commissions and with verbal instructions from the exiled King.[1] Booth, with 'about 500 horse and foot', declared for 'a Parliament freely chosen' at Warrington. The town was important because of its bridge over the River Mersey, which dominated the London to Lancaster road, as well as much of south-west Lancashire. In 1643 Warrington had endured a ferocious siege and become a Parliamentarian garrison, whilst during the Preston and Worcester campaigns, it had witnessed the defeat of invading Scottish forces. Importantly also, though the Booth estates were centred upon Dunham Massey in Cheshire, much of the political interests of the family were at Warrington and various other places in Lancashire. Whitley handed Sir George a letter from Charles, expressing his intention of crossing to join him, but in declaring for a free parliament Booth carefully omitted the King's name, feeling that more general terms might gain more recruits. Following the Charles II's instructions, the Royalists acquiesced, although their papist associates were indignant at Booth's refusal to allow them to serve under him.[2]

The main body of the rebel army (numbering a reported 3,000 men) advanced on 1 August from Warrington and across the Mersey into Cheshire, where it continued its advance towards Chester. Thomas Davenport of Halton observed 30 horsemen passing with pistols and white breastplates, and reported that a body of cavalry seen near Bridgnorth was apparently using

1 *CCSP*, IV, pp.252, 270.

2 Clarendon, *Rebellion*, VII, pp.332–3; Thomas Carte, *A collection of original letters and papers, concerning the affairs of England, from the year 1641 to 1660, found among the Duke of Ormonde's papers*, 2 vols (London: J. and P. Knapton, 1735), II, pp.242–4.

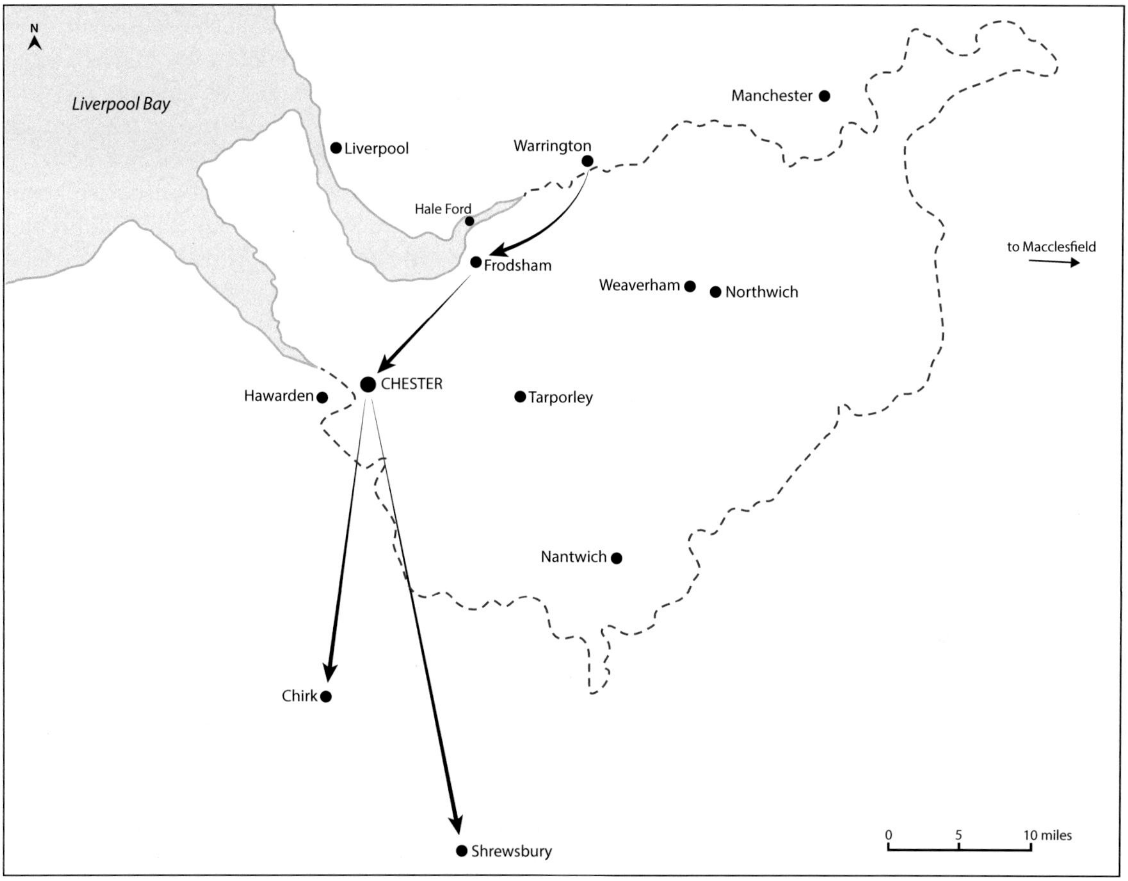

Map 1 Movements of Sir George Booth and his forces, 1-4 August 1659.

the password 'King and Parliament'. Signs that things were afoot elsewhere were indicated by the discovery of 12 cases of pistols in Wrexham by an innkeeper.[3] Baker's *Chronicle* allows some reconstruction of the movements of Sir George's troops:

> The first thing they resolved, was to march towards Chester, and the first night they marched to a place called Frodsham [an important crossing of the River Weaver, 10 miles south-west of Warrington], where they met Colonel Werden, who assured them that the gates of Chester would be opened to them. And the next day they marched thither, and took possession of the town, but the castle was defended against them by Croxton, the governor thereof for the Parliament, which had one company in it.[4]

With events swiftly unfolding, the Lancashire colonels, Thomas Birch and William West – the only other senior officers in the area other than Colonel Thomas Croxton in Chester – rifled off a series of reports, based on up-to-date military intelligence via their various mounted patrols in the locality. In his letter to the Speaker on 2 August, Birch reported that 'upon

3 *CCSP*, IV, p.306.
4 Baker, *Chronicle*, p.672.

Thursday night last' (29 July) he had requested Colonel Henry Bradshaw 'to give notice of it to the sheriff of that county [Colonel John Leigh] and to Colonel Croxton, the governor of Chester Castle, to look after the safety of that city, and to desire them immediately to give the Parliament and Council of State to know, for where I was at home'.[5] Birch, who lived just north of Manchester, had been advised, apparently by Quakers, of an uprising and named Sir George Booth as its leader. Moreover, on 30 July the Colonel had ridden cautiously into Manchester and had satisfied himself by the general atmosphere of expectation and the movement of weapons that the tip-off was precise. According to Birch, Booth's advisors in the city were the Lancashire Presbyterian officers, Ralph Assheton junior, Gilbert Ireland and Richard Holland.[6]

On 3 August Colonel Mayer, the governor of Carlisle, forwarded reports to the cautious but wary, Monck in Edinburgh, whilst assuring the General that he would 'use all means possible to secure the peace of these parts, in order to which I intend forthwith to secure most of the active and dangerous persons, and if anything of concernment happen I shall give your lordship an account of it'.[7] Enclosed with Mayer's letter was an update, probably from Colonel Birch at Manchester:

> On the last Lord's day after the latter sermon drums did immediately beat in Warrington (the only pass in London road between Lancashire and Cheshire), and a great sudden insurrection in many places of the borders of these two counties (on Monday morning) meeting at Warrington, whereas were embodied about 500 horse and foot armed, headed by the Earl of Derby, Sir George Booth, Warburton of Arley, Brooke, and other gentlemen of Cheshire and some of Lancashire, who have made them captains of men who have been in arms for Charles Stuart formerly. I being then at Wigan, eight miles distant from Warrington, where was a slender party called the county troop, and 26 horse of Colonel Saunders's regiment, and ten horse of Captain Baynes' troop of the Lord Lambert's regiment, and being desired by the Council of State to be assisting to the preservation of the peace of the county, [I] desired the officers that a party of ten might go towards Warrington to discover the truth of such intelligence received by letters intercepted at two in the morning upon the guards; and our party at Winwick, a mile [*sic* – three miles] from Warrington, met their scouts, and asking who they were for, they answered not; and to their question to ours, it was answered 'for the Commonwealth,' upon which they fired and retreated. Our scouts pursued till they discovered a troop of horse with colours advancing; which news I desire you to give an account of.

On the same day Colonel West wrote to Birch from Lancaster:

5 Bod. Lib., MS Tanner 51, fol. 108r.; *Clarke Papers*, IV, p.287. According to his testimony to the county sequestration committee shortly afterwards, William Heywood, one of the sheriffs of the city of Chester, stated that Croxton further received a letter from the county sheriff on the evening of 31 July 1659 (TNA, SP23/263, fol. 115r.).

6 Bod. Lib., MS Tanner 51, fol. 108v.

7 *Clarke Papers*, IV, p.31.

> I thank you for your care and am glad to observe Mr Mayor and your diligence to preserve the peace. The new enemy is busy raising men but come no nearer yet than Wigan with any party. I think (by what I have) they are very much short of their expectation, and their chariot begins to drive heavily. If you can by your means hasten the advance of some horse and foot or dragoons, they would hinder their increase, and secure theirs our counties, and be ready with such as shall come out of the south and Yorkshire; from both places I am sure there will shortly be sent, and they may drive them on me and you, if we have not the reputation of some force on this side of the enemy. It will concern you to have an eye on good neighbours; anything promotes at the beginning. Yesterday some good men came from York and say all is at peace there, so that I hope they will have a poor business of it, if they have not too much liberty given them.[8]

But neither the Council of State nor the local government authorities had remained immobile, partly due to the testimonies from Colonel Thomas Birch and other intelligencers. Birch and his officers were right to remain vigilant – it was later revealed by an informer, Thomas Greenhalgh of Brandlesholme, that on 6 August he had received a warrant from Colonels Assheton and Holland in Lancashire to raise 60 armed horsemen to appear at Bury two days later. He was also granted a commission from both officers to be their captain, although he 'refused to act when he heard that Parliament had declared against Sir George Booth'. Greenhalgh further admitted that he 'was misled by reports of some ministers that religion was in danger, and that the undertaking was only against Quakers'.[9] In Cheshire, meanwhile, the insurrection gathered pace. Colonel Thomas Croxton, the governor of Chester, realising that the sympathies of the preponderance of the city authorities were with Booth, had informed the mayor and aldermen of his intentions, before withdrawing into the citadel to await events. A resident of Chester reported to the later parliamentary commission:

> on the last day of July, in the morning at the mayor's house [he] was present with the mayor of the city of Chester and divers aldermen of the said city ... when Colonel Croxton, governor of the castle of Chester, did acquaint them with several letters, after that there was a rumour that there would be an insurrection in the county of Chester and other parts, wherein together that which the same thought good to acquaint him thereof, Alderman Johnson told [him] that the governor of the castle of Chester did then say that the gentlemen of the county of Chester did intend not only to possess themselves of the county of Chester, but also the city of Chester, and that Colonel Croxton offered himself to assist the citizens in the preservation of the city, or words to that effect.[10]

Thus, when called upon to surrender, the defiant Croxton reportedly answered, 'that as perfidiousness in him was detestable, so the castle which

8 *Ibid.*, p.32.

9 *CCSP*, IV, p.381.

10 TNA, SP23/263, fols 113r., 108r., 119r.; *CCC*, I, pp.751–2 ('The Council of State's proceedings of the investigation into the Insurrection of Chester, 27 September 1659').

East Gate, Chester, demolished 1766. (Author's collection)

he kept for the Parliament of England was disputable and if they would have it they must fight for it, for the best blood that ran in his veins in defence thereof should be as sluices to fill up the castle trenches'.[11]

The encouragement given towards the Cheshire rebellion by the city authorities was both significant and foreseeable. Although the Cromwellian minority on the Bench had succeeded in winning the parliamentary election of January 1659, their period of dominance, secured only by the threat of armed force during the Protectorate, was quickly diminishing. By the end of July Mayor Gerard Jones and most of the aldermen were foremost, and just waiting for a sign to proclaim themselves against the government. Localised events during the next few weeks provided them with a good opportunity to seize control of the city.[12] During the evening of 1 August Colonel John Booth entered Chester, where he met the mayor and some of the aldermen, who had decided to come over to the rebellion, and promised to receive Sir

11 *Mercurius Politicus*, 29 July–5 August 1659.

12 A.M. Johnson, 'Politics in Chester during the Civil Wars and the Interregnum', Peter Clark and Paul Slack (eds), *Crisis and Order in English Towns 1500–1700: Essays in Urban History* (London: Routledge, 1972), pp.204–36, (pp.224–5).

George the following morning. Evidence that this was the result of earlier negotiations is compelling – one of the rebel officers, Captain Daniel Bevan, was known to have entertained various aldermen at his house in the city, while William Walker, who knew John Booth from his previous Civil War service, said that he witnessed him several times the month before the insurrection 'in private discourse in the garden' with Alderman Bradshaw and the recorder, John Ratcliffe, who 'came to the house of the said colonel to speak with him in the said month'.[13]

Moreover, it had become common knowledge, perhaps as much as a week before 1 August, that Sir George Booth and his troops would be arriving in Chester and that the city authorities had agreed to assist them. Reportedly, in the early hours ('between four and five o'clock') of the following morning the captain of the city watch, Sheriff Heywood – under orders from the mayor and accompanied by two leading aldermen – met Sir George at the head of his own troop of horse in the Foregate Street, part of the eastern suburbs of the city, and duly opened the adjacent Eastgate to him. Located at the site of the primary ingress to the Roman settlement, the medieval gate (the most important entrance into Chester, and depicted in Braun's map of 1572 and Speed's schema of 1610) comprised a tall rectangular tower with octagonal corner turrets, whilst at its flanks were lower towers which also had octagonal structures. During archaeological excavations in 1972 a segment of the northern flanking turret was found to consist of cream-coloured sandstone, thus implying that it possessed a distinctive appearance. Further work in 1991 revealed the presence of three defensive ditches outside the Eastgate, an area that was devastated by the Civil War.[14] The structure, sketched by Randle Holme in the early 1640s, was demolished and replaced in 1768.[15] Shortly afterwards, the traveller Thomas Pennant remembered it as 'a lofty square tower with many apartments erected according to tradition by Edward III', while in his city guide, published in 1828, John Seacome described that:

> it consisted of a beautifully formed Gothic archway flanked by two massive octagonal embattled towers connected by a substantial building two storeys in height over the gateway the roof of which was raised to a level with and embattled in the same manner as the flanking towers to which it formed the centre. From the bearings on four shields which ornamented the front of this gate it is conjectured to have been erected during the reign of Edward III in 1270.[16]

If Baker's timescale for the movements of Sir George Booth's force from its starting point at Warrington and north-eastern parts of Cheshire on 1 August 1659 is accepted, then it seems entirely possible that the troops pushed on towards Chester the remaining 11 miles or so from Frodsham overnight,

13 TNA, SP23/263, fol. 111r.; *CCC*, I, p.751.

14 P.H. Alebon, P.J. Davey and D.J. Robinson, 'The Eastgate, Chester 1972', *JCAS*, 59 (1976), pp.37–49; Simon Ward, *Chester: A History* (Bognor Regis: Phillimore, 2009), pp.39–42.

15 BL, MS Harley 2073, fol. 22r.

16 Thomas Pennant, *A Tour in Wales*, 2 vols (London: Henry Hughes, 1778), I, p. 157; John Seacome, *The Chester Guide or, a Walk Round the Walls, and Through the City* (Chester: John Seacome, 1828), p.87.

Chester Cathedral by Thomas Wiltshire, 1847. (Author's collection)

possibly with a largely or wholly mounted force. An eyewitness reported 'there came to the said city several gentlemen and others on horseback with their swords drawn, and did so ride up and down streets, crying the town was their own'.[17] The main body, comprising most of the foot companies, may have taken up their march at first light on 2 August, and rendezvoused at Rowton Heath, later that morning. The town crier of Chester, Robert Moulson, stated later that he 'was called out of his bed by a soldier, being upon the watch to come to open the city gates … being at the Newgate then to the Eastgate, then to the Northgate, then to the Watergate, then to the bridge, [and before Moulson had opened the last gate] Sir George Booth and his confederates were entered the city and a high shout was made in the city'.[18] About eight or nine o'clock, after the most of the insurrectionaries were in, the mayor, recorder and several of the aldermen were ordered to the Pentice, where Sir George declared his reasons for taking up arms. Booth and his officers were subsequently entertained with wine and biscuit, but shortly afterwards he departed. Various witnesses stated that 'there was a friendly compliance' between Booth and the city authorities, who acquiesced to the publication of his *Declaration* at the High Cross, barely feet from the Pentice itself.

There were upwards of 500 rebel soldiers within Chester's walls by this point – the well-informed Ludlow related that 3–400 horse had entered the city with Booth – although within a short time they would be bolstered by another 200 foot of the city's trained band, and two companies under Captain Bevan and Colonel Whitely.[19] Most of these troops would remain in the city until the third week in August when they were ejected by Parliamentarian

17 TNA, SP23/263, fol. 109r.

18 TNA, SP23/263, fol. 112r.; *CCC*, I, pp.751–2.

19 Ludlow, *Memoirs*, II, p.108.

St Peter's Church and Ancient Pentice, showing nineteenth-century alterations. (Author's photo)

forces under Major General Lambert. Writing slightly optimistically to the ambassador to France on 6 August Major General Deane reported, 'Sir George Booth, Colonel Brooke, Sir Thomas Myddelton, and others of repute, and by the help of some ministers, and the treachery of two of our county troops whom they seduced to their party, they got together 1,000 horse and foot'.[20] It was further conveyed by Sheriff Heywood that 'Colonel John Booth, who was called the governor of the city and expressed the place of the governor, was observed by [himself] to be often with the mayor and aldermen of the city of Chester in conferences with them at the Pentice'.[21] This was without the endorsement of the authorities, and certainly without the approval of Colonel Croxton, who remained ensconced in the castle. Moreover, the former Royalist mayor, Randle Holme III, noted how on Sunday 7 August 1659 'Governor John Booth, with all the rebellious commanders and captains went into St Werburgh's Church, where Mr Rawson, the minister, preached for Charles, King of England'.[22]

---

20 *CSPD 1659–60*, p.88.

21 Though some of the depositions are muddled and tend to conflate timings, those of William Wright, John Witter and William Heywood are particularly relevant (TNA, SP23/263, fols 108r., 111r., 115r.–19r.; *CCC*, I, pp.751–2).

22 BL, MS Harley 1929, fol. 21r.

Significantly, it was not until after the defeat of the rebels and the occupation of Chester by the triumphant John Lambert a few weeks later, that Mayor Jones claimed to the Council of State, rather implausibly, that the insurgents 'appointed a governor of the city without our consent'.[23] As with much of the county of Cheshire, various Presbyterian ministers in the city encouraged the uprising. William Cook, curate of St Michael's, played a part in persuading the citizens to yield up the city, and he and at least one other minister prayed openly for the exiled King.[24] Cook was a staunch Royalist, but was ejected from his living in 1662. Similarly, Philip Henry, according to his own diary, 'preached the lecture at Chester soon after [the end of the rebellion], just at the time when Mr Cook, an eminent minister in Chester, and several others were carried prisoners to London for their agency in the late attempt'. His son also reported, 'He was a hearty well-wisher to the return of the King … and was much affected with the mercy of it … He was very industrious to quiet the minds of some who were uneasy at that great revolution'.[25] Such cases are compatible with Giavarina's comment of 15 August:

> The ministers or preachers of the country render the rebels great assistance, as in a very large number of parishes they have read in the pulpit, when most people were present, the declaration issued by the Presbyterians, blowing up the fire kindled and preaching nothing but war, urging that if the present parliament is not cast down the Gospel is lost; that to die for this cause is true martyrdom and so forth, which uttered by such folk cannot fail to make a great impression on the people.[26]

In response to Sir George Booth's proposal to the mayor of Chester that three companies of trained band foot should be mustered 'for the preservation of the city' – something of a paradox given the function of Colonel Croxton's garrison – Captains William Wright and John Witter were ordered to take command of their respective units, but refused to do so. They were duly arrested, although under pressure from the Assembly they agreed to muster their men a few days later.[27] Wright and Witter, with Lieutenants Richard Bridge and Thomas Fernihaugh, and Ensigns Edward Burroughs and William Street, were compelled to petition the authorities, declaring that in taking such actions, they 'had had no aim but obedience to the city'.[28] On 9 August it was decided by the mayor and his 'brethren' that a third militia company should be raised and placed under the command of

23 *Clarke Papers*, IV, p.294.

24 Scott S. Cooper, 'Extracts from the Churchwarden's Accounts and Vestry Minutes of St John's Chester', *JCAHS*, New Series, 3 (1890), pp.48–70, (p.57); Samuel Palmer (ed.), Edmund Calamy, *The Nonconformist's Memorial* (Liverpool: Button & Son, 1802), I, pp.326–30.

25 H.D. Roberts, *Matthew Henry and his Chapel, 1662–1900* (Liverpool: The Liverpool Booksellers Co., 1901), p.27.

26 *CSPV*, p.56.

27 CRO, ZA/B/2 (Chester City Assembly Book, 1 April 1656–31 October 1659), fols 124v.–25r.; TNA, SP23/263, fols 101r., 112r., 114v.–15r., 117r. See also CRO, ZA/F/37b/8 for an Attendance List, which notes the order for the raising of three companies.

28 CRO, ZA/F/37b/10.

Jonathan Ridge, the Cromwellian MP and militia commissioner, but in his own evidence to the commissioners he stated that when obliged to accept the command he 'utterly denied to accept the post', despite coercion from the city's recorder and other aldermen.[29] Sergeant Major Jolly and Lieutenant Jonathan Godson were subsequently given the command, but there is no evidence that this additional unit actually materialised. When later asked by the commissioners investigating the insurrection about the trained bands, Samuel Elcock, a loyal citizen, provided much detail about its composition and role, before adding 'That it could not be by him, observed there was any difference between the two city companies so-called, and those of the insurrection for that they watched together, provided each other were violent against the castle and governor thereof.'

Sir Thomas Myddelton (1586-1666) Thomas Pennant, *Tour of Wales* (1778).

Significantly also, he complained that:

> William Heywood and Randle Oulton, sheriffs of Chester, did quarter many soldiers before and took in the said city to the great impoverishment thereof and straightening the funds in this insolent manner (in all probability) could not have had a party in Chester had [it] not been a receptacle for them to fly into, and have free quarter in contrary to known laws of the land'.[30]

Following Sir George Booth's entry into Chester during the morning of 2 August, his main force assembled on Rowton Heath, some two miles south-east of the city and the scene of a critical defeat for the Royalist cause in 1645 during the siege of Chester. Booth was joined by Sir Thomas Myddelton, and according to Clarendon, 'all men's spirits were raised by the action of these two gentlemen'.[31] In the preamble to his *Declaration*, which he issued before his troops, Booth declared:

> the word was given for a general rendezvous, the place appointed at Rowton Heath within three miles of Chester, and the time prefixed was on Tuesday last. Which day they accordingly met, being above 3,000 horse and foot, well mounted and armed, with drums beating, colours flying and trumpets sounding. After they were all drawn up in the heath, Colonel Brooke and Colonel Ireland divided the horse and foot into several bodies, placing them in sundry warlike figures and postures. After which, they were united and brought into one entire body, where Sir George made a speech to them, showing the grounds and reasons of their

29 TNA, SP23/263, fols 113r.–15r., 116v.

30 *Ibid.*, fol. 110r.

31 Clarendon, *Rebellion*, VII, p.322.

> present engagement and undertakings, and withal (by several specious pretences) declared for a free parliament; publishing a declaration for the same end and purpose, and several invitations for all those that way affected to join with them, they holding a correspondence with those of the same party in the city of Chester, who it is said, and frequently discoursed, set upon the city gates, and gave them admittance.[32]

Both Brooke and Ireland were men of military experience, if on a local scale – during the First Civil War the former had raised a troop of horse and regiment of foot for Parliament in Cheshire, acted as acted as sheriff and deputy lieutenant, and commanded a militia regiment in 1651; Ireland on the other hand, served as captain of horse between 1644 and 1646, colonel and commissioner for the militia in Lancashire, and governor of Liverpool from 1655. Sir George Booth's *Declaration* failed to mention the King, but focused on the unrepresentative nature of the Rump, and its insincerity in blaming Oliver Cromwell for what they were doing themselves – governing through Army interference – and called for a free parliament. Booth asserted further that destabilised by the usurpation of the Rump and the ambition of the senior officers, without this freedom there could never be any settled foundation for religion, liberty and property. Moreover, rather incongruously with his grievances against heavy taxation, he offered not only arrears but increase of pay, and future promotion to 'the undeceived part of the army' – in other words, those of the government's forces who might be encouraged to desert.

As Dore suggests though, 'It is very much a document aimed at conservative opinion, both of the gentry and of the clergy', for it spoke of subjection to the 'meanest and most fanatical spirits of a nation' and again of a 'mean and schismatical party depressing the nobility and the understanding Commons'.[33] Together with his *Declaration* was published *a Letter from Sir George Booth to a Friend*, which repeated the substance of the first appeal and laid down the same objectives, although it was permeated by a class consciousness likely to attract the nobility and gentry.[34] It claimed that 'God hath made our Lot larger than our Desires in that kind; and we suppose by that blessing, put an obligation upon us, as we are considerable members of our country, to have more sober and courageous thoughts in time of extremity than other men have'. Moreover, it asserted that the newly constituted militia subjected them to 'the meanest and most fanatic spirits of the nation'. The document concluded with the promise to lay down arms if those in authority would either admit the old members to both houses of Parliament or call a new and free parliament. Despite the implications of Sir George Booth's discouraging news from the Sealed Knot on 31 July, his success up to 4

32 *A Declaration of Sir George Booth, at the General Rendezvous on Tuesday last, near the City of Chester, with the number other Horse & Foot, their advance to the City, & the joyning of Col. Ireland with their Army. Also, the securing of the Castle, the Governor's Resolution, and the mounting of the strong Walls, Bulworks & Towers, etc.* (London: G. Horton, 1659); *CWTC*, pp.164–7.

33 Dore, 'Cheshire Rising', p.63.

34 *A Letter from Sir George Booth to a Friend of his shewing the reasons of his present engagement in defence of his country's liberties, &c.* (London: 1659); *CWTC*, pp.185–7.

Southwest prospect of Shrewsbury, after Samuel Buck, 1741. (Amsterdam, Rijksmuseum. Public Domain)

August was remarkable. By the latter he had received the support of a major part of the nobility and gentry of Cheshire and Lancashire, both Presbyterian and Anglican alike, many of whom had previously been enemies.

Sir George Booth himself possessed some military capability, but he was wholly lacking in experience of independent command. His councils of war were in utter confusion and open to any gentleman who wished to attend.[35] Baker later spoke of 'everyone aspiring to command, whilst nobody obeyed, while more recently, Dore remarked, 'too many adherents of high birth accustomed to giving and not receiving orders, could be a grave disadvantage'.[36] Perhaps Booth's worst tactical mistake lay in not seizing Chester Castle, following the entry into the city of his forces. During the Civil War siege, the stronghold had been the Royalist headquarters, with a garrison commanded from 1642 by a military governor. The citadel avoided physical damage, and in 1646 was surrendered with all its arms, ordnance, and ammunition, to become the headquarters of a parliamentary garrison under a new governor. During the Interregnum it remained a supply base for parliamentary troops in Ireland.[37] In August 1659 Chester Castle was garrisoned with 200 foot and 50 horse, and adequately supplied with arms, ammunition and provisions, which might have been distributed among the rebel army. Sometime after the fall of the city to Lambert's troops on 21 August, Thomas Silvester, a soldier in Captain John Witter's militia company admitted:

> after Sir George Booth and his party entered the city of Chester, but [he] was warned by William Baguley and Richard Taylor, constables, to go to keep the watch in the said city, wherein [he] remained each night to go after, and [he] was afterwards enlisted in Captain Witter's Company, which company was also [with]

35 *CCSP*, III, p.552.

36 Baker, *Chronicle*, p. 674; Dore, 'Cheshire Rising', p.65.

37 *CSPD 1652–3*, pp.303, 474, 478; *1655*, pp.256; 1656, 186.

> Alderman Wright's company now several times upon the guard, sometimes at the Bridgegate, sometimes at the Watergate [and] sometimes at the Rood Eye, all of them against the castle.[38]

Such measures can scarcely have amounted to a serious blockade, especially as the insurgents possessed no artillery pieces. Hence, Colonel Croxton, the well-informed governor, continued to both send and receive messages during the confinement, whilst from the castle's elevated position his gunners were able to dominate the city walls – still in partial disrepair after the Civil War siege – with their cannons. According to *The Loyall Scout*, since withdrawing to Chester Castle at the outbreak of the rebellion, the loyal troops made an irritant of themselves by repeatedly 'shooting, battering down some houses and chimney tops'.[39] Moreover, desultory musket fire was exchanged with Sir George Booth's troops, while a member of the city militia, William Street, admitted whilst at the watch, 'he did about four days after the rebels had entered, in a fowling-piece did shoot at a man in a Montero cap who was in the castle of Chester, and he did his best endeavour to kill him, although he was not killed by him'.[40] As Mordaunt informed the King:

> The not attacking that, or at least not securing it so, as no intelligence could be given to or received from it, was in my opinion one of the greatest failings of the general officers; for Sir, to the castle wall is joined a house inhabited, so that from thence intelligence was daily sent into Wales, and as daily received; and it is believed though the governor refused to surrender upon the first summons, he would have easily been persuaded to it, had he not known how ill all other risings succeeded, nor how suddenly Lambert was sent against Sir George Booth; and this place being the only magazine of those parts, the neglecting it was sure a great omission, being their only want was arms and ammunition. For had they been furnished with those, they wanted not bodies of men to have fought three such armies.[41]

Problems surrounding the adequate supply of ammunition would prove to be significant later in the campaign. But given Sir George's previous military service – albeit some 15 years earlier – it seems unrealistic to think that he would not have been cognisant of the potential hazards of besieging and assaulting fortified places such as Chester Castle. The experience at the fortress of Beeston – which held for Charles I between December 1643 and November 1645 – illustrates that a motivated and adequately supplied garrison could not only resist a siege, but the besieging forces consumed staggering resources in terms of troops, materiel and time. No such luxuries were available to Booth in 1659. Additionally, during the siege of Chester the Cheshire Parliamentarian army, even with the additional support of auxiliary forces, still did not possess enough numbers for a major assault

38 TNA, SP23/263, fol. 117r.

39 *The Loyall Scout*, 2–8 August 1659.

40 TNA, SP23/263, fol. 108r.

41 Carte, *Letters*, II, p.198; *LM*, pp.70–1; *CCSP*, III, pp.552–3.

until the autumn of 1645. The operational and logistical challenges faced by Sir William Brereton's commanders in prosecuting the siege, against a large garrison behind formidable defences, were enormous. Brereton never lost sight of the intervention by a sortie from the Nantwich garrison that delivered the final blow to Sir John Byron's besieging army in January 1644. This served as a valuable reminder of engaging any relieving force at a distance, so that the besieging troops were not attacked in the rear.[42] A further point concerns the loyalty of local garrison commanders during the Booth rebellion, and their ability to perform their duties successfully. Reece points out that 'for every seasoned regular army officer who served as garrison governor ... there was a local man, whose military experience might only have been in his county during the war, who commanded a small garrison'.[43] This would be irrefutable, however, if the nature of local or regional conflict were disregarded.

Although these apparently 'non-New Model types' were of the local gentry, and in some cases men of minimal experience, others were more inured to warfare and resolute of character.[44] Thomas Croxton, of Ravenscroft, near Northwich, had been a captain of the Northwich hundred trained bands in the early 1640s, and served as sergeant major to Sir William Brereton's own regiment of foot throughout the First Civil War. He also acted as deputy lieutenant for Cheshire and governor of Nantwich (replacing Booth's grandfather, Sir George the elder in 1644) until 1647.[45] Thomas was a proficient officer, who was highly regard by his commander-in-chief. He was promoted to colonel in late 1645, and in 1651 he raised a regiment of Cheshire militia foot that fought at the Battle of Worcester. Croxton succeeded Colonel Robert Duckenfield as governor of Chester, and in February 1656 was regarded by Major General Worsley – 'the most doctrinaire and demanding of the major generals' – as 'a good an instrument for this commonwealth as any we have in this country'.[46] Similarly, the young governor of Shrewsbury, Colonel Humphrey Mackworth, performed his duties well during the Royalist insurrections of early 1655. In a letter to Thurloe, Commissary-General Reynolds reported that Mackworth 'behaved himself very discreetly and faithfully', and Shrewsbury, 'if surprized would have proved in all likelihood once more the fountain of a war'.[47] Significantly, everything indicates that during the turmoil of 1659 the governors of local garrisons, whatever their military background and however durable their local connections, maintained a primary loyalty to the government in London that had appointed them.

---

42 BL, MS Add. 11332, fol. 35v.; *BLB*, II, 790.

43 Reece, *Army in Cromwellian England*, p.155.

44 Derek Hirst, 'Local Affairs in Seventeenth-Century England', *HJ*, 32 (1989), pp.437–48, (p.443); A.H. Woolrych, 'The Cromwellian Protectorate: A Military Dictatorship?', *History*, 75 (1990), pp.207–31, (p.217).

45 BL, MS Harley 2119, fols 211v.–13r.; *CJ*, III, p. 484; *BLB*, I, p. 29; Morrill, *Cheshire*, pp.81–3, 235–6.

46 *Thurloe*, IV, pp.189, 520; Reece, *Army in Cromwellian England*, p.156.

47 *Thurloe*, III, p.265. See also Hilda Johnstone, 'Two Governors of Shrewsbury during the Great Civil War and Interregnum', *EHR*, 26 (1911), pp.267–77; Derek Hirst, 'Local Affairs in Seventeenth-Century England', *HJ*, 32 (1989), pp.437–48.

Lieutenant-General Edmund Ludlow (1617-92) C. H. Firth (ed.), *Memoirs of Edmund Ludlow* (1891).

On 4 August, within a few days of the rising in Cheshire and Lancashire, Sir George Booth sent some cavalry from its quarters in and around Chester towards Shrewsbury. Here the insurrectionaries hoped that by capturing the town they would not only be able to establish a more direct line of communication between their compatriots in Cheshire and North Wales, but the whole county of Shropshire might adhere to their cause. Their machinations failed through the timely precautions of the governor and the authorities at Shrewsbury.

The loyal officers of the garrison had met with difficulties in raising the militia, owing to the obstructive attitude of the town officials, and Mackworth did his best to dispatch a small troop of horse to chase away the rebels. He declared not to leave the town for fear that on his return he would find the gates closed against him. The following day Colonel Mackworth junior reported to the Council of State:

> The enemy has attempted a disturbance; the magistrates here would not defend the town, so the writer could not leave. The enemy, 60 in number seven miles away, escaped. Some were stayed at Shifnall and brought to the castle. They were assured that this town would rise for them; and were commanded by one of Sir Thomas Myddelton's sons; his brother, the cornet, is a prisoner; the rendezvous was near Newport's and Scriven's houses. Sir Thomas Harris came from London on Friday but rode away again. If the enemy prevailed anywhere the county would show its hostility to writer's troops. Reports from Lancashire and Cheshire. Disaffection of professed friends. Captain Bagott by beat of drum has only raised 30 men since Monday, some being strangers. The Welshpool foot post has been killed and his letters taken. Reports that Booth intends to send to writer declaring his intentions as to a free Parliament, etc. [Mackworth] has just sent a party to Oswestry.[48]

Meanwhile, Major General Egerton advanced with two troops of horse from Chester to Chirk, where on the same day, as his soldiers occupied the castle, he was met by Sir Thomas Myddelton (who had been in prior contact with Mordaunt and had risen for Charles II) indicated that he had encountered little or no opposition in raising his relatives and friends in the locality.[49] A substantial number of gentlemen from across north-east Wales, mostly former Royalist and Parliamentarian officers (the majority being Anglican in religion) had already turned out or were in the process of arming themselves in support of the uprising. Amongst the most prominent were Sir John

48 *CCSP*, IV, p.309. For Clarendon's *Rebellion*, III, p.886.

49 *CSPD 1659–60*, p.87.

Owen of Clenennau, a soldier of considerable experience, whose service to Charles I had spanned the years 1642 to 1648.

He associated himself with exiled Royalists and was induced to join the Booth rebellion by the personal appeal of James, Duke of York.[50] Myddelton's brother-in-law, Richard Wynne of Gwydir, who had been sheriff and MP for Caernarfonshire during the 1650s, also joined him. However, another leading figure, Edward Vaughan of Llwydiarth, sheriff of Denbighshire and MP for Montgomeryshire, and former Parliamentarian official, had been suspected of disloyalty since 1651 and on 3 August 1659 was 'violently seized by a company of soldiers under Captains Sontley and Manley, rudely handled, and with two servants and horses, carried prisoner to Shrewsbury'.[51] Leaving his son in charge to defend Chirk, Sir Thomas Myddelton, who had only days before assured Lieutenant General Ludlow in person 'of his resolution to continue steadfast in the interest of the Commonwealth', hastened to Wrexham with five troops of horse and a number of foot companies, where, sword in hand, he boldly proclaimed the King in the marketplace.[52] Further reports reached Parliament that the cavaliers drank toasts to the King 'on their bare knees'.[53] But Myddelton's was a premature proclamation, which caused misgivings among the local Presbyterians that an unconditional restoration was intended. According to Mordaunt:

Richard Baker, *Chronicle of the Kings of England* (1670 edn). (Author's collection)

> Most of the gentry [of North Wales were] actually engaged; they spent the first ten days in sending out good parties of horse to countenance the well-inclined, and to strengthen themselves in numbers. Sir Thomas Myddelton appeared then so considerably and so frankly in your Majesty's score, that ministers checked at it, fearing left by his persuasion the war might have been owned [won], in order only to your restoration. I believe this caused some debates, because he was permitted to visit Wales no more.[54]

50 NLW, Clenennau letters and papers, 691–2; Norman Tucker, *Royalist Major General Sir John Owen* (Conwy: Gwasg Gee, 1963); A.H. Dodd, 'Owen, Sir John (1600–1666), Royalist commander', *DWB*.

51 *CSPD 1645–7*, pp.230–1, 441, 461, 491; *CCAM*, 995–7; *Thurloe*, I, p.749; *CSPD 1659–60*, p.159.

52 Ludlow, *Memoirs*, II, p.108.

53 Bod. Lib., MS Clarendon 63, fol. 113r.; Baker, *Chronicle*, p. 668; *CSPD 1659–60*, p.104; Ludlow, *Memoirs*, II, pp.108–9.

54 Clarke, *Letters*, II, p.196.

The kind of royal proclamations made by Sir Thomas Myddelton at Wrexham caused misgivings amongst Presbyterians that an unconditional restoration was intended by the wider rebellion. The newsbook *Mercurius Politicus* (under 11 August) reported a meeting of 40 ministers in Northampton, who debated whether 'capitulations' were necessary before a restoration could occur. Many were said to have declared, 'We have been for a king, and will live and die for a king'.[55] Similarly, the clergyman Adam Martindale was of the view that some Royalists refused to stir because the leaders did not rise for king and church.[56] According to Baker's *Chronicle*, the day after Myddelton's declaration at Wrexham, Colonel Roger Whitely captured Hawarden Castle, 'which was newly left by a party of the Parliament's soldiers that marched from thence to Denbigh Castle their next garrison, but were seized by the country, and brought prisoners to Sir George Booth's party'.[57] Similarly, Mordaunt's account of recent operations in the borders of North Wales bears comparison with the situation report of the governor of Shrewsbury, to the Council of State on 4 August 1659:

> Intelligence of the entry of horse and foot into West Chester. Sir John Coppleston's troop and the 'county troop of Wales' under Captain Zankey who quartered the night before at Oswestry, were alarmed at midnight by a trumpet who pretended to come from Sir Thomas Myddelton. Chirk Castle is in the enemy's hands. Hesitates to say that Sir Thomas gave it up, though it was taken by only two troops of horse from Chester. Captain Morgan has gone for Chester. Wales is in a sad condition and this town wholly hostile.[58]

Lieutenant General Ludlow, who had recently passed through the area on his return to Ireland in the company of Colonel John Jones, provided a detailed account of military operations in North Wales during this period. Having received intelligence 'that the small garrisons of Denbigh, Beaumaris, Caernarfon and Holyhead, were undermanned, I sent over [on 6 August] 100 foot to be distributed amongst them, which small supply came so seasonably, that it not only prevented the enemy from rising in those parts, but enabled the governors to bring in provisions for the garrisons, of which they stood in great need'.[59]

The same day, Parliament received news of the attempted capture of Shrewsbury. Lancelot Lee and other members of the Shropshire Committee informed the Speaker that in obedience of the Act for settling the Militia they had gathered the previous day in the town and had agreed that one regiment of foot 600 men, and a troop of horse and a company of dragoons, besides commissioned officers, be raised and submitted a list of elected officers.[60] Whether anywhere near this many were actually recruited, equipped and paid from the county is doubtful, however. Colonel Mackworth junior, who

55 *Mercurius Politicus*, 10–17 August 1659.

56 *Life of Adam Martindale*, pp.136–7.

57 Baker, *Chronicle*, p.672.

58 *CCSP*, IV, p.309.

59 Ludlow, *Memoirs*, II, p.107.

60 Auden, 'Shropshire and the Royalist Conspiracies', p.149.

succeeded his father in early 1655, played a crucial role in securing Shrewsbury for Parliament during the rebellion of that year. His letters to Thurloe reflect his energy and skill during this period.[61] As Hilda Johnstone highlighted in 1911, the printed *Calendar of State Papers Domestic* in their indexes and entries treat Sergeant Major Edmund Waring of Humfreston near Shifnal, Mackworth junior's successor, as already holding office from 22 August 1659 onwards.[62] Although there is no doubt that Waring was in command of a militia company in Shrewsbury at this time, on 27 September Mackworth signed a receipt for the sum of £24 19s. 4d., sent to him by a warrant of 31 August, amounting to a month's pay of himself 'as governor and those under his command in the garrison, according to the establishment commencing 15 October 1655'.[63] It is entirely likely that Waring succeed as governor either towards the end of 1659 or early 1660. As early as 28 May 1659 the Council of State had issued instructions to the county committees of England and Wales, including 'Major Waring, captain in county Salop, having heard of the enemy's preparations to disturb the public peace, and especially in the Western counties, we desire you to continue your troops some time longer'.[64] This was followed on 9 July with the warning that 'the common enemy is drawing together, we desire you assemble your troops in the most convenient place in the county'.[65]

As the rebellion began to take shape in the North West and parts of the Midlands in early August, the government, though slow to act initially, began to scale up its measures for the defence of the nation. On 4 August Sir Brice Cochrane was ordered to transport three regular foot regiments from Flanders to Gravesend, whilst various officers were authorised to raise militia forces in the south-east of England. A new commission was dispatched to Colonel Thomas Croxton as governor of Chester, while Henry Bradshaw of Marple, a Presbyterian officer of considerable experience, who had desisted from joining the rebels, received a colonel's commission 'on consideration of his past fidelity and good services [to] appoint officers, and communicate with Colonel Croxton and other army officers in those parts on occasion'. Additionally, Bradshaw was issued with blank commissions for his lieutenant colonel and major, and for nine captains, lieutenants and ensigns in his regiment.[66] Bradshaw, the elder brother of John, the MP and regicide, had previously been sergeant major to Duckenfield's regiment in Sir William Brereton's forces, a sequestration commissioner for Macclesfield hundred, commanded one of the four regiments of Cheshire infantry raised in 1650, and sat at the court martial of the Earl of Derby.[67]

61 *Thurloe*, III, pp.209, 215–6, 244–5, 265; IV, pp.393–4, 413.

62 Johnstone, 'Two Governors', pp.267–77, (p.276). The mistake was repeated by H. Owen and J.B. Blakeway in *A History of Shrewsbury* (London: Harding, Lepard & Co., 1825), I, p.476, and J.E. Auden in 'Shropshire and the Royalist Conspiracies between the end of the First Civil War and the Restoration, 1648–1660', *TSANHS*, 10 (1910), pp.87–168 (pp.152–3).

63 Johnstone, 'Two Governors', p.276 (citing 'Commonwealth Papers, Exchequer, no. 117').

64 *CSPD 1658–9*, p.360; *CSPD 1659–60*, pp.152–3, 156.

65 *CSPD 1659–60*, p.139.

66 *Ibid.*, p.74.

67 Bod. Lib., MS Top Cheshire e. 3, fol. 1r.; A. Craig Gibson, 'Every-Day Life of a Country Gentleman of Cheshire in the Seventeenth Century', *THSLC*, 15 (1862–1863), pp.67–92.

On 4 August 1659 President Whitelocke informed Colonel Croxton in Chester Castle:

> On intelligence this day from Chester, though the enemy be scattered and greatly prevented in those parts, Council thinks it necessary that you execute your former order to seize and secure all suspected and dangerous persons, their horses and arms, and also to enlist and arm all the well-affected who offer to serve with you, for the safety of the city and public peace, if there be any insurrection, or preparation for it. And that nothing may be wanting that Council can contribute to your safety, you are also empowered to raise three companies of well affected volunteers from the citizens, for which they send you nine blank commissions to fill up with suitable names; they thank you for your care and desire its continuance. With note of three blank commissions for captains, lieutenants, and ensigns, for three foot companies for Chester.

To the mayor and aldermen of the city, who had sided with Sir George Booth and facilitated the admittance of his troops, Whitelocke appealed:

> Council hears that there are designs on foot to surprise and seize Chester. This time of eminent danger requires from you, and all the military officers with you, the utmost care for the preservation of the place. Council therefore desires you to assist Colonel Croxton, on occasion, and to list, arm, and employ such well-affected citizens as shall volunteer, for your better security, and also that you will keep vigilant watch at the gates and in the city, as the discharge of your trust and faithfulness to Parliament and the State requires.[68]

On the same day, Colonel Ireland – who had been made governor of Liverpool four years earlier, promising Oliver Cromwell his diligent support – declared for the King and persuaded some of the town's militia to desert their colours.[69] Yet increasingly ominously, with barely the addition of a few minor gains in North Wales, no other success outside of Cheshire was achieved by Booth's troops. On 7 August Colonel Henry Bradshaw, who had received a commission from the government as colonel of a militia regiment in Cheshire days before, wrote to Sir George Booth:

> The undeserved respect which my late father and his family have formerly had for your late renowned grandfather, and that which I have hitherto experienced from your honour, has laid such an obligation upon me and mine as will never by me be forgotten, and I am confident had you been acquainted with any [such] design of any under your command against me, I should not have had my unfinished house so rifled, and my estate so carried away, my poor wife, children and family so a frightened as they were upon Friday night last by persons calling themselves soldiers sent by Colonel Holland, as their captain alleged. Sir, I had not nor have in the least measure advised, acted or consented unto anything against you or any in your army, or that hath relation to you, was nor am privy to any plot contrivement

68 *CSPD 1659–60*, p.73.

69 *Ibid.*, pp.24, 114, 147; *CCSP*, IV, p.312; Underdown, *Royalist Conspiracy*, p.274.

> or raising of men either directly or indirectly against you or the cause you have in hand ... and being so minded therefore had and yet hope of your continued respect and protection.

Two days later, however, he advised in a somewhat darker tone:

> I have received certain intelligence of a considerable army coming from the Parliament towards our county and beseech you to give me leave to entreat you that you would seriously consider of the cause thereof of your public intentions, and actions and the consequence thereof and in time desist and submit to the all-seeing decree and providence of a merciful God ... That he alone may be your counsel, guide and governor, is the hearty prayer of, Sir your thankful humble servant. Be pleased to take notice that our county and Lancashire are the only disturbing unsettled ones.[70]

In the event, this warning was needless. By now Booth had become exceptionally downhearted, having realised (probably too late), much against his expectations that his rising was but part of a larger apparatus of rebellion, that assistance was unlikely to reach him. Colonel Edmund Temple, who had been waiting at Chester to take ship to Ireland when the rebellion began, and was detained by the insurgents (but subsequently released, thus indicating a conspicuous example of Sir George's leniency towards his opponents) later recounted that on 6 August he was asked by Booth 'if he had not heard of any rising in other parts, and having informed him that he had found all quiet on the road from London, Sir George seemed much surprised and discouraged, saying that other promises had been made to him'.[71] The following day, Booth, returned to Manchester to recruit further men. Newcome reported:

> As we were at sacrament, the Earl of Derby came in with a troop of horse; and they shot off their pistols, which did somewhat disturb us, and sufficiently affect us, with the voice of the trumpet and the noise of war. At night, after sermon, we were with Sir George Booth, who, with much sorrow told us how basely he was deserted. 500 lords and gentlemen, of the best in England, were engaged, and were all either prevented or had failed their trust; and none was up but Sir Thomas Myddelton.[72]

Sir George Booth's strategy, it seems, was to adopt a defensive posture, to prepare himself for the attack that would come, in the hope that by repelling the forces of the government, others might be encouraged to revolt elsewhere. Thus, it can be said that between this point and his decision to march his troops when suddenly confronted by Lambert's troops in Cheshire on 18 August, Booth did little to improve his army's situation. According to Petty, 'from the very first Sir George Booth showed little idea of leadership in an enterprise that demanded courageous and inspiring captaincy', and 'he quite

70 Bod. Lib., MS Top. Cheshire e. 3, fol. 23r.; Ormerod, *History*, I, p.531.

71 Ludlow, *Memoirs*, II, p.108.

72 *Autobiography of Henry Newcome*, pp.110–11.

failed to realise that a quick victory is essential to success in a rebellion'.[73] One vague and unreliable newssheet reported that a council of war at Chester determined that he should march to York (and thus capture the city) while Sir Thomas Myddelton withdrew to Wales to proliferate the rebellion there.[74] Sir George, it was said, returned only on hearing of the departure of Lambert's forces from London. However, as Petty and Davies assert, this is altogether suspect and there is no corroborating evidence that he ever set out for York, and besides, it seems unlikely that Booth's hastily raised militia men were willing to leave their homes unprotected.[75] Similarly, Myddelton's cavalry had been recently worsted by two regular troops which Sergeant major Creed had sent from Shrewsbury. On the contrary, *The Loyall Scout* for 15 August declared that 'last week' Sir George Booth was in Chester, precisely the time when he would have been on his way back from York.[76]

By the end of the first week of August 1659 the government's troops were firmly on the move against Booth and his conspirators. Major General Lambert had left the capital on 6 August with 'a considerable brigade' of over 3,000 veterans, and news soon arrived that Ludlow had sent over 1,000 foot and 500 horse under Colonel Jerome Zankey (the former preaching captain of Brereton's cavalry regiment) from Dublin to North Wales. Moreover, Colonel Robert Lilburne was approaching from York, and Birch was back in Lancashire with horse from the Midlands.[77] Newcome, the Manchester minister, who was heavily involved in the preparations for the rising, related that on 5 August, 'We were at a day of prayer and were forced to break up sadly, by an alarm that Lilburne was coming towards us with his regiment out of Yorkshire. It was wonderful mercy that put him by, for he might have come on us and spoiled us without resistance, for we had nothing in readiness for him; but the Lord turned him aside, and he came not near us'.[78] Within the next 10 days, Lambert had reached Cheshire, troops had arrived from Ireland, republican ships were blockading the Dee and all the Welsh ports remained firmly in the government's possession. Desperate attempts by Mordaunt and others to spark fresh rebellions elsewhere completely failed.

Faced with this, Sir George Booth's nerve broke, and indecisiveness would characterise his actions from this point. Thus, at Manchester he issued his third manifesto, *An Express*, a strange and mendacious document, characterised by Dore as 'a counsel of despair'.[79] Addressed to the citizens of London and all other freemen, but specifically aimed at the sectaries, Booth's appeal for a 'free parliament' justified his actions as an attempt to obtain what was rightfully his: admission to the Parliament, exemption of his property

73 Petty, 'Rebellion of Sir George Booth', pp.125, 128.

74 *The Weekly Post*, 9–16 August 1659.

75 Petty, 'Rebellion of Sir George Booth', pp.127–8; Davies, *Restoration*, p. 138.

76 *The Loyall Scout*, 15–22 August 1659.

77 Whitelocke, *Memorials*, IV, p.356; *CSPD 1659–60*, pp.78, 86–7.

78 *Autobiography of Henry Newcome*, p.110.

79 *An Express from the Knights and Gentlemen now engaged with Sir George Booth; to the City and Citizens of London, and all other Freemen of England* [London:1659]; Dore, 'Cheshire Rising', p.65; Davies, *Restoration*, pp.136–7.

Chester Castle (Thomas Pennant, *Tour of Wales* (1778).

from illegal taxation, and freedom from the rule of the 'meanest and most fanatical spirits of the nation'.

It also acknowledged that as Englishmen, of whatever station and fortune, all were possessed of the same birthright, not only fitting to nature, which afforded them 'a common and equal bond of freedom and unity', but also to laws and customs, 'general, equal and impartial to all, without respect of persons, rank, quality or degree'. Essentially, Booth was prepared to defend a position akin to the constitutional position reached in 1648, in other words, the full reinstatement of the Long Parliament and his own preferences for a restoration of the monarchy as part of a negotiated agreement. Whilst not forgetting that he had fought against the King during the First Civil War and been ejected from the Commons by Pride's Purge, Sir George must have known initially that elsewhere in England Charles II would be proclaimed unconditionally. But even though Booth was ready to work with Royalists, he was clearly dismayed when some began overtly declaring for the King. When this occurred at Warrington on 3 August, 'Sir George Booth hearing of it, said it would be their ruin; they declare only for a full and free parliament, taking of the taxes, liberty and conscience, and paying the soldiers', and he also appears to have sought to counteract the move by getting the Chester Common Hall to petition for a free parliament.[80] Still, by this time Sir Thomas Myddelton had appeared at Wrexham, and on 7 August at least who clergymen in Chester had prayed for Charles, 'to the no little joy of the people which drew tears into the eyes of many'.[81]

Precisely what Sir George Booth stood for in political terms, remains problematic. Though most historians have stated his objectives as articulated in his *Declaration* and *Letter to a Friend*, they have stopped short of

80 *Clarke Papers*, IV, pp.38, 40.
81 *CCSP*, III, p. 552; BL, MS Harley 1929, fol. 21v.

explaining how he reconciled these with his commission from Charles II.[82] Dore argues that to Booth a free parliament would be one that incorporated king and House of Lords, and that he was striving for a Presbyterian–Royalist settlement.[83] Likewise, Morrill concludes that the key issue was 'not that Charles II should be King, but how this was to be brought about. Thus, Booth and his followers were particularly anxious that there should be a negotiated settlement, particularly in matters of religion'.[84] It is obvious, however, that the government itself either misunderstood or purposely chose to misrepresent Booth's aims. President Whitelocke's letters to the Rump's supporters consistently claimed that Sir George had proclaimed Charles Stuart, which he reiterated to the Commons on 9 August and in the official declaration of Booth and his leading supporters, Egerton, Werden and Myddelton as 'rebels and traitors to this Commonwealth'.[85] That this was a calculated distortion is suggested by the evidence that many other people were conscious of Booth's position. Royalist agents were clear on the situation: on 10 August 1659 Dr William Denton wrote to Sir Richard Verney, 'the only thing that looks like countenancing Sir George is the intended petition of the city for a free parliament as they say ... I do not hear of anyone cavalier in all this affair but that it lies wholly on the presbytery, and those that fought and engaged for what they call the good old cause'. Moreover, three weeks later the French ambassador reported, 'His speeches show that there was a misunderstanding between him and the other chiefs, because he refused to proclaim the king'.[86] Similarly, it appears that some of the governmental reports exaggerated the poor level of organisation, leadership, effectiveness and motives of the rebel forces in order to delegitimise their cause.

Sir George Booth's desperate throw of the dice on 7 August was to no avail. As the authorities increasingly came to realise, the insurgents were vacillating, becoming ever more isolated and alienating an important part of the clergy. Booth was now confronted with a number of stark choices: he could assemble all his forces and attempt to defeat the highly experienced and skilful Lambert, and his veteran soldiers in the field; he could storm Chester Castle, drive out Croxton's garrison, and sit out a siege in the city by defending the walls of Chester – whose Royalist mayor had come over with the entire council as soon as the serial conspirator, Colonel John Booth had entered in his nephew's name – in the hope that either Charles II would invade; or perhaps even that Monck, the commander-in-chief in Scotland, would intervene. The latter was considering an approach for support from the King, and had framed 'a declaratory letter to the Junta at Westminster', which purported to represent not only his own, but 'the nation's dissatisfaction and the long and continuous session of parliament, and desired to fill up its ranks and establish such rules that future Commonwealth governments might be

82 See Jones, 'Booth's Rising', pp.438–9; Davies, *Restoration*, pp.135–6; Underdown, *Royalist Conspiracy*, pp.275–6; George R. Abernathy, *The English Presbyterians and the Stuart Restoration, 1648–1663* (Philadelphia: TAPS, 1965), p.31.

83 Dore, 'Cheshire Rising', pp.65–6.

84 Morrill, *Cheshire*, p.321.

85 *CJ*, VII, p.754; *Clarke Papers*, IV, p.40; *Public Intelligencer*, 8–15 August 1659.

86 *CSPD 1659–60*, p.163; HMC, *Seventh Report*, pp.482–3.

secured by frequent and successive parliaments'.[87] Probably in anticipation of any move by Monck to offer material support to the insurgents in Cheshire and the north-west, on 7 August – the same day that Sir George Booth issued his *Letter* – the Council of State appealed to the general:

> You have heard that the old cavaliers have joined with many of our secret enemies, who are most dangerous because they professed to be our friends; but by God's blessing and the activity of the militia, their designs have been frustrated, and they dispersed whenever they openly appeared, and many taken prisoners, only Sir George Booth, Sir Thomas Myddelton, and many old and new cavaliers of Cheshire, Lancashire, and North Wales are in combination about Chester; but Colonel Croxton holds Chester Castle and will, we hope, be able to keep it until Major General Lambert, who is marching to his relief with a considerable body of troops, arrives. You are to instruct your troops to the greatest vigilance over the disaffected there, who may be in correspondence with those in England. You are to recruit your horse to the number of 80 in a troop, and your foot to 800 in each regiment, if you find a sufficient number of well-affected persons to recruit them.[88]

A further alternative open to Booth was for him to retreat to the Lancashire marshlands or the Welsh hills, for which his gentlemen companions possessed no appetite. Booth's advisors recommended conciliation with Lambert (who was marching against him), while Newcome remarked that Samuel Eaton, the Independent divine, 'was willing to have gone about it, and something to that end was drawn up; but the council at Chester was not for it, and so it fell'.[89] In any case, Booth's chances of military survival were very slim. As Dore puts it, 'The experience which he and others of his officers had had in the First Civil War was now rather remote, and his force was a medley of the experienced and the raw with no time to train it and insufficiently provided with ammunition'.[90] By 15 August the King had moved to St Malo on the Brittany coast, as more convenient for a ship to Chester, and the Duke of York and the French marshal general, Henri de La Tour d'Auvergne, Viscount of Turenne were lingering at Boulogne. Clarendon wrote frantically that he was unable to believe that Booth would be left unsupported, but in nothing could resurrect the rebellion. Mordaunt attempted it and for second time was forced to go into hiding.[91]

Sir George Booth's strategy at this point is difficult to fathom, but the anguish and panic of those final days, as he moved around the county as Lambert's troops grew closer, must have been palpable. Besides, it had been reported as early as 16 July that Booth had been apprehensive about government reinforcements coming from Ireland, while on 6 August one of

87 William Webster (ed.), Thomas Skinner, *The Life of General Monk, Duke of Albemarle* (London: J. Graves, 1724), pp.98–100; Peter Reese, *The Life of General George Monck: For King and Cromwell* (Barnsley: Pen & Sword, 2008), p.120.

88 *CSPD 1659–60*, p.84.

89 *Autobiography of Henry Newcome*, p.111.

90 Dore, *Civil War in Cheshire*, p.92.

91 *CCSP*, IV, pp.325–7; *LM*, pp.35–6.

Ludlow's officers had told him in Chester that he had not seen any other rebel activity in other parts of England.[92] A letter, undated (but probably a day or two before the fight at Winnington Bridge), from his leading commanders remaining in Chester, speaks volumes about the predicament in which the rebels found themselves:

> For Sir George Booth, Sir Thomas Myddelton and the rest of the gentlemen at Tarvin, Northwich and elsewhere, these, Haste, Haste.
>
> Gentlemen. We have received your letter but are much amazed to think of your drawing off so far as Northwich leaving us here. What the real cause maybe we cannot imagine, but in the meantime it still disheartens your friends and hath occasioned already many tears in this city and we have so far considered the business that we cannot imagine your return before you have engaged, neither can there any intelligence pass betwixt you and us nor can you think other than the enemy will immediately clap betwixt you and us, and thus obstruct all passages and in case you should receive any foil your retreating place is lost and we are left to stand by ourselves … We could wish we had been made known to your intentions sooner, but this sudden result and motion relisheth not well and looks with a very bad face to all and to [Lord] Brereton, John Booth, Henry Brooke [and] Peter Brooke.[93]

92 HMC, *Tenth Report, App. VI*, p.215; *LM*, p.27; Ludlow, *Memoirs*, II, p.108.

93 Bod. Lib., MS Tanner 51, fol. 138r.

5

'... like Mahomet's angelical cocks, made up of fire and snow'

The soldiers led by Sir George Booth during the rebellion were described by some contemporary observers as hastily raised, poorly equipped and commanded by a disparate cadre of officers of various experience. To Martindale, his troops were 'raw, undisciplined men, though with some good officers mixed among them, not well formed into an army'.[1] The not so well-informed French ambassador transmitted to Cardinal Mazarin on 25 August that 'The mere appearance of the troops put Booth's party to the rout'.[2] Contrastingly, Major General John Lambert, in writing benevolently following his victory at Winnington Bridge, described the rebel horse as 'a gallant body', and reportedly diverted the pursuit from Booth's infantry, saying, 'Alas! Poor men, these are forced and hired'.[3] Modern commentators on the revolt have generally accepted the government propaganda that the soldiers led by Sir George and his officers were chiefly pushed into service, whilst providing somewhat nebulous views that they were merely the tenants of the leaders and a few volunteers who 'flocked to the colours after being roused by the ministers'.[4] Jones asserted that not all were armed, 'and some at least of the tenants were there unwillingly', but conceded that 'many had service experience, and enough officers came to put them into some kind of military order'.[5] Likewise, to Davies, Booth's soldiers were 'half-armed volunteers'.[6]

Numerous recruits followed Sir George Booth and his leading commanders, who included Presbyterians from Cheshire, as well as cavaliers from the county. Among the latter were the local noblemen,

1 *Life of Adam Martindale*, p.136.
2 *CSPD 1659–60*, p.147. Author's italics added.
3 *Life of Adam Martindale*, p.140.
4 Morrill, *Cheshire*, p.315.
5 Jones, 'Booth's Rising', p.437.
6 Davies, 'Sir George Booth's Rising', p.140.

William, Lord Brereton of Brereton and Robert Needham, Viscount Kilmorey, although there were also highly experienced soldiers of the calibre of Major Generals Robert Broughton and Randolph Egerton, as well as Colonels Werden and Whitely. The composition of such a force is not entirely obvious, but as some participants later described being raised by, and serving under, certain officers, it seems likely that the foot companies – based to an extent on the hundredal trained band units – were loosely organised into regiments. These were probably led by the colonels who brought them in, such as Henry Brooke, Thomas Leigh and Henry Mainwaring, while Roger Whitely appears to have commanded much of the horse. Men who had served in the Parliamentarian forces between 1642 and 1655, such as Henry and John Brooke of Norton, William Massey of Moss House, Henry Mainwaring of Kermincham, John Daniell of Daresbury and various other lesser men, were joined by former comrades from Lancashire in the form of Colonels Gilbert Ireland, Ralph Assheton junior and Richard Holland.

With them came numbers of former junior officers of varying levels of proficiency. Critically, all recognised Booth as their leader, even the young William Stanley, Earl of Derby, accepted a lesser position. The insurgents also included men who had previously been the most bitter of enemies, and about one third of those subsequently listed as prisoners had at some stage or another been Royalist officers. However, as events would demonstrate, the very mixed composition of the rebels was not conducive to effective command and control, as political considerations among the commanders would reduce their chances of success. A close examination of the documents relating to the rebellion indicate that although some men – particularly ex-Royalists – volunteered for service, a significant proportion of the troops were probably from the trained bands of Cheshire, and to a lesser extent, of Lancashire. In a letter to the lords lieutenant of all shires in 1626 the Privy Council described the militia as 'the sure and constant bulwark of defence'.[7] During the early modern period the geographical county of Cheshire possessed two militia forces: the 'whole' militia (comprising the trained and freehold bands) and the Chester militia companies. The city energetically upheld the privilege of organising and maintaining its own units that were completely distinct to the county force. Cheshire, and in particular, its deputy lieutenants, was at the forefront of the improvements made to the militia during the reigns of James I and Charles I, although like others, suffered from the neglect of the central government during the 1630s, which were apparent in the shortcomings of the English forces mustered for the First Bishops' War and the years leading to the Civil Wars.

Despite recent research into the military organisation, finance and administration of Civil War Cheshire, understanding the survival and nature of the trained bands remains problematical. This is not assisted by references in documents to 'trained soldiers' and 'countrymen', confusion over the

7 J.R. Dasent, *Acts of the Privy Council of England*, 1626 (London: HMSO, 1938), pp.73–4.

status of volunteer and trained band units, and problems in identifying both Royalist and Parliamentarian officers in 1642.

Membership was obligatory for 'well-affected men' – able-bodied Protestant freeholders, landowners and householders. The freehold bands were regarded as an elite reserve, who saw themselves as somewhat distinct from the county force. At Warrington on 21 October 1642 the Royalist leaders agreed that the Lancashire trained bands were to be maintained by the hundreds and the freeholders by gentlemen of the county. The 'whole' or 'county' militia remained the largest force and were expected to assemble in time of war. One specific aspect of the trained bands, however, was their general unwillingness to serve away from their home areas. In mid 1642 it was Sir William Brereton who saw in the Militia Ordinance a means to maintain local peace and order in Cheshire. The trained bands of five of the seven hundreds (Bucklow, Eddisbury, Nantwich, Northwich and Macclesfield) were mobilised, and later brought under the command of Brereton and the deputy lieutenants of the county. Although the survival and function of the 'country companies' in Brereton's army is not wholly clear, there were attempts to assemble the militia at Northwich, Stockport, Nantwich and elsewhere in 1642.

On 30 June, at the instigation of the Sir George Booth and other deputy lieutenants, the head constable of Bucklow summoned the trained band to

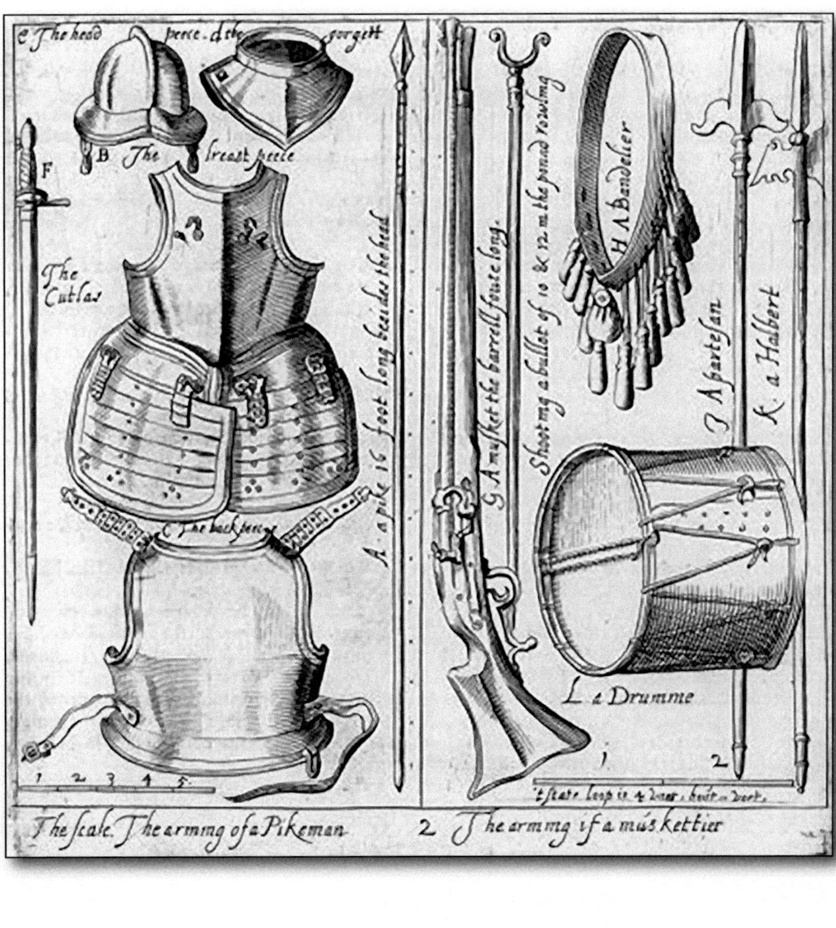

Equipment of pikemen and musketeers, Henry Hexham, *The Principles of the Art Militarie practised in the Warres of the United Netherlands* (1637). (Author's collection)

appear at Knutsford.[8] In command of the force was Captain Hugh Leigh of High Leigh. It was later reported by Parliamentarian sequestration officials:

> That the said Henry Leigh in the beginning of these distractions, being captain of the trained and freehold band with the hundred of Bucklow in the said county did call together the said trained and freehold band, and did by virtue of commission or other authority from the Commissioners of Array in the said county, exercise and lead them as captain, and afterwards, when the distractions of this county did increase, and that the honourable Sir William Brereton came down to put the militia in execution for the Parliament, the said Mr Leigh did go from his dwelling house in the country, unto the city of Chester, and was there a lieutenant colonel under the command of Colonel Marrow, a man who was a great enemy and did much damage unto this county, and formerly a commander in Ireland.[9]

A few days after the Knutsford assembly Sir William Brereton held two successful musters, probably in Macclesfield and Bucklow hundreds. He later noted that in turning out, 'they having more appearance in one hundred than the commission of array had in four and they had more volunteers three to one than the commissioners of array had'. Following a further muster at Northwich, Brereton recounted:

> So soon as we were assisted by the addition of some other deputy lieutenants to join in the other hundreds we proceeded to assemble the hundred of Northwich upon Tuesday last at Northwich, where there was a full appearance about three hundred and twenty musketeers and four score pikemen well-armed, and near six hundred other volunteers, who, thought they brought not arms so complete yet I believe their hearts as well affected as the other to the safety and peace of the King and Parliament. And though the number was not so great as in the former hundreds, which were much larger and more populous than this, wherein divers of the trained bands and some others charged with arms absented themselves by reason of their relation to the commissioners of array, that the number of those that were completely armed was double to those that are ordinarily charged with arms, besides the other 600 volunteers; so as you may be confirmed in the assurance of the good affection of many in this country if they receive encouragement and protection, and many more I am confident would discover themselves if they were not enawed by their remoteness from your assistance and exposed to more than ordinary peril in regard to the disaffected in Wales, Lancashire, Nottinghamshire, and some other neighbouring counties.[10]

The relationship between the leaders of the uprising and the officials of local Cheshire communities was vital to the mustering, payment and equipping of soldiers. Morrill maintains that a study of the quarter sessions petitions for Michaelmas 1660 (October) and Epiphany 1661 (January) arising from the events of August 1659 – relating mainly the northern and eastern townships

8 *LJ*, V, pp.200, 204.

9 TNA, SP23/183, fol. 529v.

10 HMC, *Thirteenth Report, App. I*, pp.46–7.

of Cheshire – 'reveals an unsuspected depth to the support of the movement'. He added that 'if we map those areas that we know responded to the warrants ... support came from the north and east of the county in a broad arc. That arc has the appearance of being cut from a circle centred on Manchester'.[11] Thus, in at least eight townships the constables and other inhabitants met to discuss their reaction to the warrants and call to arms from Sir George Booth's officers, although the nature of the evidence makes it impossible to determine exactly how many troops were raised by this method. Such an interpretation is challenged by Anderton, who asserts that because most of the records were:

> appeals, or petitions, to magistrates for orders to authorise the collection of levies in certain townships to pay money to individuals who claimed they were owed pay for serving as soldiers for Booth. Some petitions came directly from ex-soldiers themselves; some came from constables or ratepayers who had found sufficient cash at the time to make down payments to recruits in advance of the collection of a township rate. In both cases, the petitioners to quarter sessions had found it impossible to obtain what they said had been agreed in good faith in August 1659. In all the townships concerned, ratepayers refused to pay without at least having new orders from the Justices. Such eagerness to backtrack hardly suggests deep support for the cause of Sir George Booth.[12]

There is some merit in this, yet some of the claims of petitioners have the ring of special pleading about them, in that township officials may have been reluctant to show much acknowledgement of any support for the defeated insurrection.

Despite assertions that Sir George Booth's troops were largely forced into service, he succeeded in exploiting the traditional machinery of government to recruit troops from each township by sending warrants to local constables from named gentlemen who were known to be magistrates or militia officers. No original warrants have survived, but it would seem likely that they specified the number of men required, and had an authoritative appearance. Moreover, the township officials contributed their militia men or their substitutes in response to what appeared to be official warrants, as loyal members of the Commonwealth should have done. As Morrill suggests, 'Such a system of recruitment had many advantages, the most important being that it would help to produce men who had had some military training. But it also laid the burden of maintaining the troops in the townships'.[13] An impression of how the system operated in practice in one township comes from the testimony of the constables of Kettleshulme:

> Petition and information from the inhabitants of the township of Kettleshulme in Macclesfield hundred, that at about the beginning of August in the year 1659

11 Morrill, *Cheshire*, p.315.

12 Paul Anderton, 'The Booth Uprising in Cheshire, 1659: Another Look at Some of the Evidence', *CH*, 39 (1999–2000), pp.7–14, (p.7).

13 Morrill, *Cheshire*, p.315.

> there came a warrant, directed to the constables of Kettleshulme, commanding them to Wilmslow to find able men of the township for the use of the present service then in being, upon the receipt of the said warrant the constables did call the said inhabitants of the township together, for the most of them, who did give their consent, and agree, that all such sums of money as soldiers' laying out, and disbursed for the hiring of five to go upon that present service should be levied and gathered throughout the whole township, and for the rate of the late six months' pay. In obedience to the said warrant the constables brought to Wilmslow five able men to serve under the command of Thomas Leigh of Adlington: William Egerton, to whom John Ely paid £3 4s.; William Fletcher, to whom Thomas Stark paid £3; William Lynch, to whom Thomas Gaskell paid £2 4s.; George Scholes, to whom John Wilson paid £2 10s.; and Humphrey, to whom George Brocklehurst paid £2 10s., and 14s. to others of these soldiers for a fortnight's pay. Also several soldiers being added together is in total £22 8s. Petitioners add that the inhabitants who supported these five soldiers were from Stockport and acknowledge that many in the township are reluctant to pay their share of the cost.[14]

The proceedings by the Cheshire sequestration committee in October 1659 against Dr Peter Harrison, Presbyterian minister of Cheadle, also reveal the mechanics of the recruitment and arming of soldiers, and procurement of horses – in some cases, forcibly – by insurgent officers. In response to accusations of 'aiding and assisting and adhering to Sir George Booth and his confederates in the late rebellion and insurrection, in the time of the late rebellion', Harrison stated that he was served with a warrant by Thomas Owen, high constable of Macclesfield hundred (via one of the constables of Cheadle) on 16 August, instructing him to send an armed foot soldier to Macclesfield by 10:00 a.m. the same day. He was subsequently served with another warrant by the Cheadle constable, compelling him to send a man, horse and arms to John Bromley's house in Cheadle by 4:00 p.m., and the same night was ordered by Thomas Browne of Cheadle Hulme, another of the constables of Cheadle, to direct a man and arms to Wilmslow the following day. Harrison added that such demands were made:

> with intimation of great threats of plundering to him and others parishioners then present, in case they should fail, and also having seen another warrant, pay or order, shown to him by the said Thomas Brown, on the same Wednesday afternoon, which paper or order was signed by Colonel Nathaniel Booth, wherein it was ordered that fifteen footmen, armed, should be sent out of the said parish of Cheadle to Bowden Downs the next day, being Thursday the eighteenth day of the said month of August, in which order it was particularly expressed thus, for the parson one, and in is much as Humphrey Bulkeley of Cheadle, esquire, who was then in arms, had sent [Harrison] several messengers, with whom he refused to speak, and had by himself in language harsh enough, and by gestures, speaking, threats, required him to send in a man, horse and arms, the said Peter

14 CRO, QJF/88/4/40.

> Harrison being in a great fright for his present safety, did promise the said Mr Bulkeley to send in a horse and arms to him that night, but quickly after repented of that promise, as he manifested to some of his most considerable neighbours, to whom, before he came to his own house, he affirmed that he would do nothing, notwithstanding his promise; neither did he ever fulfil that said promise, but moved his parishioners to also stand out against him, and not to send in the horses and arms required of them by his warrant.[15]

Additionally, both constables of Cheadle Hulme (Robert Bancroft and Richard Downes) testified that 'Mr Nathaniel Booth and Mr Davenport of Widford, did threaten the country to plunder it if they did not send in their men to them [and were present] when Major Humphrey Bulkeley did demand a man and horse, and Mr Bulkeley laid his hand upon his sword and said that was his authority.' Harrison's protestations, given that he was complicit in the promotion of Sir George Booth's rebellion by means of his preaching, can be interpreted as hollow and self-serving. Ultimately he failed to convince the Parliamentary authorities. Yet if only partly true, his testimony and that of others, suggests that despite the initial mustering of a sizeable force during the period leading up to 1 August, within a fortnight or so the leaders of the uprising had resorted to threats and intimidation in their seemingly frantic attempts to raise further troops as Major General Lambert's brigade was arriving in strength in Cheshire. The township of Leighton received a warrant to provide two soldiers, fully armed; John Ingham, husbandman, enlisted under Captain Lieutenant Davis of Sir George Booth's regiment for the township of Millington; William Whitelegg of Northenden hired four soldiers for the township of Northenden under the command of Colonel Leigh of Adlington; George Hale of Lower Knutsford and Hugh Woodward of Bexon 'were hired soldiers under the command of the right honourable Sir George Booth'; Isaac Gee of Werneth and John Reed of Hattersley testified that 'forth of their fidelity and loyalty to the beloved prince and anointed sovereign in or about August 1659 did put themselves about, enlisting soldiers under the command of Colonel Thomas Leigh of Adlington, esquire, for the township of Hattersley'.

The head constable of Northwich received an order at Adlington (the home of Colonel Thomas Leigh) to raise two men 'in his Majesty's behalf'; similarly, Ralph Burgess of Adlington was charged with 'the raising of the militia in the late engagement of Sir George Booth, to serve himself or to find a soldier to serve him in the said service'.[16] In all, over 60 recruits can be identified from the quarter sessions material as being enlisted into the rebel forces from parishes and townships in the north-eastern and eastern hundreds of Macclesfield, in addition to Northwich and part of Bucklow.[17] There were clearly more –several constables reckoned to have been compelled to provide

15 TNA, SP23/263, fols 82r.–83v.; Earwaker, *East Cheshire*, I, pp.227–8.

16 CRO, QJF/88/3/21, 24–5, 28, 32; 88/4/31, 50, 56.

17 CRO, QJF/88/3/21, 24–6, 28, 32, 38–40, 43, 46–8, 68, 75; 88/4/23–4, 32–3, 49–50, 53, 55–6, 60–4.

Stefano della Bella, *Soldaat met geweer* (c. 1640). (Amsterdam, Rijksmuseum. Public Domain)

unspecified numbers of men. In obedience to their warrant the Norbury officials were 'required to send foot soldiers to serve under the command of Sir George Booth' for the township, while nearby Lower Withington provided soldiers under Colonel Leigh and paid them £6 6s. each. Likewise, the constables of Nether Alderley reported that they had been charged with finding men to serve under Leigh.[18] It remains distinctly possible that similar recruitment was achieved in other parts of Cheshire, such as Eddisbury and Nantwich hundreds, as well as western Bucklow – from which soldiers under the command of Colonels Brooke and Mainwaring in particular were drawn – but no documentary evidence has been found for this.

As well as drawing from the county militia (which except for the cavalry troop had largely forsaken government orders to muster in favour of Sir George Booth's warrants), tenants of the leaders of the rebellion – usually freeholders or their sons – were sometimes answerable by the terms of their 'leases' (contracts or indentures) for military service. However, not every soldier provided by such means was necessarily pressed. During the First Civil War several volunteer and 'country companies' were maintained from the area of the Booth family estates, and other parts of eastern Cheshire as part of the Cheshire Parliamentarian army. In 1645 the trained bands were occasionally reluctant to march to the siege of Chester and beyond their own county because of a lack of pay. On 9 November old Sir George Booth reported to Sir William Brereton from Dunham Massey his 'endeavours to advance the service' in attempting to muster Captain Alcock's soldiers at Wilmslow and Captain Grantham's men in Bowden parish, and to muster 200 of his tenants 'by covenants in their leases' under their assigned captains. A few

18 CRO, QJF/88/3/22, 28, 35–6.

days later Booth outlined to Brereton some of the difficulties in providing such men for the army in Cheshire, stating that a leaseholder of his:

> upon knowledge of my letters and warrants for the calling of Captains Walker and Weld with 200 of my tenants by covenants in their leases and others in Ashton [-under-Lyne] parish to repair unto the said siege [of Chester] and further as they should be required, publicly declared before the congregation on the Sabbath day after my directions were read by Mr Harrison that the said service was not for the king's war, and my letters and warrants were such as were never heard [before] and that he for his part would not send forth any man.[19]

The evidence relating to the August 1659 rebellion indicates that various tenants of Booth and his commanders were called to arms in support of the uprising. Thus, in Pownall in Lower Knutsford – of which Sir George was lord – some inhabitants maintained that they were ready 'to have laid their hands under the feet of him the said Sir George Booth at that time', whilst John Burgess of Styall testified 'being tenant to the right worshipful Sir George Booth in August 1659 (in promotion of the design then on foot) sent forth his eldest son and a horse to wait on Sir George Booth to be ready for what service he should be commanded'.[20] Furthermore, Thomas Greenhalgh of Brandlesholme in Lancashire, received a warrant on 6 August from Colonels Assheton and Holland to raise 60 cavalry to assemble at Bury. He was also granted a commission as captain from both officers, but 'refused to act when he heard that Parliament had declared against Sir George Booth'.[21] As for funding his troops, experience had shown Booth that any attempt to impose a general excise on the population or to claim free quarter would be both time consuming and unpopular. But local communities might be more amenable to the notion of supporting men whom they knew. Hence, an occupant of Northenden undertook to provide the four soldiers from the township 'to pay £3 10s. to every of them did at the time of their going forth pay each of them £1 15s. and furnished them with arms'. The three hired in Newton in Mottram were promised by the constables £3 10s. a man advance money and 12d. a day, while other townships (such as Aston and Pownall) pledged their soldiers six months' pay, or a lump sum of either £4 4s. or £5.In one known instance, on 7 August 1659 Colonel Henry Mainwaring issued a warrant for the imbursement of a fortnight's pay of 14s. to one of his soldiers, Matthew Miller of Hattersley, near Mottram in Longdendale.[22]

The tenants and friends of other leading insurgents certainly came in. The Earl of Derby and Sir Thomas Myddelton led their own troops of horse (the latter observed to be 60 troopers strong), and it is probable that others – including the ex-Parliamentarian colonels – raised cavalry units and foot companies from this source. Lady Eleanor, widow of Robert, second Viscount Kilmorey was later accused by the authorities of encouraging some of her

19 BL, MS Add. 11332, fols 71v., 123r.; CRO, DDX/428, fol. 88v.; *BLB*, I, 182; II, 846, 934.

20 CRO, QJB/88/3/71, 26.

21 *CCSP*, IV, p.381.

22 CRO, QJF/88/3/25, 47; 88/4/60.

Major-General John Lambert (1619-84). (Britton-Images. Public Domain)

tenants in Dutton to join the Booth rebellion. She was not arrested, although her sons were.[23] The same is possible with other former Royalists, including Thomas and Francis Cholmondeley of Vale Royal, as well as members of the gentry of north-east Wales, such as Thomas Baker of Wrexham and Myddelton's own tenant, Richard Dutton. If volunteers, tenants and militia soldiers received an initial payment upon their enlistment, in addition to a certain number of days' money (with promises of more), Booth's greatest problem was the procurement of arms and ammunition. Mordaunt later lamented that the rebels' 'only want was arms and ammunition. For had they been furnished with those, they wanted not bodies of men to have fought three such armies'.[24] Likewise, Lambert implied that many of his foes at Winnington Bridge on 19 August 1659 were poorly equipped, and evidence shows that Sir George, who seems to have been determined not to act indiscriminately against neutrals, sanctioned the appropriation of horses and weapons.[25]

It might be assumed that a certain quantity of arms was furnished by those tenants who were liable for military service (at either the expense of their own or their lord's pocket). Three early eighteenth-century surveys and rentals of the Booth family's estates in Cheshire and Lancashire show that Sir George's great-grandson, the second Earl of Warrington, could raise over 700 armed men, equipped with muskets, bills, halberds, pikes and corslets, with approximately two pieces of armament for every three tenants.[26] Though rather outdated by the 1650s, this possibly represented an issue of arms which was established in the 1620s and 1630s during the general rejuvenation of the militia. Alternatively, it might have been instigated at the time of the Monmouth Rebellion of 1685 or the Glorious Revolution of 1688, in which Henry Booth was heavily involved. Although the figure of around 700 soldiers (based on the number of arms each tenant was expected to produce) from the Booth lands alone sounds impressive, a note of caution should be sounded.

---

23 CRO, QJF/88/3/47; ZCR/63/2/129.

24 Carte, *Letters*, II, p.197; *LM*, pp.70–1; *CCSP*, III, pp.552–3.

25 *The Lord Lambert's Letter to the Right Honorable the Speaker of the Parliament, concerning the Victory which it hath pleased God to give the Forces of this Commonwealth over the Rebels under Sir George Booth in Cheshire. Read in Parliament, Monday, 22 August, to which is added a List of the Officers which are Prisoners, with the number of Soldiers and Colours taken, according to the Relation made by Captain Brown who was present in the Fight* (London: Thomas Newcombe, 1659); *CWTC*, p.170; Mahler, *The History of Chirk*, p.190.

26 JRL, EGR1/1–3; Joyce Littler, *Protector of Dunham Massey: Dunham Massey Estate in the 18th Century – A Study of the Management Carried Out by George Booth, 2nd Earl of Warrington* (Altrincham: Joyce Littler Publications, 1993), pp.79–82; G.P. Higgins, 'The militia in early Stuart Cheshire', *JCAS*, 61 (1978), pp.39–49.

During the summer of 1628 the Cheshire county militia was one of the few that mustered complete, which they did at Northwich at a cost of over £4,000. Cheshire's force of horse and foot had three days' training, either from gentlemen with overseas experience or from local men whom these 'sergeants' had coached. The trained bands were habitually chosen from sons of freeholders, being also young men of sound religion. Responsible for their attendance, pay, equipping and training, the deputy lieutenants conducted a complex plan of organisation, including marking their arms CR, and threatened to take sworn statements as to their being borrowed or not. The officials suspected that they were sometimes misled, and wished they had authority to impose stricter questioning.[27] Improvements were such, however, that by the following year calivers had been wholly replaced by 700 muskets, compared to 280 in 1613.[28] An inventory of the goods of the Cheshire Royalist, Edmund Jodrell of Yeardley, taken on 28 April 1643 contains a range of items pertaining to a gentleman, such as personal weapons, horses, saddlery and silverware.[29] But also included were equipment of a military nature, meant for the defence of the house, but which might potentially have been issued to trained bandsmen or volunteer soldiers.

These were: a stoned horse, valued at £20; a nag at £10; one musket, one head piece and bandolier, worth £1 6s. 8d.; two fowling pieces; four longbows with three sheaves of arrows; three watch bills; one set of armour; a drum; two buff coats; two riding coats; a pair of wrought hangers and a girdle, leather sword belt; two rapiers; daggers; three swords; two great saddles; four hackney saddles and horse cloths; bridles with bitts and swaffles; a saddle cloth; a powder flask for a dragoon; one pair of bullet moulds and two pistol barrels. Probably more relevant to the present study is the inventory of the weapons and armour taken at Wythenshawe Hall on 25 February 1644.[30] The owner was Robert Tatton, a pre-war captain in the Macclesfield hundred trained bands, who withstood a siege by parliamentary forces for three months in 1642–3. He was subsequently one of the defenders of Chester and Royalist sheriff of the county for 1644–5. Towards the inventory is a detailed list of weapons and military items:

Arms in the house:
The ensign.
One large drum with Mr Tatton's coat of arms and three other drums.
Two halberds.
One complete lance.
Six corselets with headpieces and swords.
Three headpieces for musketeers.

---

27 R.R. Steele (ed.), *Tudor and Stuart Proclamations 1485–1714* (Oxford: Clarendon, 1910), I, 1541; Lindsey Boynton, *The Elizabethan Militia* (London: Routledge & Kegan Paul, 1967), pp.250, 258.

28 TNA, SP14/72/94, unfol.; SP14/72/125, fols 95r., 143v.; CRO, ZCR 63/2/6, fol. 46r.

29 JRL, JOD/62c; Malbon, *Memorials*, pp.245–7.

30 JRL,TW/287; CL, CPP/5/81–2 ('A particular of the real and personal estate of Robert Tatton, Esq., discovered by himself, and so put into the Committee [for Compounding with Delinquents] at Goldsmith's Hall', dated 5 December 1646).

Twenty-two pikes.
Thirty-two muskets with bandoliers and rests.
Four long fouling pieces.
Six lesser pieces.
Two carbines and one caliver.
Four cases of pistols with holsters.
Twelve bills, pole-axes and half pikes.
A steel rack bow and a steel crossbow.
Eight longbows and two quivers of arrows of five dozen.
1 cwt of powder with match and bullets answerable.

Although some of these weapons would have been outmoded by the Civil War period, and certainly by 1659, a closer inspection of the list makes it possible to discern a clear division between the arms of the gentry and weapons for the soldiers. However, most of the arms – the muskets, pikes, drums, colour, halberds and powder – were military items, and could be distributed to the troops enlisted in Sir George Booth's cause. Although the Macclesfield trained bands were absorbed into the Cheshire Parliamentarian army in 1642, it is likely that the Royalist Robert Tatton retained such equipment at Wythenshawe. According to the 1609 *Boke of Ye Trayned Bandes* of Cheshire, the local townships of Northenden and Etchells in the parish of Stockport should have produced three corslets, two calivers and seven men. The total compliment of muskets for Macclesfield hundred was 30.[31] The broader question of why such gentlemen as Tatton, even as an officer in the trained bands, should have had ready access to its arms is relevant. He obtained weapons via his tenants. According to five leases, two wills and two inventories from the 1630s, in return for reducing the boons and services on tenements with rents above a certain amount, some tenants were to provide, at their own expense, trained-band arms, such as muskets and pikes.[32] Such tenants were to have weapons 'ready to serve our sovereign, the lord king's Majesty, his highness's heirs and successors in the time of wars and trouble so often as the said Robert Tatton, his heirs or assigns shall be appointed or commanded to serve or show his arms in anywise'. Though some of the arms at Wythenshawe were purchased by tenants at the instigation of Tatton, they were considered the tenant's property by probate assessors. He did not participate in the Booth uprising, but his sons William and Robert both served as officers, probably under Colonel Thomas Leigh of Adlington. The constable of nearby Northenden was also charged with raising four soldiers under the command of Leigh.[33]

How well-equipped Sir George Booth's soldiers were in 1659 remains unclear, although it would be unwise to imagine that they were all 'poorly armed', especially the troops of horse. Colonel Thomas Birch, having arrived back in Manchester on 29 July, reported to the Speaker:

31 JRL, TW/282.

32 JRL, TW/1071–3, 1431–2.

33 CRO, QJF/88/3/25; W.H. Shercliffe (ed.), *Wythenshawe: A History of the Townships of Northenden, Northen Etchells and Baguley* (Didsbury: E.J. Morten, 1974), pp.116–7.

> I came into the next confines of Lancashire upon Thursday night last, where by a Quaker that followed and called after me I was informed obscurely of great preparation of arms, and that Sir George Booth and some other gentlemen of Lancashire and Cheshire, who live next bordering upon the confines of both counties, were endeavouring an insurrection. At home my wife told me that the same man and some others had been the day before at my house with the same relation, expecting to have found me at home. Upon the Friday I went to Manchester, where I was much more confirmed in the truth of it; and that night I heard of some cart loads of arms carried from Manchester to Sir George Booth's house in Cheshire.[34]

This information reveals further that a nucleus of Booth's force of horse and foot – probably chiefly his own tenants and volunteers – had been mustered well armed at Dunham Massey for some time. Newcome's comment, that at the rendezvous at Warrington three days later, 'the gentlemen met; and the next the town engaged and mustered 500 men in arms', confirms this. Similarly, a more detailed report (probably also from Birch) mentions:

> On the last Lord's day after the latter sermon drums did immediately beat in Warrington (the only pass in London road between Lancashire and Cheshire), and a great sudden insurrection in many places of the borders of these two counties (on Monday morning) meeting at Warrington, whereas were embodied about 500 horse and foot armed, headed by the Earl of Derby, Sir George Booth, Warburton of Arley, Brooke, and other gentlemen of Cheshire and some of Lancashire, who have made them captains of men who have been in arms for Charles Stuart formerly.[35]

It appears that the warrants issued by Booth and his officers – though legally dubious – had some basis in, or intentionally aped pre-existing methods of obtaining money and equipment, and hence provide a sense of how the rebel troops were supplied. Although during the First Civil War the Parliamentarian army in Cheshire under Sir William Brereton received much of its resources from London, the local sequestration committee authorised a system of fixed contributions by the constables of several townships towards the payment and outfitting of the Parliamentarian army in the county.

Accordingly, Church Lawton in Nantwich hundred was responsible for maintaining two soldiers at 1s. a week, while in late 1642 they paid 15s. 8d. 'for a sword and belt, and bandolier for one or two trained-band soldiers'.[36] Likewise, the constables of Hollingworth kitted out a dragoon, except for his musket. This included a horse, costing £5, and 'a saddle, bridal, stirrups, boots, spurs, sword, girdle and other furniture for a rider to the said horse', at a further cost of £4. Moreover, the institution of short-term loans and direct taxation levied on the local population by Parliamentarian forces expedited the flow of warlike material. In early 1643 Hugh Leigh contributed of a horse

34 MS Tanner 51, fols 108r.–v.; *Clarke Papers*, IV, pp.287–8.

35 *Autobiography of Henry Newcome*, p. 109; *Clarke Papers*, IV, p.31.

36 BL, MS Harley 1943, fols 2r., 3r., 6r., 8r.

worth £8 10s. to Colonel George Booth's troop, while in the year following the sequestrators of Northwich hundred paid £14 for maintaining seven horses and arms. Likewise, the constables of Lymm accounted for '26 horses [taken] by Colonel George Booth out of the township for his troop, worth £48'.[37] Also, the following year the constables of Mere in Bucklow hundred disbursed to Colonel Henry Brooke 'towards a horse, arms and rider', while the same amount was paid for a horse and arms for his troop by the neighbouring constables of Lymm.[38]

Although there is little widespread evidence for it, some funds were disbursed by Booth's subordinates out of their own pockets for the maintenance of their troops. Such a practice had been commonplace during the Civil Wars, often with the expectation of reimbursement at a later stage. Sir Thomas Myddelton's 'Disbursements in the Cheshire Expedition', occasioned between his declaration for the King at Wrexham and the weeks leading up to the overthrow of the insurgents by Lambert's troops, detail a series of payments for military equipment, provisions and the quartering of horses. On 1 August 1659 Myddelton paid 5s. 6d. 'for a new lock to the old Spanish piece of 1558 mark'; at Farndon-on-Dee three days later the sum of 7s. 6s. was spent on 'a breastplate, bitt and collars' for his own horse; on 5 August Sir Thomas laid out 10s. for an ensign staff and girdle for Thomas Grosvenor, possibly an officer in Captain Thomas Baker's company; 2s. 6d. was given 'to Sir George Booth's man for a blank commission'; on 13 August a pair of holsters was purchased for 7s. 6d. for himself, and 10s. 'to Colonel Broughton what he laid out for information'. During his stay of two nights in Chester (16–17 August) Sir Thomas Myddelton made various payments to Captain Baker of Wrexham, a Royalist officer who had helped to defend Chester from 1643 to 1646. During the Booth uprising he raised a company of foot from Wrexham town, which served alongside other forces commanded by Myddelton. Baker obtained a total of £22 7s. 9d. 'for quartering at the time of the Cheshire rising', while his men received what was probably an advance of 20s. in pay. Sir Thomas' accounts also show that this officer was reimbursed 9s. for a musket, while 36 pairs of shoes were procured for his soldiers from Randle and Richard Bennett, shoemakers of Chester, at 3s. 4d. per pair.[39]

As previously noted, Sir George Booth allowed the appropriation of horses and weapons by his officers. Only a few days before the fight at Winnington Bridge 'a party of horse and foot, about 100, under the command of Captain Shepley and Captain Shenton' quartered overnight at the house of John Brereton, minister at Wilmslow, on the banks of the River Bollin. The following morning the troops marched to Handforth Hall, home to Sir William Brereton, where they took his horses – some of them reportedly

37 BL, MS Harley 2128, fols 41v., 43r., 49r., 60r.; 2137, fol. 115r.

38 BL, MS Harley 1970, fols 60r., 49v.; 2137, fol. 200v.

39 W.M. Myddelton, *Chirk Castle Accounts, AD 1605–1666* (Privately published: 1908), I, pp.82–4; A.N. Palmer, *A History of the Older Nonconformity of Wrexham and its Neighbourhood* (Wrexham: Woodall, Minshall and Thomas, 1888), p.38; Norman Tucker, *Royalist Officers of North Wales 1642–1660: a Biographical List* (Denbigh: Gwasg Gee, 1961), p.12.

'of great value'. Booth's men also plundered mounts from Sir William's neighbours, William Barrett of the Grove and John Astle of Cheadle. It is difficult not to conclude, however, that such acts of thievery and intimidation were also politically motivated, in that they were aimed towards Brereton (perceived by the insurgents as a key symbol of Parliamentary authority in the county) and his associates. A witness to the events later testified that 'having that evening some private conference with the said Mr Harrison, and telling him that he heard that the late rising was intended to obstruct Sir William Brereton, who was then expected to come to Cheshire to settle the militia'.[40]

In terms of the acquisition of provisions for Sir George Booth's soldiers and horses, even less is known. The author of *Another Great Victory* described that as Lambert's troops were marching out of Nantwich on 18 August they discovered 'by some warrants of theirs [Booth's men], by which they had required provisions to be brought to them that morning for 5,500 foot and horse, that they were for a march'.[41] During the period leading to this Sir Thomas Myddelton spent over £60 on horsemeat, bread and cheese for his soldiers, and it is likely that other leaders made similar hurried and localised outlays.[42] While beef, cheese, bread and beer were the backbone of the diet of the seventeenth-century British soldier, food supplies were affected by availability and season, and were contingent on whether units were in garrison or in the field. A warrant for the supply of foodstuffs for the English army in Ireland, drawn up on 7 February 1642, directed the commissary for victuals to provide for the magazine at Chester provisions 'for 10,000 men for three months, at the rate of 4d. the day for every man, in bread, beef, butter [and] cheese. Wherein you shall be careful of the goodness and wholesomeness of the provision; and likewise of the prices, that they be as cheap as the markets will afford'. As near as prices would allow, each man was to be given daily 1lb of bread, 1lb of beef, or, in lieu thereof, ½lb of cheese, or fish, and ¼lb of butter.[43]

Estimates of the strength of Sir George Booth's forces are varied. Royalist propaganda tended to over-estimate the figures. Baker stated that 500 rebel soldiers rendezvoused at Rowton Heath on 2 August, but the army rose with a few days to a strength of 3,000.[44]

On 8 August an unnamed Royalist newsletter described that in Manchester the rebels 'had raised three or four troops of horse, and that three counties did rise with them, viz. Staffordshire, Cheshire, and Lancashire, that

40 TNA, SP23/263, fols 84r.; Earwaker, *East Cheshire*, I, p.230.

41 *Another great Victory obtained by the Lord Lambert against Sir George Booth, on Sunday morning last; with the manner of his taking the city of Chester and throwing open the gates; the taking of 500 prisoners and divers eminent commanders, viz. Major General Egerton, The Lord Kilmorey, Colonel Brooke and Sir William Neal. Also another Desperate Fight at Liverpool, the taking of the town, the beating and pursuing of the enemy towards Wales; and the Escape of Sir George Booth with 200 horse, to Chirk Castle* (London: Edward Horton, 1659); *CWTC*, pp.176–81.

42 Myddelton, *Chirk Castle Accounts*, I, pp.82–4.

43 *CJ*, II, p.417.

44 Baker, *Chronicle*, p.573.

they had raised 7 or 8,000 horse and foot'. Likewise, the Venetian Resident exaggerated somewhat when he told the Doge, 'it is known that the Royalists, consisting of 10,000 armed men, have captured the city of Chester'.[45] On the other hand, the Parliamentarian Colonel Birch reported that upon his return to Manchester on 29 July he received intelligence that Booth's force totalled 1,500 men, 'but within this week they [had reached] I believe, 3,000 or thereabouts'.[46] In his *Declaration*, which he issued on 2 August, Sir George Booth acknowledged that 'the word was given for a general rendezvous, the place appointed at Rowton Heath within three miles of Chester, and the time prefixed was on Tuesday last. Which day they accordingly met, being above 3,000 horse and foot, well mounted and armed, with drums beating, colours flying and trumpets sounding'.[47] The rebel horse, which Lambert described after the fight at Winnington Bridge as 'a gallant body', was estimated by him to be 1,700–1,800 in number. Yet although Booth's entire army was most probably about 4,000, the Parliamentarian commander declared that 'in our view, [there] never appeared above two thousand', although he may only have been talking about the forces that appeared at Winnington Bridge, there having been the '700 of their best foot' which Mordaunt claimed to have been left behind in Chester. This would compute then, to upwards of 1,500 foot under Booth's command being present at the battle.

45 *CSPV*, p.54.

46 MS Tanner 51, fol. 108v.; *Clarke Papers*, IV, p.288.

47 *Declaration*; *CWTC*, pp.166–7.

6

The Council of State and its Response

On the surface it might have appeared that during July and August 1659 the government would collapse before any formidable opposition. But though the Rump was weak and unpopular, it was vigilant. Exactly when the Council of State, via its network of spies and local informers, learned of the general conspiracy is uncertain. Under the energetic leadership of John Mordaunt, by July 1659 the scheme had gathered considerable momentum. From mid July, prominent Royalists and Presbyterians were detained on suspicion of involvement in the plot. Although the spymaster Thomas Scot made much use of informers, intercepted correspondence gave him abundant evidence to take measures. On 9 July – the same day that Mordaunt and other leading conspirators met in London to complete plans for the uprising – the Council sent warnings to 'the colonels, majors or captains of militia forces in the several counties [that] the common enemy is drawn together with designs against the peace', and to muster the troops under their command, to pay them the same as regular soldiers and to report their place of rendezvous.[1] As the Council received more definite information, further measures for the safety of the country were put into place. On 30 July 1659 Vice-Admiral John Lawson, commander of the fleet in the Narrow Seas, was ordered to embark with a squadron for the purpose of watching the Flemish coast. Additionally, the Council requested on 12 August that the Admiralty Committee keep in correspondence with him, 'desiring his vigilance over Ostend and the coast of Flanders, to prevent transport of soldiers thence'.[2]

The intervention of Lawson and the fleet would play a decisive role in the political events of December, which precipitated the demise of Lambert's cause and the hastening of the return of the monarchy to England. The significance of the need to safeguard key ports against the insurgents was not lost on Francesco Giavarina, Venetian Resident in England, who reported to the Doge and Senate on 19 August:

1 *CSPD 1659–60*, pp.15–16, 24, 38–40.
2 *CJ*, VII, p.708; *CSPD 1659–60*, pp.52, 101.

> It is very important for the Royalists to have a seaport in their hands to facilitate the landing of their supporters from Flanders. They were not able to do anything at Bristol but enjoyed better fortune at Chester. Although that is not so convenient for the passage it is on the same coast and is of almost more consequence because of its relations with Wales and its proximity to Ireland where Royalists abound.[3]

Earlier that month, in response to the immediate threats posed by the uprising in the north-west of England, two warships were sent to blockade the Dee, to prevent any provisions reaching Sir George Booth and to seize any rebel ships which might approach. Since the Roman period, Chester – and later, but to a lesser extent, Liverpool – had been an important anchorage, although by the late Middle Ages the silting of the Dee had reduced its commercial viability. A temporary revival was brought about in the early 1640s by the war in Ireland, when the city was used as a base for reinforcing the armies with men and stores. Trade prospered with the influx of troops and travellers, but the citizens complained of the lawlessness of the soldiers and the damage they inflicted, and there were further outbreaks of plague. There is clear evidence of sensitivity in Cheshire towards ill discipline amongst troops passing through the county and the port of Chester to Ireland during the early months of 1642. On 22 April the mayor of Chester, Sir William Brereton (as MP for the county) and others told the Speaker, 'We understand from their officers that several more regiments will soon pass this way and we have received divers complaints from the city and the country [county] that several sums of money are still owing, although some have been discharged, and there have been robberies and violence committed by soldiers who were put upon [quartered on] some persons without their consent'.[4]

Yet the greatest hardship suffered by the city and port of Chester during the century was the damage and loss of trade during the First Civil War, when it was besieged by Parliamentarian forces and finally surrendered. A few decades later the French traveller, Albert Jouvin de Rochefort give a robust account of the city:

> Chester lies at the mouth of the river Dee, where it enlarges itself into the form of a gulf, in which by the assistance of the tide vessels come up to the town. On this account it may be reckoned among the good sea-ports, since it is the ordinary passage of the packet-boat, messengers and merchandise, going from England to Ireland. The plan is nearly formed by two great streets, which cross each other in the middle, and as they are very broad at this crossing, they make a fine and spacious area, which serves for the marketplace, in which is the town house. Turning on the right hand, the way leads to the great church, where I saw a tomb worth remarking. The wall on the bridge is very agreeable; the gate which shuts it in is like a strong little castle; there is then a suburb. Chester is esteemed one of the strongest towns in England, on account of its fine high walls, the many towers by which it is defended, and its strong castle, standing in the highest part

---

3 *CSPV*, p.54.

4 HMC, *Thirteenth Report, App. I*, pp.32–3; BL: MS Add. 11333, fols 130v.–4r.; *BLB*, II, pp.539–40.

> of the town, which it commands. It has been much damaged during the late wars. Under the usurpation of Cromwell the town was almost entirely ruined, after having sustained a long siege. The first thing I did on my arrival at Chester was to learn when the packet-boat would sail for Dublin; it had set off some days before; but I found a trading vessel laden with divers merchandises, in which I took my passage for Ireland. This vessel was at anchor in the gulf, near the little village of Bagillt, eight miles from the town. Here are some large storehouses for the keeping of the merchandise to be embarked for Ireland, as is generally done every month from hence to Ireland, and reciprocally from Ireland to England, from whence all the letters, the messengers, and vessels that are to pass go first to the village of Holyhead, which is in the island of Mona or Anglesey, as a place of rendezvous, there being a very good harbour, from whence a boat commonly sets out for Dublin.[5]

Between 1643 and 1646 the Parliamentarian army in Cheshire had been extensively supplied by sea. According to Dore, 'The evidence shows that there was considerable maritime activity in the north-west during the Civil War. Both sides spent energy and resources in trying to control the sea approaches to Chester and Liverpool, the Royalists sporadically and with only limited temporary success, the Parliamentarians throughout and with increasing effectiveness as the war progressed'.[6] It is clear that Parliamentarian commanders attached great significance to this mode of supply and that the Royalists were keen to prevent it by capturing the Lancashire port. During the winter of 1643–4 the governor of Chester highlighted its importance to Ormonde, while in April 1644 Sir John Byron informed Rupert that the seizure of Liverpool would be the chief benefit of the Prince's march to Lancashire.[7] From Plymouth on 8 August 1659 Captain Henry Hatsell informed the admiralty commissioners:

> I have just returned from Brent, to dispatch the *Gainsborough* and *Sapphire* for Chester Water. [Orders enclosed by Captain Hatsell] of an order from the admiralty commissioners, to Captains Richard Heaton and Robert Clay, commanders of the said ships, to lie at Chester Water to prevent any provisions going into Chester, and to seize all vessels going in thither. Council being informed that some persons have risen, and are in arms, and proceeding there. Also to give notice of their arrival in Chester Water to Colonel Croxton at the castle, or to Colonels Berry or Lilburne, who are on their march thither, and whose orders they are to observe.[8]

By 21 August 1659 the naval blockade of Chester and the Dee was firmly in place, with the admiralty agent Richard Dermott confirming to commissioners:

---

5 Albert Jouvin de Rochefort, *Description of England and Ireland under the Restoration* (Paris, 1672), pp.409–10.

6 R.N. Dore, 'The Sea Approaches: the importance of the Dee and the Mersey in the Civil War in the North West', *THSLC*, 136 (1987), pp.1–26, (p.19).

7 Carte, *Letters*, V, p. 525, VI, p. 10; BL, MS Add. 18981, fol. 137r.

8 *CSPD 1659–60*, p.88.

> The *Gainsborough*, *Oxford*, and *Greyhound* have arrived, the *Greyhound* and *Oxford* riding at Dawpool, and the other at the point of the Ayr, in the roadway, where none can pass either out of Chester Water or the Welsh side, but they can command them, nor come in but by their permission. They all three arrived from Plymouth the 15th instant and found this poor country in a sad condition.[9]

As Bernard Capp's study of the Cromwellian navy shows, it was developed by the Rump into a potent European force. Traditionally the wartime English navy had consisted of merchant vessels hired from their owners and ships captured from the nation's enemies, but during the Anglo-Dutch war a large number were constructed, so that by 1653 the Rump possessed a huge fleet of 180 craft, far more than its French and Spanish rivals.[10]

To counter the threat of Royalist risings (both real and perceived), between May and August 1659 the new government increased the strength of the land forces based in England, in addition to conveying five regiments of foot and 500 horse from Scotland, Flanders and Ireland. Fourteen new regiments of foot were ordered to be raised in different parts of the country, while more were authorised later. Within three months around 8,000 additional troops had boosted the military establishment in England from about 14,000 to 22,000 men.[11] Alongside the growth of the standing army came a further expansion of the military's responsibility for government in the localities. A sign of the emergency was that the colonels were given the right to nominate their own officers, a privilege hitherto denied the colonels of the established army.[12] New militia regiments were raised in London – despite the hostility of the majority of the citizens – while the regiments in the French service who were garrisoned in Flanders were recalled.[13] Similarly, the mobilisation of the militia and the reinforcement of strategic garrisons around the country was ordered. As Reece points out, the basis for garrisoning certain towns and fortifications requires little justification. Hull, Dover and Portsmouth were traditional strongholds, whilst Berwick and Carlisle were essential safeguards against the Scots.[14] Given the military commitments of the Commonwealth and Protectorate, many garrisons, such as Bristol, Liverpool and Chester, acted as magazines and were utilised as arms stores for Ireland in 1649. Even those garrisons housing small magazines could be used for the distribution of weapons to local militias in times of emergency.[15]

In addition, serving regular army officers were ordered to return from England to their commands in Ireland, and like instructions were issued for the regiments in England and Scotland soon afterwards. All 'excepted' persons were banished from London, while measures, such as the prevention

---

9 *Ibid.*, p.133.

10 Bernard Capp, *Cromwell's Navy: The Fleet and the English Revolution 1648–60* (Oxford: Oxford University Press, 1989), pp.5–6.

11 *CJ*, VII, pp.627–31; *CSPD 1659–60*, pp.49, 58; *Clarke Papers*, IV, pp.15, 45.

12 *Clarke Papers*, IV, pp.71–4; Wanklyn, *New Model Army*, II, pp.114, 132, 255.

13 Whitelocke, *Memorials*, IV, p.682; *Clarke Papers*, IV, pp.38, 40; *Mercurius Politicus*, 4–11 August 1659.

14 Reece, *Army in Cromwellian England*, p.81.

15 Ive, 'Local Dimensions', pp.114–25.

of horse racing and the watching of inns was enforced. The Council of State was empowered to arrest and detain suspects, whose houses were searched. Orders were also sent to officers in all parts of the country to seize the arms and ammunition of suspected persons, whilst 600 horses were secured, which were later reused to mount six companies of dragoons. Other quickly passed bills called on householders to supply details of their lodgers' horses and arms, and another, which equated soldiers departing from their colours as high treason.[16] Although such military preparations proved more than satisfactory against the largely weak attempts at Royalist insurgence in August 1659, when the army failed to find 'the enemy answerable to his boastings', neither the Rump nor the revolutionaries attracted civilian support in much numbers. Traditional members of the county and urban elites regarded the new government with little eagerness. The spectre of renewed social and religious upheaval conjured up by the radical chorus that had greeted the Rump's return was given solid form by the appointments to the militia in July 1659. Radicals, sectaries, even Quakers appeared in enough numbers to cause marked disquiet in traditional circles.[17]

Yet such concerns did not translate into support for Royalist risings. So long as the standing army remained united and maintained order, the propertied classes were not prepared to search for an alternative. Hence, calls for 'all honest men to appear and not stand newter', to respond were generally met with silence. On 31 July, the clergyman and cavalry officer, Sergeant Major Nathaniel Barton had informed Colonel Thomas Sanders in Derbyshire of his hearing 'that some of the Council intend to command you and I to attend the service in Derbyshire and Staffordshire – I hope the commission will act thoroughly for it is not a time to dally and I hope the Godly ministers and others about you are not wanting in managing our spiritual militia'. Four days later Barton further lamented:

> a cloud of disturbance seems to hover over Lancashire and Cheshire – it is reported that Tuesday last was to be a rendezvous at Rowton Heath near Chester and that divers persons of quality and divers ministers are engaged thereabouts. I have much wondered that any Godly Presbyterian ministers should ever expect or have reason to believe that the cavaliers could forget old hatred – this alarm from Cheshire has I suppose wrought your parts by now – there are orders issued to Colonel Lilburne's regiment and other forces that lie that way, to immediately draw into those parts and several regiments of horse are to be in readiness – I am sorry that friends in Derbyshire are so shy.[18]

But although such measures were implemented for the broader defence of the country, the immediate need was for a potent force to confront the menace of Sir George Booth in Cheshire. The Council of State, after some hesitancy, appointed Colonel John Lambert as commander-in-chief of an

16 *CJ*, VII, pp.709, 739, 744; *CSPD 1659–60*, pp.48–50, 54–6, 114, 124–5, 128.

17 Morrill, *Cheshire*, pp.258–9; Barry Reay, 'The Quakers, 1659 and the Restoration of the Monarchy', *History*, 63 (1978), pp.193–213, (pp.200–1).

18 DRO, D1232/083; D1232/086.

expeditionary force sent from London, with a temporary commission as major general. He was the obvious choice, not only because of his personal ability and experience, but also his great popularity with the army. Civilian republicans profoundly distrusted him, while Colonel John Hutchinson, perhaps hostile to the Protectorate, opposed the nomination in Parliament, warning the House that Lambert's ambition might soon lead them to repent of their choice. Moreover, according to Clarendon, 'There were many officers whom they would much rather trust than Lambert, but there was none they thought could do their business so well'.[19] But the fact that two of the leading councillors of state, Sir Arthur Haselrig and Sir Henry Vane, were willing to approve Lambert's appointment clearly illustrates how seriously the Booth rebellion was taken. Lambert had informed Vane that the Royalists had offered great rewards to his wife if she would persuade her husband to refuse such a command, and this may have swung the decision.[20] The Major General's principal commission, issued on 5 August, authorised him to direct military operations in the counties from Chester to Lincoln and in the six northern shires, to command a brigade consisting initially of his own regiment of horse (under Sergeant Major Richard Creed) and that of Colonel Robert Swallow, and two regiments of foot – Lambert's own and Colonel John Hewson's.

In several contemporary sources the term 'brigade' was applied to the main force that marched from London. During the first half of the seventeenth century the term usually referred to a battlefield formation, especially one following Swedish drill and tactics. However, in Lambert's case, it was used in the modern context of a self-contained and self-supporting composite organisation. In Lambert's brigade this included infantry, cavalry, dragoons and artillery units. In addition to the four regiments advancing from London, Colonel John Biscoe's foot (which was disbursed among garrisons in the eastern counties) would rendezvous with the main force *en route*. The combined formation would also include three troops from Colonel Robert Lilburne's regiment of horse, presently marching westwards towards Lancashire from Yorkshire. Although Lilburne (a long-time adherent and friend of Lambert's) received orders to recruit his troops up to 80 troopers, and marched towards Cheshire, he would remain in Manchester, though three (unnamed) troops of his regiment did come up in time. On 8 August 1659 John Lambert understood from President Whitelocke that Lilburne had in addition 'mounted and sent away two companies of Colonel Ashfield's regiment as dragoons, and some other forces to meet you'.[21] As to the prospect of gaining further local reinforcements upon his arrival in the North West, the Major General was informed by the same source that 'the lieutenant of Colonel Croxton's militia troop in Cheshire having gone over to the enemy, Council appoints Captain John Carter, the bearer of this, to his place, and has given him a commission; and to George Gleave to be quartermaster, both being highly recommended, and their knowledge of Chester county may be of use'.

19 Lucy Hutchinson, *Memoirs of the life of Colonel Hutchinson* (London: H.G. Bohn, 1863), p.382; Clarendon, *Rebellion*, V, p.120.

20 Ludlow, *Memoirs*, II, pp.111–2.

21 *Ibid.*, pp.86–7.

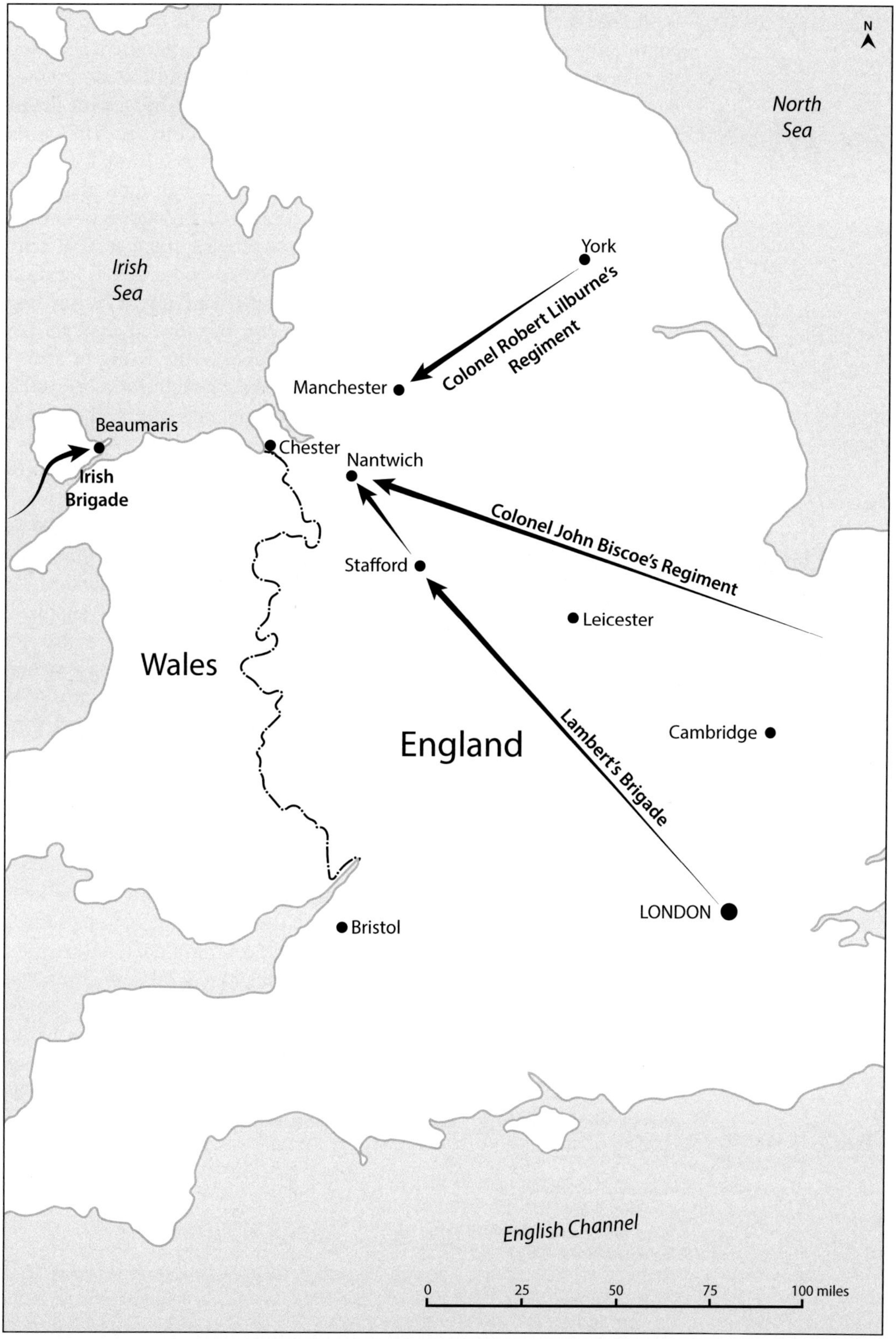

Map 2 Movements of Parliament's Forces, 6-15 August 1659.

It seems clear that the government, acting on the advice of the army's commanders, envisaged a fast-moving, mobile response to insurgent threats. On 13 August Whitelocke informed the 'militia commissioners of the several counties', that the 'Council think that horse and dragoons rather than foot will be most of use in the present emergency'.[22] Lambert's force was composed of veteran officers and soldiers, inured to arduous military service. Initially it numbered about 3,500, but upon arrival in the North West 10 days later, the brigade's combined strength had swollen to 1,200–1,500 horse and 3,000 foot.[23] Accompanying them was an artillery train of eight cannon, with 'gunners and matrosses entertained for it, [and] 45 barrels of powder from Windsor'. Moreover, Parliament had instructed the governor of Stafford that upon reaching the town Lambert's troops should not only receive local intelligence reports, the fixing of arms and extra supplies of ammunition, but equipment suitable for siege-work, in the form of drawbridges, shovels, spades, and pickaxes.[24] The supply of ammunition in particular – musket and pistol bullets, cannonballs and mortar bombs – from Stafford and the surrounding area, is unsurprising, especially given the alacrity with which Lambert's troops were dispatched from London. During the First Civil War the Parliamentarian forces of Staffordshire, Shropshire and Cheshire procured significant quantities of artillery ordnance, manufactured by Hough furnace, near Stafford, while during the siege of Chester in 1645 the Mereheath foundry supplied Sir William Brereton's army with 53cwt of cannon rounds. Moreover, from 1643 onwards Brereton maintained a powder mill in Stafford, having poached Sir John Gell's gunpowder maker at Derby.[25]

Major General Lambert was also empowered to summon to his assistance any other forces he might require, and to grant commissions to such as he deemed faithful to raise additional regiments, troops or companies. On 4 August 1659 the Council instructed that three regiments of foot to be transported from Dunkirk to Gravesend, and the following day ordered Monck in Scotland, to send two regiments of foot and two of horse, but according to Ludlow, 'he excused himself, under colour of the enemy's strength and inclination to revolt, though there were not wanting some who then thought that his engagements with the common enemy were the true reasons of that refusal'.[26] At the same time, Major General John Disbrowe was given command of the forces in the South West, South Wales, Gloucestershire and Worcestershire.[27] The divergence between Army and Parliament, which had become acute during the months leading up to August, was smoothed over temporarily by the necessity for unity caused by the threat posed by Sir George Booth's rising. Lambert and Disbrowe's commands – to operate in the

22 *Ibid.*, p.106.

23 *Clarke Papers*, IV, pp.38–9n.

24 *CSPD 1659–60*, pp.76, 192.

25 TNA, SP28/36, fol. 405r.; SP28/35/5, fols 751r., 754r.; Peter Edwards, 'Turning Ploughshares into Swords: The Arms and Military Equipment Industries in Staffordshire in the First Civil War, 1642–1646', *MH*, 27 (2002), pp.52–79.

26 *CSPD 1659–60*, p.74; Ludlow, *Memoirs*, II, p.112.

27 *Clarke Papers*, IV, pp.75, 92–3. 120; Davies, *Restoration*, p.139.

Jan van de Velde, Artillery on the march (1632). (Amsterdam, Rijksmuseum. Public Domain)

North and North West, and in the South West and South Wales respectively – were regions in which they had both worked before. The former, and some of his cavalry officers (including Captain John Hodgson) were familiar with Cheshire and the northwest through their previous military service. After the relief of Nantwich in 1644 Lambert was praised by Sir Thomas Fairfax for his good service, and he accompanied the general at the siege of Lathom House. His leadership during the Preston campaign contributed greatly to the New Model's victory. On 17 August 1651 Lambert was with his cavalry at Knutsford Heath, where he wrote to the Speaker to hasten General Cromwell, before playing a prominent role in defeating the Scots at Worcester.[28]

On 5 August 1659, the day before Lambert's brigade commenced its march, the Council of State issued various last-minute instructions. The treasury commissioners were instructed to pay £1,000 each to Lambert and Hewson's foot, who were in dire arrears, although it is unclear if they received anything before leaving the capital.[29] Lambert was given command of the northern forces, whilst he and Desbrowe were provided with 100 blank commissions for the commissioning of offers and raising of local troops along their line of axis. Lambert's commissions were particularly intended for the Parliamentary forces of Cheshire, Lancashire and Shropshire, in order to ensure that the regular troops were aided in the North West and border regions by effective and properly trained local units.[30] Prior to embarking from London, the sum

28 Farr, *Lambert*, pp.34, 42–3, 90–1.

29 *CSPD 1659–60*, p.75.

30 *Ibid.*, pp.74–5, 92–3.

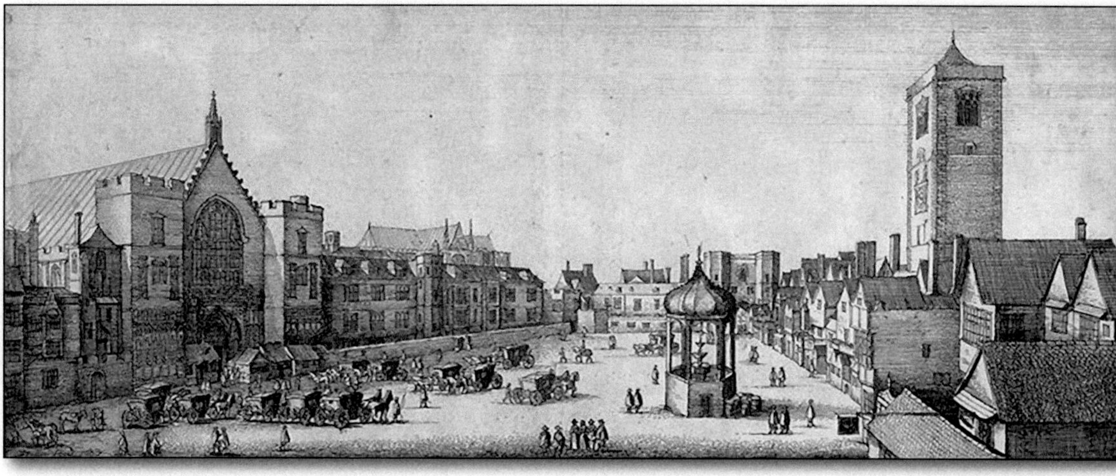

Wenceslaus Hollar, *New Palace Yard and Westminster Hall*, 1647. (Minneapolis Institute of Art. Public Domain)

> As the post is interrupted by the enemy's possession of Chester, we send an express to tell you that is the only place where they have been successful, notwithstanding their designs to rise in almost every county, their rendezvous being discovered and prevented, themselves scattered, and several ringleaders taken. At Chester they took but the town, Colonel Croxton valiantly holding the castle. Major General Lambert is marching towards them, and we believe their own fears will disperse them when they hear the near approach of his army, seeing that the rest of the country is quiet, and the expectations of the conspirators disappointed therein.[37]

Having been sent ahead of the army with part of Lambert's cavalry regiment, Sergeant Major Creed quickly reached the Midlands. The nature of the fast-moving military campaign is evident from the content of the frequent and hastily written intelligence updates sent back to London by mounted couriers (which were of a generally high quality). On 13 August 1659 one report from the Council of State stated:

> Yesterday a letter came from Major Creed, that he hath lately taken a sergeant and six private soldiers of the enemy, by whom he understood that Sir George Booth was marched towards Liverpool to possess himself of some great guns, with other arms and ammunition. That he hath a 1,000 horse, but for the number of his foot he cannot learn. Other letters say that Sir George Booth hath sent a party to North Wales, another to Shropshire, another to Lancashire, and that their rendezvous is appointed at Branden Moore, twelve miles from Chester. The Lord Lambert lay at Coventry last Wednesday, and at Whitchurch this night. Major Creed endeavoured to engage them at Nantwich, but the enemy marched away in a disorderly manner towards Liverpool.[38]

Creed's mounted force was augmented by cavalry drawn from Lancashire and Yorkshire. They kept watch on the movements of the rebels, but avoided bringing on an engagement until the arrival of Lambert with his foot. On 8

37 *Ibid.*, pp.90–1.
38 *Clarke Papers*, IV, p.42.

August the Major General, who had been recently apprised of the situation by his subordinate, was prompted by President Whitelocke to 'look after the safety of Shrewsbury in your march to Chester, as the enemy aims at its possession. Though no efforts should be spared to check the enemy at the beginning, yet we hope Major Creed will not engage with them at too much disadvantage before he is reinforced by you, but we refer him to you for directions'.[39] Creed did not have long to wait, for making good time Lambert arrived with his redcoats to meet him at Market Drayton on 14 August, eight days after his departure from London.[40]

The march of Lambert's brigade had been the subject of predictable rumour. Greatest among them was that the foot refused to progress much further than London, and that their stubbornness was overcome only when Lambert turned his cavalry on them. The cavalier politician Sir Edward Nicholas stated on 8 August, 'The common soldiers, though encouraged with free quarter and plunder, show little alacrity to the service. Hewson's regiment on Saturday last refused to march against Sir George Booth are Some of Lambert's forces were reported to have mutinied for lack of pay on their way out of London to suppress Booth's rising'.[41] Similarly, an intercepted letter from Brussels to the King's agent in Paris (dated 20 August) recounted, 'Lambert's forces mutinied on the way and refused to march, so that there was a great conflict among them, and many killed or wounded, but at length they were forced to march, though with grumbling'.[42] Two further, and more detailed, reports were made by Francesco Giavarina, Venetian Resident in England, to the Doge and Senate. On 22 August he wrote of Lambert's soldiers:

> What service these troops will render cannot be known, but it is fairly safe to predict that it will not be much, as besides showing a great reluctance to march, it is known that the infantry stopped several times on the road protesting that they would not advance unless they were paid what was due, as they did not receive a penny before they started. They were induced to proceed with fair words and promises after the mutiny had lasted some hours, the men absolutely refusing to go on as they did not wish to fight those whose opinions did not differ from their own, as they themselves claim a free and lawful parliament. When the cavalry, commanded by Anabaptists dependent on this parliament, tried to force the infantry to advance, a conflict ensued in which several infantrymen were wounded, who have been brought to London in a serious condition. The others resumed their march, but grumbling and very dissatisfied, especially as the march is long and toilsome and they are harassed by terrible winds, very unusual for the season, and by rain which has fallen almost incessantly since they started. The news is very bitter to them here and they greatly fear that when these troops arrive near to the enemy a large part of them will go over to the other side, especially as it is asserted that Sir [George] Booth, Lieutenant General of the rebels, in Chester,

39 *CSPD 1659–60*, p.86.
40 *CWTC*, p.168.
41 *Nicholas Papers*, IV, p.178.
42 *CSPD 1659–60*, p.132.

> has offered four months' pay down to every parliamentary soldier who joins him, and whatever is due to him. This inducement may attract many and if this army, thus weakened, tired by the long march and its hardships should meet the enemy at some narrow pass or river, as is practically certain, they are fearful of the issue.

Seven days later, Giavarina elaborated:

> Until the meeting of the parliamentary army under General Lambert and the Presbyterian led by Sir George Booth in the county of Chester no definite judgment can be formed of the affairs of England. The rebels continue their conquests in that and other neighbouring counties, but these being of little consequence can bring them no great profit. Other counties are in arms but before going on they apparently want to see the issue of a fight between Lambert and Booth. It is impossible to say when this will happen, for the parliamentary army has been hampered by floods due to the incessant rain, the men in some places being up to the middle while they find all the bridges broken by the enemy. These consist mainly of cavalry who are raiding in all directions, and everywhere they burn the books of the customs and other taxes, promising that there shall be no more taxes. They comfort the people with this and urge them to join and follow them. This has delayed the march extremely, and though the army started from here a fortnight ago we do not yet hear that it has reached its destination. The delay is also due to two mutinies, between the cavalry and infantry, some hundreds of soldiers losing their lives, besides the wounded reported last week. As the infantry continues to clamour for a free parliament there is great apprehension about its loyalty when it comes near the enemy.[43]

It must be concluded, however, that such reports were grossly inaccurate and propagandist in nature. These were undoubtedly the product of misinformation propagated against the Parliament by Royalist and to some extent, Presbyterian agents. One of these was Major Robert Harley, son of Sir Robert Harley of Brampton Bryan, Herefordshire, who had fought against Charles I in the Civil Wars, but from 1657–8 had engaged in negotiations between the Presbyterians and cavaliers for the restoration of the monarchy.[44] On 2 May 1659 John Mordaunt confided in Nicholas that Harley junior had exerted considerable influence over the Presbyterian faction.[45] He was brought before the Council of State on 19 July on charges of spreading sedition; he confessed that he 'lately had conference, and held correspondence, with Major General Massey'.[46] The rumours and propaganda that spread about Lambert's enterprise against the Cheshire rising were one thing, yet the Council of State was kept in more certain knowledge. It knew that there was no discontentment among the army's ranks and that the only obstacle they met with was heavy rain and flooding. President Whitelocke reported that Whitehall received intelligence from the marching troops 'twice or thrice

43 *CSPV*, pp.56, 61.
44 *CCSP*, IV, pp.155, 195.
45 *LM*, p. 10 and note 2; *CCSP*, III, pp.459–61.
46 *CJ*, VII, p. 724; *CSPD 1659–60*, pp.32, 567.

James, Duke of York (1633–1701). (Emmet Collection, from The New York Public Library. Public Domain)

a day', learning from them of their arrival at Coventry and Lichfield on 10 August, and of the rendezvous with Creed on the 14th.[47]

Across the English Channel on 24 July 1659 Charles II's brothers, James, Duke of York and Henry Stuart, Earl of Gloucester had been summoned from Breda to Brussels, but they arrived after the King's departure.

By then, however, Major General Browne, won over to the notion of an immediate rising, attempted to galvanise London. The citizens were overawed by the Council of State's preparations – which included the mustering of redcoats and city militia at Whitehall – and therefore no uprising transpired.[48] An immediate threat to the government was the altogether more serious rebellion in the West Country led by the leading Presbyterian-turned-Royalist, Sir Edward Massey. Reports from Gloucester, delivered to the Speaker on 27 July, indicated that the situation there was severe. There was a strong cavalier party and even the colliers from the Forest of Dean being expected to rise, while the troops quartered in the city were dispirited due to their lack of pay.[49] But on 30 July, the Sealed Knot dispatched messengers warning the conspirators that the situation throughout England was unpromising, and that the uprising should be abandoned. Garrison commanders throughout the country were alerted and troops of horse marched out to rendezvous. Yet from the letters that passed between the commanders and the government during this period, it is obvious that they were still in the dark about many locations and individuals, and that in more distant places, such as Cheshire, small bodies of soldiers stood among a population suspected of hostility. The highest military authority in the county at this point was the governor of Chester, Colonel Thomas Croxton. As Reece mentions, 'For every seasoned regular army officer who served as a garrison governor for an extended period … there was a local man, whose military experience might only have been in his county during the war, who commanded a small garrison'.[50]

In the South West, on 31 July 1659 a party of 100 troopers ventured along one bank of the Severn towards Gloucester in pursuit of Massey's co-conspirator, Lord Herbert, while other troops scoured the opposite bank for other leaders. In a streak of good fortune, the first body not only captured Herbert, but detained Sir Edward himself. Of the subsequent events, Whitelocke recalled:

47 Whitelocke, *Memorials*, IV, p.356; *CSPD 1659–60*, p.101.
48 *CJ*, VII, pp.753–4; *CCSP*, IV, p.313.
49 *CJ*, VII, p.744; *Clarke Papers*, IV, p.35.
50 Reece, *Army in Cromwellian England*, p.155.

> Massey was taken in Gloucestershire, and mounted before a trooper to take care of him, and to bring him prisoner to Gloucester; but riding down a steep hill, the weather being wet, and a dark night, in a great wood, the horse slipped and fell down (which Massey caused by checking of him), and being dark crept into a bush, and the whole troop could not find him out; but he escaped, and got the next morning to a friend's house, where he was concealed about a fortnight after.[51]

Rumours surrounding Massey's arrest, and the aggressive prosecution of operations by the government forces, soon brought about the dispersion of the Gloucestershire rebels, especially as he was recaptured near Bristol two days after his escape.[52] The testimony of John Penny of Hannington, Wiltshire, given before the local sequestration committee on 4 August 1659, reveals that four days previously he and others had met 30 horsemen at Lansdowne, near Bath, whilst a similar group assembled at Malmesbury. Penny related that they 'were waiting for Massey and two troops of horse from Bristol; on hearing he was taken, [their leader, William Basset] dismissed them'.[53] Lieutenant General Edmund Ludlow added later, 'Some of these, with others from the borders with Hampshire, went and joined the body that was commanded by Sir George Booth'.[54] On 4 August the Council of State prepared itself for further trouble in the West country by appointing Major General Disbrowe as commander-in-chief there.[55]

The situation in neighbouring Shropshire also called for immediate action. With Lambert's army leaving London for the north-west of England, Captain William Botrell, the governor of Ludlow and MP for Shropshire in the 1653 Parliament, was advised by the Council of State on 5 August 'to apply to Major General Lambert, who commands in Salop and other northern counties, and is now marching on Chester, and he will give you the commissions for your officers, and orders for such other supplies as he finds requisite for the safety of your garrison'. Similarly, four days later Captain Richard Bagott, having provided Parliament with a situation report from Shrewsbury, received its gratitude for enlisting a company of 60 foot, and was told that Lambert would 'satisfy your desire concerning your lieutenant and ensign, as he has the conduct of the forces in Shropshire and all the northern counties'.[56] Likewise, on 27 September 1659 the keeper of the magazine at Chester Castle was ordered to deliver 50 pikes and 30 firelock muskets to Major Waring, for the arming of a foot company in the Shrewsbury garrison.[57] The rebel commanders in the Midlands, encouraged by a report that insurgents had captured Coventry, hoped that this would divert any forces sent from London. But the report was untruthful. The governor of Warwick had wavered in his fidelity to the Parliament, but

---

51 Whitelocke, *Memorials*, IV, p.355. See also *Mercurius Politicus*, 28 July–4 Aug 1659; *CCSP*, IV, p.313.

52 *CCSP*, IV, p.315; *Clarke Papers*, IV, pp.35–7.

53 *CCSP*, IV, p.309.

54 Ludlow, *Memoirs*, II, p.108.

55 *CSPD 1659–60*, pp.72 115; *Mercurius Politicus*, 4–11 August 1659.

56 *CSPD 1659–60*, pp.92–3; *CWTC*, 175–6.

57 *CSPD 1659–60*, p.227.

Colonel William Purefoy, the veteran regicide, and active member of the Rump and the Commonwealth's Council of State took command, and kept Coventry and the surrounding area loyal to the government.[58] In his support, Purefoy had on 7 August received the Council's recognition of his raising of four companies of militia foot, who would be remunerated at the same rate as the regular army for the term of their engagement. He was urged to be 'vigilant over the enemy and seize all disaffected persons'.[59]

In Derbyshire plans for the rebellion were coordinated by Colonel John Frescheville, a former commissioner of array and captain of horse in the Royalist army, and Philip Stanhope, Earl of Chesterfield. They appear to have been materially aided by the high sheriff, who was later indicted as 'a principal encourager of Sir George Booth's rebellion in county Derby'.[60] Early on 12 August Lord John Byron – whose attempt to recover weapons left at Colonel John Hutchinson's house at Owthorpe was largely foiled by the watchfulness of the latter's wife, and despite the treachery of some of his servants – and Colonel Charles White concentrated a body of 60 to 80 men from Nottingham in Sherwood Forest and attacked the local militia, who put up a determined resistance. The rebels fled rapidly through Nottingham to Derby, where they caused a tumult in the marketplace, 'some crying a king, others a free Parliament'.[61] Command of this group was briefly offered to Colonel Thomas Sanders, a regular army officer of considerable Civil War experience, and currently the commanding officer of a regiment of horse stationed in Scotland. Whatever his sympathies, he declined to declare for the insurgents, and was therefore allowed to depart to his home at Little Ireton. Sanders was, nevertheless, later charged with aiding the rebels and possessing prior knowledge of the risings in a broader sense. Something of the confusing events at Derby may be gleaned from the various letters and other documents of some of the local military officers who had remained steadfast. On 12 August Lieutenant William Broadhurst gave evidence against the commander of his own militia troop, Captain Samuel Doughty, who as county treasurer caused the church bells to be rung and promised that £4,000 would be given to the insurgents from recently levied taxation:

> coming to Derby from Mercaston, he understood that one Colonel White had made a tumult in Derby. He rode down to Corn Market and meeting Colonel White demanded of him who he was for. White said he was for a free Parliament and that he declared against Charles Stuart, whereupon Captain Doughty said 'we are all friends'. Broadhurst wished White to go with him to the Commissioners for the Militia, which he did. Afterwards Broadhurst came to Colonel Sanders in a chamber in the George Inn and told him he perceived the business had no bottom, that the tumult was only a confused party and that he conceived the best

58 Ludlow, *Memoirs*, II, p.109.

59 *CSPD 1659–60*, p.84.

60 *CPCC*, V, p.3249.

61 Hutchinson, *Memoirs*, pp.348–51; *Clarke Papers*, IV, pp.44–5; *CSPD 1659–60*, pp.119–20; *CCSP*, IV, p.325; Brian Stone, *Derbyshire in the Civil War* (Matlock: Scarthin Books, 1992), pp.113–4.

> course would be to draw them out of town to Nuns's Green, and delay them to prevent a leading of them into town by any disaffected party. He asked Sanders to get on horseback and lead them out of town. Sanders said he would not engage with them but after Broadhurst had been to the marketplace again and seen what posture the people were in, he persuaded Sanders to mount his horse, ride with him to the marketplace and so draw the party to Nuns's Green. After Sanders was at Nuns's Green he denied to head them in any way of command and would have gone home, pretending he was unwell but Broadhurst persuaded him to stay, for while Sanders was present, no other dared lead them. After a while the party was persuaded to come into town and lay down their arms.[62]

Yet uncertainties surrounding the conduct of Sanders, as 'a person engaged in promoting the late insurrection', persisted, causing one Needham to write to Thomas and his fellow officer, Nathaniel Barton on 30 August:

> on Friday a letter was read in the House from Captain Tomlinson who, I understand, commands your Derbyshire troop, giving an account of the insurrection in Derby, in which some reproach is cast upon yourself and Major Barton. He claims that you forbad Captain Thorpe to charge the enemy. It exalts the other party who rejoice at the humbling of men of your persuasion. The House referred the letter to the Committee of State. It will be a wound to your reputation until the matter is cleared. It is the opinion of all you or your major should hasten speedily to satisfy the Council. I entreat you to write to me narrative of the business.[63]

Resistance ended when Colonel William Mitchell, who had marched from Hull with three companies of foot, and joined by the militia from Leicestershire and Nottinghamshire arrived to quell the uprising.[64] Colonel White, the hitherto rebel, escaped to Uttoxeter, where he recited Sir George Booth's *Declaration*, but any local support for the rising evaporated when most of the militia changed sides. White was duly captured and incarcerated. The only other significant flicker of a rising occurred at Leicester. It was reported in Parliament that on 15 August, Henry Grey, Earl of Stamford, father-in-law to Sir George Booth, assembled 200 men in arms. They drank the King's health and quickly disbursed when experienced troops from Colonel John Biscoe's regiment of foot approached. Stamford then quietly surrendered.[65]

Later depositions taken at Chester, whose authorities had gone over to Booth's uprising, revealed that 'upon 13 August the mayor, recorder and aldermen commanded by the constables every person to make bonfires and shout for joy, Derbyshire, Leicestershire and five other counties had declared for them'.[66] Such celebrations were somewhat premature, because almost everywhere the rebellion collapsed. When the government issued proclamations against its

---

62 DRO, D1232/0/103.

63 DRO, D1232/0/89. For further, more official, enquiries into the conduct of Sanders and others, see D1232/0 90–6.

64 *Mercurius Politicus*, 10–17 August 1659; Bod. Lib., MS Tanner 51, fol. 144r.–v.

65 *CCSP*, IV, p.325;*CSPD 1659–60*, p.120.

66 TNA, SP23/263, fol. 110r.; *CCC*, I, p.751.

leaders, John Mordaunt, with his fellow exile, the Earl of Lichfield, and a group of supporters made a final attempt at an uprising in favour of Charles II in Surrey during mid August, but it came to nothing. Mordaunt took refuge in London and in the November he fled to France.[67] On 17 August 1659, a few days after the capitulation of Stamford and his adherents in Leicester, President Hesilrige reported to Monck, who was observing events from Edinburgh:

> Last Sunday we heard how the Earl ofStamford declared for the king, and with Major Babington, gathered together 200 or 300 in arms, but hearing that Colonels Biscoe and Salmon's regiments, on the march towards Major General Fleetwood, were quartered near, and with some militia horse were making towards him, the whole company dispersed, and the earl is now prisoner in Leicester. At the same time Lord Byron, Colonel White, and others gathered together 120 horse in Sherwood Forest near Nottingham, but were fallen on and dispersed, their colours taken, and they pursued twelve miles by the county troop. White and some few that escaped came to Derby, and on market day declared for a free Parliament, and thus deceived some into joining them; but on Lambert's sending towards them a troop of horse, they also dispersed, and now the country is everywhere quiet save at Chester. Lambert will be there today, with eight regiments of horse and foot, and if he succeed, we doubt not the troubles in England will speedily be over, and we in a capacity to help you, if there is any rising in Scotland.[68]

The situation in Cheshire and the North West of England during the early weeks of August 1659 is admirably summarised by the broader report written by Colonel George Thomson, the MP, member of the Committee for Intelligence, to Ambassador Lockhart, the same day. If overly optimistic concerning troop numbers, and taken from a London perspective, it gives an impression of confusion and confidence in the ability of Lambert to put down the rebellion:

> Since my last to your excellency of the 8th present, some further designs of rising have been discovered and prevented, others disappointed ... Those in Cheshire fly before Major Creed, who possessed some of Sir George Booth's quarters, but forbore to engage, his force being only horse. Lord Lambert not being come up to him; it is supposed that both horse and foot, under Lord Lambert, joined yesterday, or will this day, near Chester, and an engagement like to be today, if Sir George Booth will stand. There is no news of any in arms against the Parliament but Sir George Booth, and Myddelton's party in divers parts about Cheshire and those about Derby, and with the Earl ofStamford, which it is said are not great numbers ... Just now there is news that some horse and dragoons from Lord, Lambert reached Derby the 13th instant, but those that had been in arms had laid them down and gone home. The revolt which was said to be general in England, is reduced to two counties, Lincolnshire [*sic* – Lancashire] and Cheshire, where Sir George Booth – a gentleman who has 200,000 livres rent and lately born arms for this very Parliament – is at the head of 10,000 or 20,000 men. He is a great

67 *CCSP*, IV, p.333; Baker, *Chronicle*, p.668.
68 *CSPD 1659–60*, p.120.

> Presbyterian, and for politic reasons has not yet declared for the king, but for a Parliament freely chosen. Major General Lambert has gone with 6,000 men, and others are to join him *en route*, to suppress this rebellion. They are now near each other. If Lambert can beat them, this disorder will contribute much to the establishment of the republic; but if he were beaten, great changes would happen.[69]

On 5 August 1659 President Whitelocke had assured Colonel Thomas Croxton, the governor of Chester, that the Council:

> hearing both from yourself and others of the preparations of the enemy against Chester, has ordered Major General Lambert to begin marching to your relief tomorrow, with a considerable force, and some have already started. They desire your utmost resolution and courage to withstand the enemy, who has in every attempt elsewhere been frustrated, and you are to report constantly your condition to Council and Lord Lambert.[70]

Government Forces Deployed to Counter the Booth Rebellion

Major General John Lambert's Brigade:

Major General John Lambert's Regiment of Horse
(as of 28 May 1659)[71]

Colonel John Lambert's own troop
Captain Lieutenant Thomas Spilman
Cornet John Holdsworth
Quartermaster Isott

Sergeant Major Richard Creed's troop
Lieutenant Thomas Ince
Cornet Matthew Brandon
Quartermaster Cuthbert Creed

Captain Adam Baynes' troop
Lieutenant Page
Cornet George Thomlinson
Quartermaster Matthew Strigley

Captain John Hatfield's troop
Lieutenant Thomas Davies
Cornet [??]
Quartermaster Ashton

69 *Ibid.*, p.113.
70 *Ibid.*, p.78.
71 *Clarke Papers*, III, pp.113–14, 132, 196, 215; *CJ*, VII, pp.668, 680; Wanklyn, *Reconstructing the New Model Army: Volume 2: 1649–1663* (Solihull: Helion and Co., 2015), pp.130–1.

of £10 was granted 'to buy colours for the foot regiments that are to march'.[31] These were presumably Lambert's and Hewson's, who may have already had them issued, the purchase equating to 20 items at £1 (20s.) apiece. In 1643 the Staffordshire Parliamentarian commander, Colonel Jackson spent £2 12s. on having his standards made (for his own company) at Uttoxeter, disbursing a further 1s. 6d. for the staff and head to mount them on. Moreover, the sum of £14 3s. 6d. was paid out for colours for the Cheshire regiment of Colonel James Lothian in August 1648.[32] By comparison Alexander Venn, ensign maker, was contracted by Parliament in 1645 to provide 'drums, colours, halberds and partizans for the furnishing of Colonel Aldrich's regiment, viz., for eight new ensigns made of blue Florence sarcenet with distinctions of gold-coloured laurels with tassels to them … at the rate of 45s. apiece'.[33]

In addition to the purchase of new colours, the Tower ordnance officers – responding to a warrant from the Council for the arming of troops to face the current emergency – issued 400 pikes and muskets to each of the infantry regiments commanded by Lieutenant General Fleetwood, Major General Lambert, Colonels Hewson, Sydenham, Morley, Mosse, and Biscoe, and the Tower regiment. Swords were also delivered 'in proportion to the pikes, and bandoliers in proportion to the muskets, while those already delivered were to be accounted part of the number'.[34] The two infantry regiments that marched from London and who benefitted from this issue of arms and equipment (Lambert's and Hewson's), would unite with the cavalry units of Colonel Swallow and Sergeant Major Creed at Market Drayton, Shropshire, on 14 August, whilst Biscoe's companies joined them soon afterwards. Regarding the progress of this impending relief force, President Whitelocke reassured Colonel Croxton in Chester Castle on 5 August that 'Council, hearing both from yourself and others of the preparations of the enemy against Chester, has ordered Major General Lambert to begin marching to your relief tomorrow, with a considerable force, and some have already started. They desire your utmost resolution and courage to withstand the enemy, who has in every attempt elsewhere been frustrated, and you are to report constantly your condition to Council and Lord Lambert'.[35]

Lambert was overjoyed to be taking to the field once more. As he passed out of London with his troops he was reported to be 'obviously high' against cavaliers and Presbyterians, and exclaimed that 'he will perish or not allow life to any gentleman engaged or above £200 per annum to any of that party or persuasion surviving'.[36] Three days later the commissioners in Ireland, and Lieutenant General Ludlow, commander-in-chief of the forces there were informed:

31 *Ibid.*, p.76.
32 TNA, SP28/134/2, fol. 23v.; SP28/346/1, unfol.; SP28/128/13, fol. 23r.
33 Gerald I. Mungeam, 'Contracts of the Supply of Equipment to the 'New Model Army' in 1645, *JAAS*, 6 (1968–70), pp.53–114, (p.75).
34 *CSPD 1659–60*, p.103.
35 *Ibid.*, p.78.
36 *Nicholas Papers*, IV, pp.177–8.

Captain John Pockley's troop
Lieutenant John Hodgson
Cornet Thomas Paul
Quartermaster Robert Gledhill

Captain Robert Salmon's troop
Lieutenant Henry Webley
Cornet Digles
Quartermaster Charles Stoddard

Surgeon John Hodgson

Colonel Robert Swallow's Regiment of Horse
(as of 11 July 1659; by 5 August Captain William Evanson, who had lost his place in the July shake-up, had been reinstated)[72]

Colonel Robert Swallow's own troop
Captain Lieutenant Nathaniel Holt
Cornet Thomas Bidley
Quartermaster John Pitts

Sergeant Major Thomas Chamberlain's troop
Lieutenant Anthony Lacon
Cornet Francis Howe
Quartermaster Thomas Huckle

Captain Daniel Dale's troop
Lieutenant Richard Ireland
Cornet George Ash
Quartermaster Jacob Peck

Captain Joseph Sabberton's troop
Lieutenant Thomas Steward
Cornet Thomas Rendall
Quartermaster Timothy Thornborow

Captain William Granson's troop
Lieutenant John Dew
Cornet David Camby
Quartermaster John Harrison

Captain John Wright's troop
Lieutenant John Pitchford
Cornet Richard Gilder
Quartermaster William Shepherd

72 *CSPD 1659–60*, pp.8–9; Firth and Davies, *Regimental History*, I, pp.228–9; Wanklyn, *New Model*, II, pp.113, 130, 283–4.

Colonel Robert Lilburne's Regiment of Horse
(as of 31 May 1659)[73]

Colonel Robert Lilburne's own troop
Captain Lieutenant John Turner
Cornet George Denham
Quartermaster George Aston

Sergeant Major George Smithson's troop
Lieutenant William Wheatly
Cornet John Thicket
Quartermaster Robert Harrison

Captain William Peverell's troop
Lieutenant Robert Crooke
Cornet [??]
Quartermaster Robert Nicholson

Captain Thomas Strangeways' troop
Lieutenant Thomas Elliot
Cornet William Smith
Quartermaster Thomas Hawson

Captain John Groves' troop
Lieutenant Walter Merry
Cornet John Bradford
Quartermaster John Belley

Captain Francis Wilkinson's troop
Lieutenant Richard Skipper
Cornet Thomas Randolph
Quartermaster Thomas Redford
Surgeon William Dodd

Major General John Lambert's Regiment of Foot
(as of 1 August 1659)[74]

Colonel John Lambert's own company
Captain Lieutenant Thomas Hooper
Ensign Samuel Rigge

Lieutenant Colonel Jeremiah Campfield's company
Lieutenant John Lakin
Ensign William Page

---

73 *CJ*, VII, pp.669, 682; Firth and Davies, *Regimental History*, I, pp.264–75.
74 Clarke, *Papers*, IV, p.19; *CSPD 1659–60*, pp.216–7, 226.

Sergeant Major Christopher Skipper's company
Lieutenant William Cash
Ensign William Scudamore

Captain John Lambert's company
Lieutenant John Young
Ensign Johnson

Captain Edward Bradshaw's company
Lieutenant Richard Hogg
Ensign Abraham Read

Captain Thomas Fryer's company
Lieutenant Richard Bradley
Ensign Enoch Greenleaf

Captain Thomas Axtle's company
Lieutenant Samuel Foster
Ensign William Atkinson

Captain Walter Brocket's company
Lieutenant [?]
Ensign William Newhouse

Captain William Elwan's company
Lieutenant Richard Hanley
Ensign Clark

Captain Isaac Haugh's company
Lieutenant James Thomas
Ensign Richard Elton

Chaplain George Fryers
Surgeon Anthony Devizes
Surgeon's Mate William Swadlin
Quartermaster and Marshal John Southern

Colonel John Hewson's Regiment of Foot
(as of 13 June 1659; second formation, some original companies remaining in Ireland)[75]

Colonel John Hewson's own company
Captain-Lieutenant Israel Bolton
Ensign Robert Goodall

75 *CJ*, VII, pp.682–3.

Lieutenant Colonel John Duckenfield's company
Lieutenant Daniel Webb
Ensign Leonard Brotherton

Sergeant Major Edward Hoare's company
Lieutenant Abraham Hoare
Ensign Borne Pave

Captain Samuel Bennett's company
Lieutenant John Newton
Ensign Thomas Bailey

Captain Robert Smith's company
Lieutenant Matthew Scott
Ensign Robert Gay

Captain Edward Turner's company
Lieutenant Alexander Fry
Ensign Henry Risby

Captain William Duckenfield's company
Lieutenant Edward Birtles
Ensign Thomas Howley

Captain John Hardier's company
Lieutenant Stephen Coone
Ensign Andrew Faith

Captain Richard Goodwin's company
Lieutenant Andrew Farnham
Ensign John Lloyd

Captain Robert Brown's company
Lieutenant Henry Gooch
Ensign Robert Sutcliffe

Quartermaster William Pritchard
Chaplain John Faldo
Surgeon Jeremiah Higgs
Surgeon's Mate Nathaniel Harris

Colonel John Biscoe's Regiment of Foot
(as of 13 June 1659)[76]

Colonel John Biscoe's own company

76 *CJ*, VII, p.682; Wanklyn, *New Model*, II, pp.118–19.

Captain Lieutenant Thomas Andrews
Ensign Robert Treswell

Lieutenant Colonel William Styles's company
Lieutenant John Fairfax
Ensign Matthew Whiteside

Sergeant Major Matthew Cadwell's company
Lieutenant Edward Jones
Ensign John Knight

Captain John Groome's company
Lieutenant Thomas Baxter
Ensign Joseph Archer

Captain Stephen White's company
Lieutenant Henry Read
Ensign William Baddeley

Captain Samuel Wise's company
Lieutenant Edward Read
Ensign Stephen Lyman

Captain John Styles' company
Lieutenant Robert Grubb
Ensign John Leake

Captain Daniel Nicholls' company
Lieutenant Rowland Williams
Ensign Joseph Jones

Captain Benjamin Gifford's company
Lieutenant Richard Hamlin
Ensign George Smoute

Captain Hannibal Vivian's company
Lieutenant Benjamin Ruddier
Ensign John Shelton

Surgeon Edward Atkinson Surgeon
Surgeon's Mate John Fairfax
Quartermaster and Marshal George Atkinson

Colonel Richard Ashfield's Regiment of Foot
(as of late September 1659)[77]

77 Wanklyn, *New Model*, II, p.116.

Colonel Richard Ashfield's own company
Captain Lieutenant Weare

Lieutenant Colonel William Symonds's company
Sergeant Major Henry Dorney's company
Captain Robert Baynes's company
Captain Thomas Heyrick's company
Captain William Fitch's company
Captain Jones's company
Captain William Hooper's company
Captain William Davies's company
Captain John Radlee's company

Lieutenant John Radford – received his commission with Captains Hooper, Davies and Radlee when the four of them were in London on 9 July 1659.[78]

The Irish Brigade in England 1659–60

On 30 July 1659 Lieutenant General Edmund Ludlow, commander-in-chief of the forces in Ireland, was ordered to send over 500 horse and 1,000 foot 'under the conduct of able officers'.[79] He was to land them near Chester, at Liverpool or Beaumaris. The Irish brigade consisted of eight troops of horse and 11 companies of foot under the overall command of Colonel Jerome Zankey (who was appointed at the suggestion of the commander-in-chief of the army, Lieutenant General Fleetwood, and who also led the horse), while Colonel Daniel Axtell was placed in charge of the infantry.[80] Jerome Zankey – an officer of considerable experience – was described by Richard Gough as 'a person of a mean stature, mild disposition, and accounted a very religious man', whereas he was noted in Royalist propaganda as a preaching captain and nicknamed 'the little pope'.[81] Dore described Zankey as 'a colourful and energetic man who had a remarkable career'.[82] He served as captain lieutenant to Sir William Brereton's troop in Cheshire during the First Civil War, before leading 400 Cheshire horse in North Wales under Colonel Mytton in 1646. Jerome later served with distinction in Cheshire and Ireland, rising to the rank of colonel.[83]

Each unit in the brigade drawn from a variety of standing regiments in Ireland, and were not – as imperfectly described by Baker – Zankey's and Axtell's own regiments.[84] As Firth and Davies state, the figures given with a list of troop and company commanders in *Calendar of the State Papers*

78 *CJ*, VII, pp.710, 713.

79 *CSPD 1569–60*, pp.54, 73, 90.

80 Ludlow, *Memoirs*, II, pp.110–12; *Clarke papers*, IV, pp.68, 146.

81 Razzell (ed.),*Myddle*, p.220; *Mercurius Aulicus*, 3 July 1643.

82 *BLB*, I, 186, n.1; J.E. Auden, 'Sir Jerome Zankey (or Sankey), of Balderton Hall, co. Salop, and of Coolmore, co. Tipperary', *TSAS*, 50 (1939–40), pp.171–8.

83 BCA, MS 595611, pp.24, 26, 67–7; *CSP Ireland, 1647–1660*, p.750.

84 Baker, *Chronicle*, p.674.

Relating to Ireland of 474 cavalry and 875 represent troopers and common soldiers mustered for duty on 11 April 1659.[85] By the time the force crossed the Irish Sea in early August, some of the brigade's officers had changed. According to Ludlow's account of the subsequent campaign:

> Lieutenant General Fleetwood having in a letter to me desired that Colonel Zankey might command the forces to be sent from Ireland, I readily consented to it, having no suspicion of any design concealed under that request; and being informed by Colonel Axtell that he also had some important affairs in England, which he had left unsettled, I appointed him to command the foot. Lieutenant colonel Walker, Major Rawlins, Major Bolton, and Major Godfrey were the rest of the field-officers. I ordered that the party to be transported to England should be drawn to Dublin; and as soon as a considerable number of them were arrived there, orders were dispatched for their transportation, on assurance that the speedy landing of our forces from Ireland would tend to the discouragement of our enemies, and great encouragement of our friends. Having drawn the first party, which was to be embarked, to the waterside, consisting of about four hundred, we caused two months' pay to be advanced to them, one to enable them to pay their debts in Ireland, the other was put into the hands of Lieutenant colonel Walker, who commanded them, to be delivered to them as soon as they should arrive in England. The officers and soldiers undertook the service with all imaginable cheerfulness; and one of the vessels that was appointed to carry Captain Jeacock and his company not being able to approach so near the shore as to make it convenient for the soldiers to embark, the captain put himself into the water, which his men seeing, they soon followed his example, and all together, with the sea almost up to the shoulders, marched through from the ship. They had a very favourable passage, and landed seasonably in England: for it happened that the third day after their arrival Lieutenant colonel Walker took up his quarters at a town in Caenarfonshire, where many disaffected gentlemen and others of those parts had appointed to rendezvous the next day; but fearing he might ruin the country, if they appeared in arms, they quitted their design, and kept themselves at home.
>
> The second party I sent for England was commanded by Colonel Axtell, and the third by Colonel Zankey, to whom I gave also a commission to command the whole brigade of horse and foot, requiring him to take all advantages against the enemy, to relieve our friends, and to obey all such orders as he should from time to time receive from the Parliament, the Council of State, Colonel Lambert, or me. Thus the whole number of the forces demanded by the Parliament was shipped off within ten days after I had received their order, though some of them were quartered at a great distance from Dublin; and both horse and foot landed very seasonably in England, though not without a sad loss. For the ship wherein Major Bolton and Major Rawlins, with above thirty private soldiers, had embarked, sprung a leak in her passage, and sunk down. The Irish Brigade being joined and arrived at Chester, they sent to Colonel Croxton, to let him know, that

85 *CSPI 1647–60*, p.686; Firth and Davies, *Regimental History*, II, p.614; Wanklyn, *New Model*, II, pp.261–2.

> if he should be driven to extremity before any relief should come to him from London, they had resolved to attempt it themselves.[86]

During the voyage, another vessel, the *Flower of Liverpool*, foundered with the loss of Sergeant Major Bolton, Sergeant Major Rawlins and over 30 soldiers; the former was replaced by Sergeant Major Godfrey as senior officer of the horse, in the absence of Zankey. Concerned for the welfare of his men and also the families of the drowned soldiers, from Chester on 6 September Jerome wrote to the president of the Council of State, 'Stating the loss of a ship on the passage from Ireland with Majors Bolton and Rawlings on board and other officers and men, the hardships and dangers suffered by the other troops in their passage from a storm, and their activity in the Parliament's service, and asking that the widows and children of those who were lost should be provided for, and six weeks' pay given to the troops'.[87] Even though two months' pay had been advanced to the troops before embarkation for England, on 9 September Parliament ordered that 'the just debts due from the State to Major Boulton and Major Rawlins, and the other officers and soldiers cast away in their coming from Ireland, be paid. And also to consider the necessities of their wives and children; and present to this House what they think fit to be done for them'.[88] Furthermore, 'the officers and soldiers that came out of Ireland, to suppress the rebellion in Cheshire, and those parts' were to have six weeks' wages paid to them. The sum of £1,800 was immediately forwarded to them in part pay, whilst Zankey received 'the Parliament's Acceptation of the good Affection and Service of the Officers and Soldiers which came out of Ireland'.

But although the brigade participated in the siege operations at Chirk Castle (at the end of which their commander acted as a commissioner for its surrender), and the troops were ordered to return to Ireland on 3 September, they were destined to play an important part in the political affairs of the nation. Following the signing of the Derby Petition, in December 1659 it was ordered to march to London, before heading to the north of England in support of Lambert, and did not return Ireland for a considerable period.[89] During the campaign in England and Wales during August–September 1659 the Irish Brigade comprised:

The Horse
Sergeant Major Francis Bolton's troop (Colonel Henry Pretty's regiment)
Sergeant Major John Godfrey's troop (Colonel William Allen's regiment)
Sergeant Major William Meredith's troop (Colonel Peter Wallis' regiment)
Captain John Stroud's troop (regiment unknown)
Captain Richard McLaughlin's troop (Colonel Daniel Redman's regiment)
Captain Thomas Aske's troop (Colonel Jerome Zankey's regiment)
Captain Thomas Walcot's troop (Lieutenant General Ludlow's regiment)

86 Ludlow, *Memoirs*, II, pp.110–13; HMC, *Thirteenth Report, App. I*, pp.684–6.
87 HMC, *Thirteenth Report, App. I*, pp.685–6.
88 *CJ*, VII, p.776.
89 *CSPD 1659–60*, pp.54, 73, 166, 181; Ludlow *Memoirs*, II, p.110–1, 447.

Captain Valentine Disbrowe's troop (possibly Pretty's regiment)

The Foot

Lieutenant Colonel Walker – not with his company (Colonel Thomas Sadler's regiment)[90]
Colonel John Clarke's company (his own regiment)
Sergeant Major Thomas Rawlins' company (Lieutenant General Ludlow's regiment)
Sergeant Major Samuel Bonnell's company (Colonel Robert Barrow's regiment)
Captain Benjamin Woodward's company (Colonel Thomas Sadler's regiment)
Captain Richard Hannay's company (regiment unknown)
Captain Alexander Barrington's company (Colonel Robert Phayre's regiment)
Captain Thomas Shepherd's company (Colonel John Hewson's regiment in Ireland)
Captain Mark Mould's company (Ludlow's regiment)
Captain John Bridges' company (Independent company)
Captain Radford's company (Phayre's regiment)
Captain Quelch's company (Hewson's regiment in Ireland)

90 *CSPI 1647–60*, p.692.

7

Winnington Bridge: the Battle and its Outcome

On 15 August 1659, after a forced march of nine days, Major General John Lambert arrived with his brigade at Nantwich. This represented a considerable achievement, particularly given the adverse weather conditions. Lambert reported, 'it proved very unseasonable for rain, yet judging your service required expedition, and finding a great resolution in the soldiery to encounter all difficulties'.[1] The Venetian Resident reported that during the passage their 'march is long and toilsome, and harassed by terrible winds, very unusual for the season, and by rain which has fallen almost incessantly since they started'.[2] Likewise, the Presbyterian minister Martindale spoke of similar conditions affecting Sir George Booth's recruits, during which 'God seemed to frown upon them, the weather being so very foul, in the midst of summer, that many were thereby discouraged from going to their musters, and those that came were scarce able to stand upon the ground, much less to exercise with firearms'.[3] In August 1648 during the Preston campaign the unusually cold and wet conditions deterred potential English volunteers from leaving their firesides, while at the same time encouraged large numbers of Scots to desert and return home. Lambert wrote of 'miserable marches' and 'illness of weather', while of 18 August Cromwell described 'twelve miles of such ground as I ever rode in all my life, the day being very wet'.[4] Except as then, in 1659 the veteran troops were habituated to harsh conditions and arduous marches, whilst they were led by determined and resourceful officers.

Initially numbering about 3,500 men when it left London, upon its arrival at Nantwich Lambert's brigade was reinforced by four companies of Colonel Biscoe's regiment and a troop of the Major General's own horse, probably that of Captain Adam Baynes.[5] Lambert now had 1,200–1,500 cavalry and 3,000

1 *Lord Lambert's Letter*; *CWTC*, p.168; Mahler, *History of Chirk*, p.190.

2 *CSPV*, p.56.

3 *Life of Adam Martindale*, p.136.

4 John Rushworth, *Historical Collections of Private Passages of State* (London: D. Browne, 1722), IV, p.1218; Cortez (ed.), *Writings and Speeches of Oliver Cromwell*, I, p.636.

5 *Clarke Papers*, IV, pp.32, 38, 46.

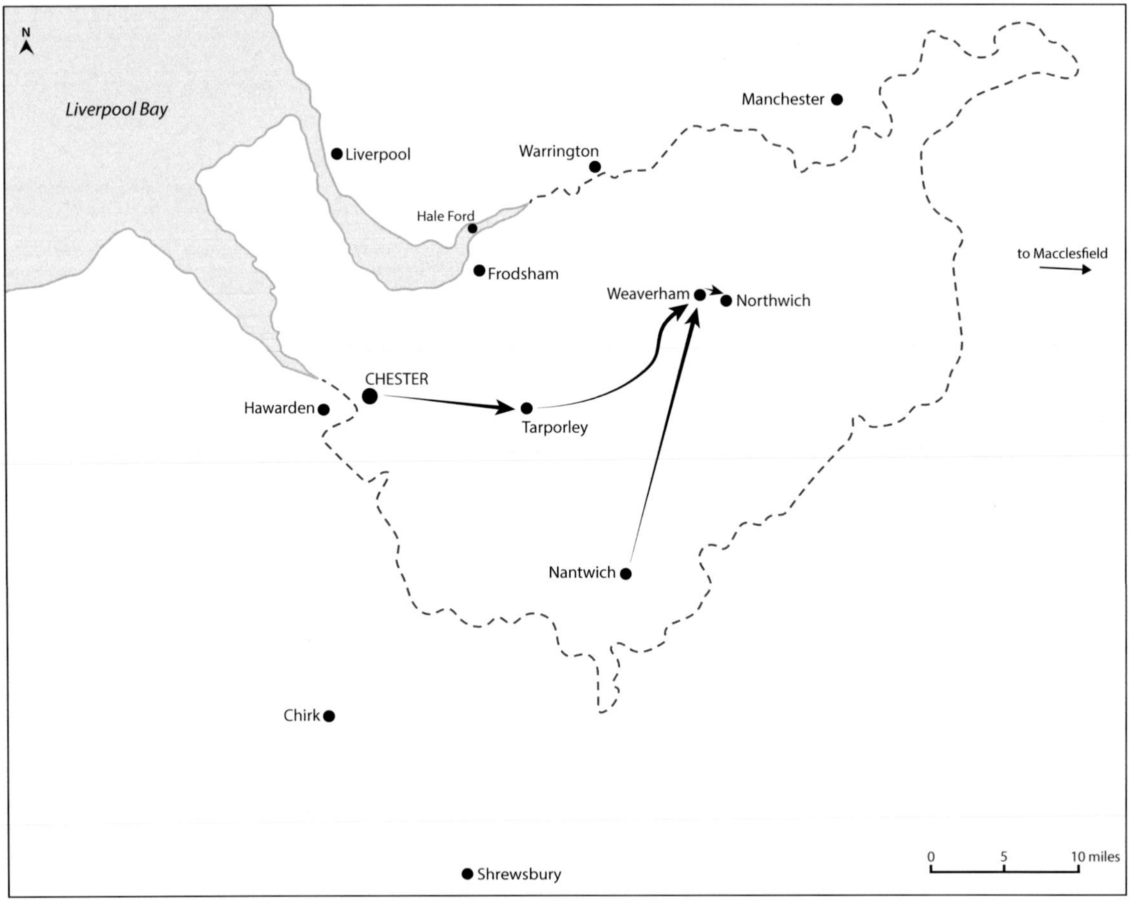

Map 3 Military Operations in Cheshire, 17–18 August 1659.

infantry directly under his command in Cheshire, in addition to militia units in the adjacent counties of Lancashire and Shropshire.[6] It may be assumed that the artillery train of eight guns that had accompanied the brigade northwards, in addition to the ordnance supplied in Staffordshire, were present. Moreover, it was reported that on the same day that the expeditionary force reached Cheshire, the force sent from Ireland – consisting of 500 horse and 1,000 foot – disembarked in North Wales, bringing the overall number of troops available for immediate deployment against the rebellion to about 6,000 (2,000 horse and 4,000 foot).[7] Nantwich was the second town in Cheshire in size and importance, and a far better communications centre than its only rival, Macclesfield. As Chester was in Royalist hands during the First Civil War, Nantwich had been the only viable alternative as a permanent headquarters for the Parliamentarian forces commanded by Sir William Brereton. His troops subsequently 'fortified all the town round-about with strong trenches, and mud-walls of clods of earth' and the location proved to be a formidable stronghold.[8]

6 *Ibid.*, pp.38–9.
7 Ludlow, *Memoirs*, II, p.113; HMC, *Thirteenth Report, App. I*, p.686.
8 Malbon, *Memorials*, p.38; Eliot Warburton, *Memoirs of Prince Rupert and the Cavaliers*, 3 vols (London: Bentley & Fley, 1849), II, pp.355–6.

Having reached Nantwich on 15 August 1659 Lambert allowed his soldiers a rest of three days. One member reported, '[we] stayed for some time there to refresh our men, and the coming up of the rest of our foot'.[9] Both armies passed through the town during the campaign, with both commanders being entertained at Townsend House by the Presbyterian gentleman, Roger Wilbraham. Of Booth's visit his diary records:

> 1659 Aug. 11. Sir George Booth (being after Lord Delamere) being then in arms to restore King Charles II, took up his quarters at my house for one night. The Monday following [15 August] Major General Lambert, who was sent with forces to suppress the rising in Cheshire and Lancashire, took up his quarters at my house, which was filled with officers, and were the more straightened my wife lying in at that time of her third child. After three nights' stay to refresh his men, he marched towards Northwich, and met Sir George Booth's forces upon the skirt of the forest of Delamere, which were easily dispersed, wanting arms, ammunition, and experienced officers to lead them, 19 August 1659.

Further details of Lambert's activities at Townsend were supplied by Wilbraham's daughter:

> Monday 15 August 1659. General Lambert with his army, consisting of 5,000 men, horse and foot, came to Nantwich and stayed therein till Thursday 18 August. The general, Adjutant-General Northrop, Colonel Swallow, one Lister, brother-in-law to the general, and one Friar, chaplain to the general, and their servants and horses quartered at my house. At meals there was for the most part as many as the table would hold, viz. Colonel Briscoe, Colonel Ashley, Major Creed and others of the principal officers, all upon free quarter, for which the general gave my servants 24s. They went hence the same month in which the Scotch army came hither eight years before.[10]

With Lambert's troops now concentrated and revitalised, events began to develop expeditiously in Cheshire. Sir George Booth, at the head of his core forces, began moving from the Chester–Tarvin area, during Wednesday 17 August. However, because of his inability to post adequate patrols – one mounted guard belonging to Sir Thomas Myddelton's troop had been positioned at Hatton Heath (five miles west of Tarporley) the previous day – it would appear that Booth and his commanders remained remarkably oblivious to the nearness of Lambert's troops quartered at Nantwich.[11] The antagonists were barely 15 miles apart at this stage. It was Mordaunt who reported:

> [The insurgents] divided and left 700 of their best foot in the town, and march towards Nantwich; but want of intelligence ruined them; and though they knew how strong Lambert was, they never knew what marches he made, nor where

9 *Another great Victory*; *CWTC*, p.178.

10 CRO, DBW/P/J/10, unfol.; James Hall, *A History of the Town and Parish of Nantwich, or Wich-Malbank, in the County Palatine of Chester* (Nantwich: Privately published, 1883), p.193.

11 Myddelton, *Chirk Castle Accounts*, I, p.84.

> he quartered. This appears by their neglect in gathering their troops together, for there were 500 Lancashire foot within a day's march, and 600 more near Warrington, and my Lord of Derby not yet joined with them. Wednesday they reached Nantwich, and the first alarm they had was by a lieutenant colonel, who bringing up the rear saw some troops he mistrusted; he rode to them, and finding them the enemy, he fired his pistol and galloped back to acquaint the general officers with it; this gentleman, formerly been a good fellow, his intelligence was not credited. And here the mistrust of a truth, proved more prejudicial than if they had believed a lie.[12]

If this was indeed the case, such a catastrophic failure of military intelligence gathering and poor level of tactical awareness on the part of Booth and his officers (some of whom were highly experienced in combat) is incredible by any standard. It also begs any number of questions about the quality and cohesiveness of the rebel leadership, as well as Sir George's own seemingly narrow awareness of the events that were about to engulf him. News of Lambert's movements from London had begun to arrive in Cheshire and the North West more than a week earlier. Moreover, Sir George Booth had been made aware by at least 7 August that his position was perilous, owing to a lack of Royalist support from other quarters, which even in a general sense, he must (or should) have known about. There seems little wonder that his senior commanders in Chester had recently expressed towards him their dismay at his lack of strategy and communication, warning:

> We cannot imagine your return before you have engaged, neither can there be any intelligence passed betwixt you and us, nor can you think other than that the enemy will immediately clap betwixt you and us, and so obstruct all passages, and in case you should any foil your retreating place is lost and we left to stand by ourselves.[13]

Exactly what Sir George Booth was trying to accomplish remains incomprehensible, but a significant rift had clearly occurred between himself and his leading supporters over the strategic aims of the rebellion. It was later reported by the French ambassador to Cardinal Mazarin, that whilst being interrogated by government commissioners following his capture:

> He ingenuously confesses having treated with Mordaunt, the king's agent, and his wife's having received a letter from the king. He has discovered the whole design, but without naming the authors, having begged not to be pressed to do a thing which would wound his honour. Hitherto they have had the courtesy to receive what he has voluntarily confessed. His speeches show that there was a misunderstanding between him and the other chiefs, because he refused to proclaim the king; that against his advice they drew near the Parliament army and engaged in fight, and that before he arrived at the head of the troops, those who had so stubbornly wished to attack Lambert had fled. That he tried to rally

12 Carte, *Letters*, II, pp.194–200; *LM*, pp.70–1; *CCSP*, III, pp.552–3.

13 Bodl. Lib., MS Tanner 51, fol. 138r.

> them in Chester, and defend the town, but they refused to bear arms longer for a cause that they said was abandoned of God. Parliament has found out from him and other prisoners that many other persons of condition had promised to follow this example.[14]

A further possibility which has not been considered by historians of the rebellion, is that Booth was persuaded to march his troops away from Chester by the discovery of elements of the Irish Brigade in the vicinity of the city. The question of exactly when Colonel Zankey's units landed from Ireland, as well as the practical military details, such as rates of marching for seventeenth-century cavalry and infantry, is potentially fundamental to any understanding of the broader campaign in the region. Lieutenant General Ludlow stated, 'the whole number of the forces demanded by the Parliament was shipped off within ten days after I had received their order [dated 30 July 1659]'.[15] There seems no reason to doubt the word of Richard Dermot (the well-informed muster-master of ships), who informed the commissioners of the navy, 'The army that came from Dublin, both horse and foot, were landed at Beaumaris on the 15th, conveyed thither by the *Paradox*'.[16] Although Ludlow's narrative provides the main source for the progress of the brigade in England and Wales, various newssheets reported on its movements. Hence, it was recounted on 20 August, 'Since my last there is come over from Ireland 1,000 foot under Colonel Axtell's command, and 500 horse under Colonel Zankey, and by this time they are marched from Holyhead to West Chester, before which the Lord Lambert is set down to refresh his army'.[17]

Even so, the chronology and details of the Irish Brigade's movements remain hazy. The statements, 'The Irish Brigade being joined and arrived at Chester, they sent to Colonel Croxton, to let him know, that if he should be driven to extremity before any relief should come to him from London, they had resolved to attempt it themselves' (Ludlow), and 'they are marched from Holyhead to West Chester, before which the Lord Lambert is set down to refresh his army' (newssheets), suggest that Zankey's troops marched with some alacrity – and presumably without interference – from Anglesey to within close proximity of the city following their assembly. Moreover, both sources indicate that the arrival of the brigade (or advanced elements of it, probably the horse) before Chester and the delivery of the promise of relief to the garrison, occurred either before or during Lambert's initial encounter with Sir George Booth's forces near Tarporley on 17 August. If this was the case, Zankey's soldiers – given that the city was in the hands of the insurgents, and the northern and eastern environs of Chester were theoretically controlled by Booth's forces also – may have reached the Saltney–Handbridge area located to the south of the Dee, across from Chester. Thus, communication with Colonel Croxton's garrison within the castle would have been possible,

14 *CSPD 1659–60*, pp.162–3.

15 Ludlow, *Memoirs*, II, p.113; HMC, *Thirteenth Report, App. I*, pp.686.

16 *CSPD 1659–60*, p.133.

17 *Mercurius Politicus*, 11–18 August 1659; *Public Intelligencer*, 15–22 August 1659; *Clarke Papers*, IV, p.45.

especially as the well-informed governor had sent and received messages from at least 4 August, partly by way of his soldiers swimming the river.[18]

On 17 August, in sudden realisation of the closeness of Lambert's troops to his own forces, Booth attempted a hurried negotiation. He wrote to the Major General, saying he was 'surprised to see him at the head of an army against him, who had only declared for a free parliament, offering to confer on an accommodation.'[19] Lambert replied unequivocally that he had been ordered to force the rebels into submission, and bloodshed could only be prevented by the laying down of their arms. Martindale, who claimed to have been dismayed by both Sir George Booth's promised manifesto of toleration and Sir Thomas Myddelton's declaration for the King at Wrexham, remarked that during the parley, 'one of Lambert's messages was very fair and moderate, carrying an olive branch of peace in its mouth, in the opinion of the general and other learned gentlemen alive ... but others were of another opinion, putting a harsh construction on it, and so the war went on.'[20] In making such a comment, albeit at second hand and some period after the event, Adam was probably anxious to deflect direct criticisms of Booth's own – it has to be said, somewhat puzzling – conduct. A further approach was made by two Presbyterian ministers, but this proved fruitless when the Major General informed them, as the insurgents had taken up arms against authority, he was 'commanded by the Parliament to reduce them to obedience, which he is by God's assistance he is resolved to do.'[21] Such overtures only served to persuade Lambert that Booth's force was in a desperately disorganised and unprepared condition.

The stark reality of the situation was that had it not been for a rapid decision by Colonel Roger Whitely – the 'lieutenant colonel, who bringing up the rear saw some troops he mistrusted' of Mordaunt's account – who, having accidently encountered one of Lambert's mounted patrols during the afternoon of 17 August, and whose report was ignored, the insurgents would probably been routed on the spot in the fields around the area of Tarporley and Little Budworth. The following morning, in pouring rain, Lambert's brigade, believing that the main rebel force lay to its north and west, began to probe towards Chester. This is confirmed by a later account, based upon the text of follow-up letters sent to Parliament by Lambert, sent on 19 August 1659:

> Yesterday we marched from Nantwich (having stayed for some time there to refresh our men, and the coming up of the rest of our foot) intending to march to Tarporley within seven miles of Chester: but understanding by some warrants of theirs, by which they had required provisions to be brought to them that morning for 5,500 foot and horse, that they were for a march, and having certain intelligence they marched towards Northwich, my lord altered his first intentions, and marched after them over the forest of Delamere.[22]

18 *CSPD 1659–60*, pp.73–4.

19 *Ibid.*, p.136; Whitelocke, *Memorials*, IV, p.358.

20 *Life of Adam Martindale*, p.139.

21 *Clarke Papers*, IV, pp.45–6.

22 *Another great Victory obtained by the Lord Lambert against Sir George Booth, on Sunday morning last; with the manner of his taking the city of Chester and throwing open the gates; the taking of 500 prisoners and divers eminent commanders, viz. Major General Egerton, The Lord Kilmorey,*

Before Lambert's troops had covered five miles, scouts brought the news that an enemy force (estimated by them at nearly 5,000 men) was advancing in an arc, eastwards and at some distance ahead of them towards the town of Northwich. Altering his line of march, Lambert advanced in the direction of Delamere Forest, along which the rebels were progressing. As he reached the forest Lambert received intelligence that his forward units had closed to within three miles of his foe. He later reported that his troops 'marched with that cheerfulness, that had we had day enough, we should in all probability have engaged them before they had reached Northwich, but do what we could, we only gained a view of their rear-guard in the dusk of the evening, and took three or four prisoners'.[23] Moreover, a somewhat overlooked, yet valuable account 'sent from a surgeon in the army, to his friend in London' – possibly John Hodgson of Lambert's regiment of horse – enclosed with *Another great Victory obtained by the Lord Lambert*, recalled, 'We had a force march upon Thursday, but God carried us through all; and with that courage and alacrity, that I have not seen. Our men went on with such shouts and acclamations, that I think astonished the enemy. The terror of the Lord of Hosts was surely upon them'.[24]

Any comparisons between Lambert's well-organised and motivated force, capable of adapting effectively to up-to-date intelligence with quick decision making and tactical changes, and Booth's units at this point are meaningless. As darkness came on, the rebels quartered at Northwich, as their adversaries paused for the night at the village of Weaverham, some 2½ miles to the west. As Mordaunt stated:

> Thus that night past, some over-secure, others too apprehensive, and some hours in the morning, before it was generally believed the enemy was so very near them; yet in order to their own security they had commanded three troops of horse to defend a pass upon the river, and had sent some 160 foot to another bridge a mile off, where they apprehended the enemy might endeavour to force his way.[25]

During the First Civil War Weaverham was plundered by Royalist troops, while Northwich – like other Parliamentarian garrison towns in Cheshire –

Colonel Brooke and Sir William Neal. Also another Desperate Fight at Liverpool, the taking of the town, the beating and pursuing of the enemy towards Wales; and the Escape of Sir George Booth with 200 horse, to Chirk Castle (London: Edward Horton, 1659); *CWTC*, pp.176–81.

23 *Lord Lambert's Letter*; *CWTC*, p.170; Mahler, *The History of Chirk*, p.190.

24 *Another great Victory*; *CWTC*, p.180. The author's additional comment in the text that 'My Lord marches tomorrow to Chester, and also sends a smart party to Warrington and Manchester' confirms that the report was penned on 19 August, probably shortly after the action at Winnington Bridge. On 28 May 1659 when the list of Lambert's regiment of horse was agreed in the Commons John Hodgson 'surgeon' was 'excepted' to and appears to have lost his place, for there is no mention of him being readmitted when Captain John Hatfield, the other officer 'excepted' to, was given his commission later on 11 June (*CJ*, VII, pp.668, 680). Hodgson was in London again in August. In his memoirs he stated that he received his commission from the Speaker on 3 August (J. Horsfall Turner (ed.), *Memoirs of Captain John Hodgson of Coalley-Hall, near Halifax; Touching his conduct in the Civil Wars, and his troubles after the Restoration* (Brighouse: 1882), pp.49–50; David Farr, 'John Hodgson. Soldier, Surgeon, Agitator and Quaker?', *JFHistS*, 58 (1999), pp.220–34.

25 Carte, *Letters*, II, pp.194–200; *LM*, pp.70–1; *CCSP*, III, pp.552–3.

Church of St Mary, Weaverham. (Author's photograph)

had been fortified by a system of earthworks. In 1643 the constables of Nether Whitley, who were specifically charged with the expense of maintaining the garrison, contributed 4s. 'for making of mud walls at Northwich'.[26] However, it is possible that the town may no longer have been garrisoned (and perhaps its fortifications abandoned) by November 1645, when Sir William Brereton informed the Speaker that the Royalist prisoners taken at Denbigh Green 'doth much add to our trouble and charge, having not only so many as all our prisons and garrisons are capable of, but we are forced to disburse them to several towns and parishes upon open quarters, as in Stockport, Grappenhall, Middlewich, Northwich and Congleton'.[27]

The two principle accounts of the fighting at Winnington Bridge the following day – Lambert's initial dispatch to Parliament on 20 August, and that of Mordaunt (who was not present, but relied on the eyewitness testimony of Colonel Whitely) – are highly important, although a series of further reports by Lambert and some of his subordinates sent to Parliament, as well as some tangential, second-hand narratives offer relevant details.

26 BL, MS Harley 2127, fol. 45r.; 2128, fols 41v.–43r.; Malbon, *Memorials*, p.38.

27 HMC, *Thirteenth Report, App. I*, p.304; BL, MS Add. 11332, fol. 59r.

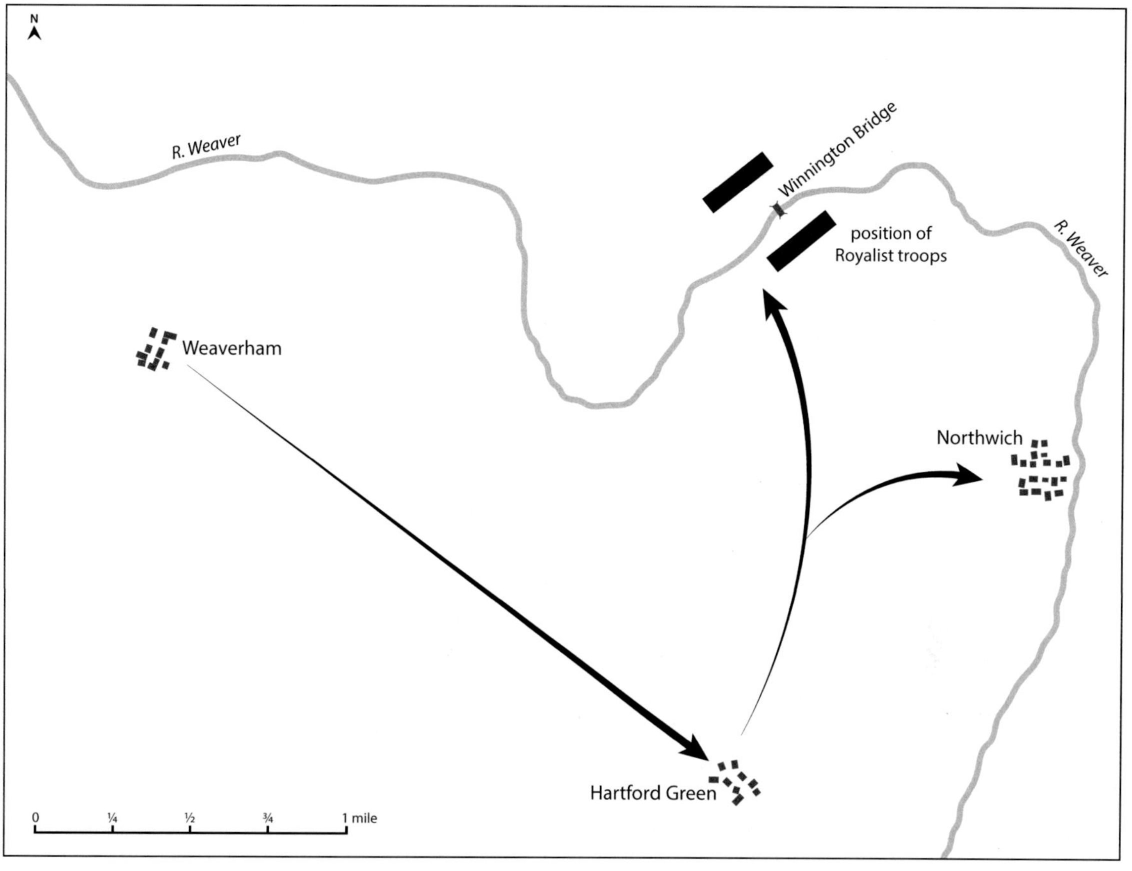

Map 4 Direction of Lambert's attack, 19 August 1659.

Early on the morning of 19 August, Major General Lambert, in continuing to dictate the tempo of operations, ordered his troops to resume their march. By all accounts this came as a complete surprise to their opponents. Except for some agricultural land and a modern golf course in the vicinity of Hartford Green the location of the ensuing battlefield has been obliterated by nineteenth-century industrialisation and urbanisation. Additionally, the area located immediately adjacent to Winnington Bridge – where most of the action occurred – is lost to the 'Winnington Village' property development. Dominating the terrain is the River Weaver, which runs at its lower reaches for more than 50 miles in a curving route across the Cheshire salt-producing area. In its natural configuration it courses through a series of bends to the east of Weaverham. Authorised improvements (augmenting the river with the new Weaver Navigation) completed by 1732, included the construction of 11 locks and weirs, and to the north-east of Weaverham. Barnton Cut sits immediately above the original line of the river.

Additionally, a series of weirs separated the Weaver and Cut to the north of Winnington, with the original bridge thus spanning the river. In 1908–9 Winnington Turn Bridge was installed over the Weaver Navigation, being a cast steel construction with a pedestrian walkway fixed to the western bridge elevation in the later twentieth century. Nevertheless, the documentary sources and remaining topography allow a reasonable interpretation of the fighting on 19 August 1659, as well as the follow-up operations of the succeeding days. Having advanced less than a mile from their overnight quarters at Weaverham, Lambert's forward units rounded the Weaver, but here they encountered a body of Sir George Booth's infantry arrayed in defensive order in the enclosed terrain. Lambert later explained, 'This morning we drew out as soon as we could see, and gave them a great alarm, and [they] drew into battalia upon Hartford Green, between Weaverham and Northwich towards us, as though they would have fought'. Moreover, a paraphrased account given in another letter of the commander added that the rebels:

> drew out of the town amongst the enclosures, where it was impossible for horse to do service, and not without difficulty for the foot to break through. Nevertheless the Lord Lambert presently drew out a party to engage them, and after a short dispute, and some small skirmishes (but gallant volleys), they quitted their grounds, and retreated from hedge to hedge, yet in that order as they suffered very little damage, it being impossible for our horse to fall in amongst them.[28]

This appeared a sound tactical deployment, seemingly organised hastily by Colonel Roger Whitely, in which the rebels' advanced foot – evidently companies or detachments of commanded musketeers from Sir George Booth's own regiment and that of Colonel Henry Mainwaring – were advantageously positioned among the hedgerows, especially to hinder the progress of Lambert's cavalry. During the encounter at Rowton Heath on 24 September 1645, commanded bodies of Parliamentarian musketeers had disrupted Sir Marmaduke Langdale's Royalist advance under cover of the hedgerows and 'so galled their horse, that the rear fled, perceiving their loss by them, upon whom they made no execution'.[29] Likewise, when Colonel Robert Lilburne's troopers were attacked by the Earl of Derby's forces at Wigan Lane on 25 August 1651, the Cheshire foot companies accompanying him stood fast, 'our horse not being able to do any service but in lanes'.[30] Of the close combat amongst the obstacles on Harford Green Lambert later reported:

> it was impossible for horse to do service, and not without difficulty for the foot to break through. We presently engaged them, and after a short dispute they quitted their grounds, and retreated from hedge to hedge, yet in that order as they suffered very little damage, it being impossible for our horse to fall in amongst them, and at length came to Winnington Bridge, behind which they retreated, without any other loss than that of reputation, and discouragement in meeting with those whom they found of equal courage, but engaged in a better cause.[31]

---

28 *Another great Victory*; *CWTC*, p.179.

29 Rupert H. Morris, *The Siege of Chester 1643–1646* (Chester: G.R. Griffith, 1924), p.119.

30 *A Great Victory by the Blessing of God obtained by the Parliament's forces against the Scots forces, commanded by the Earl of Derby, on the 25 of August 1651, near Wiggon in Lancashire, certified by a letter from Col. Lilburne and two letters from Chester, also a letter from Col. Birche to Mr Speaker* (London, 29 August 1651); *Two Letters from Colonel Robert Lilburne*.

31 *Lord Lambert's Letter*.

Terrain around Hartford Green. (Author's photograph)

Though Lambert would later stress that Booth's foot 'suffered very little damage' against his attacking cavalry troopers, their outposts were soon driven back – having come up to join the horse, the forward infantry, probably of Colonel John Hewson's veteran regiment, led by Lieutenant Colonel John Duckenfield had engaged the rebels in a brief, yet one-sided fire-fight. Hewson's soldiers were credited with performing the chief service during the battle and would subsequently dislodge Booth's men from their main defensive positions later in the battle. During the initial action at Hartford Green George Hale of Lower Knutsford and Hugh Woodward of Bexon, 'hired soldiers under the command of the right honourable Sir George Booth', were among the casualties. Hale was 'wounded and put to great want', whereas Woodward was 'shot at the onset of Winnington Bridge'. Similarly, Richard Poulson of Middlewich later recounted that as a soldier under the command of Colonel Mainwaring he 'was shot at that skirmish to the great danger if his life and lay under the surgeon's hands for many weeks together, not being able to move without crutches, nor to get anything towards the relief of his wife and children'.[32] Though suffering from a lack of effective intelligence – a persistent deficiency among the rebel commanders – the experienced and enterprising Colonel Whitely realised from his position on the hill above the crossing of the River Weaver at Winnington Bridge,

32 CRO, QJF/88/3/32; QJF/88/3/39.

Plaque at Winnington Bridge. (Author's photograph)

that the government forces were now advancing with speed. He hurried to the town, whereupon 'the order was given to draw out their foot, which they did in the nearest closes to the town, and after this their horse'. Amidst much confusion the main body of the rebel foot, under the command of the Royalist veteran Colonel Edward Broughton, drew up in the fields before the crossing.

In his initial letter to Parliament Lambert related, 'Their next endeavour was to secure that bridge', and that 'they quit their station and gave way, for both horse and foot to march over. Our horse, which hitherto had been useless to us, advanced over the bridge, together with some foot'. Moreover, his later account reiterated that the insurgents 'drew back to Winnington Bridge, behind which they retreated' and 'they drew up their foot on both sides, and their horse upon a hill behind them'. Crucially, though narrow, the river was too deep to ford, and the crossing was flanked at the far end by a low ditch. Moreover, the precipitous hill could only be traversed by cavalry via a narrow side path. This, it might be assumed, was a robust defensive position, overlooking the narrow bridge over the Weaver, and backed by high ground. However, as the result of a further, and somewhat major oversight on the part of Booth's officers, the rebel soldiers where now separated from their main supply of ammunition, which was stored in Northwich, or had been left behind in Chester. As Mordaunt put it, most of the foot 'had no match, others no ball'. Booth's troops attempted to hold the bridge, but their own bewilderment and inexperience was no match for the proficiency of their opponents. When the first two or three volleys failed to check the advance of Lambert's foot – mainly Hewson's companies, who led the assault – the rebel formations crumbled away.

Lambert's own and Swallow's regiments of horse were now ordered to attack the enemy cavalry (commanded by the former Royalist, Major General Egerton). The infantry, so resolute during the crucial encounter at the bridge, kept their formation as they charged up the hill. Lambert reported:

High ground north of Winnington Bridge. (Author's photograph)

> Our horse, which hitherto had been useless to us, advanced over the bridge, together with some foot. The horse made towards a party of theirs, which I judged was of their choicest, and came to secure the retreat of their foot; and the foot scrambling up the hill after their retreating colours, our horse charged, but by reason of the narrowness of the way, in small parties. To speak truth, that of the horse was performed on both sides like Englishmen; but ours got the better, and the enemy turned their backs.

According to Captain Robert Brown of Hewson's regiment, who took Lambert's letter to Parliament, the cry of Booth's men was 'Have at all', and the Parliament's 'God with us'.[33] Although Lambert reported afterwards that the horsemen on both sides 'performed like Englishmen', other accounts speak of the rebel cavalry making little resistance and abandoning the infantry.[34] Even Mordaunt admitted that as the foot attempted to save themselves, 'the horse trotted away, which is the civilest term'.[35] As the defeat quickly became a rout the remains of Booth's infantry fled about 400 yards northwards to the relative safety of more enclosures, where for the moment Lambert's troopers could not reach them, and before his foot came up.

This was not to last, however, and when the redcoats attacked again, the overwhelmed insurgents were scattered in all directions. The Major General's surgeon testified, 'they were quickly beat, and put to a total rout, throwing down arms and colours, and we had the pursuit of them a great way in lanes and enclosures. Their foot are all broke and disbursed. If it had been a champion country, few of them had escaped to carry home news'.[36] Lambert

33 *CWTC*, pp.171–2.
34 *CSPD 1659–60*, pp.133, 136.
35 Carte, *Letters*, II, pp.199–200; *LM*, pp.70–1.
36 *Another great Victory*; *CWTC*, p.180.

is reported to have diverted the pursuit from Booth's infantry, saying, 'Alas! Poor men, these are forced and hired.'[37] As a professional soldier, he may well have desired to avoid the abhorrence which a massacre of common men would have attached to him. Nevertheless, except for the brief, yet momentarily spirited resistance by elements of the rebel foot in the hedges about Hartford and before the river crossing at Winnington Bridge, the defeat of Booth's forces was rapid and decisive. The only conclusion to be reached is that Sir George was from the beginning of the rebellion and subsequent military campaign, considerably outmanoeuvred by the swiftness, determination and coordinated strategy of his highly proficient opponents. Thus, he and his troops were summarily trapped, with very few options left available to them, other than to either surrender or suffer complete defeat. So decisive did the overthrow of the rebels appear that on 2 September a Royalist correspondent could report, 'Sir George Booth … is poorly come off, and all his glorious pretext of a free parliament and the subjects' liberty, which in his forehead he carried, is all ended under a wench's petticoat, which makes many conclude him to be either a fool, knave or coward'.[38]

All that day Lambert's troopers chased the flying multitude, mainly the cavalry, along the roads to Warrington, Frodsham and Manchester. Newcome recalled that news of Booth's defeat reached Manchester about noon, while he saw people crying in the streets. The next day a throng of beaten soldiers arrived in the town, but Colonel Birch, the Parliamentarian commander, saw to it that the inhabitants were not treated badly.[39] According to the author of *Another great Victory obtained by the Lord Lambert*, 'Sir George Booth flying with some horse toward Chester, was pursued by Major Creed within two miles of the city', while more escaped to Warrington, where they were blocked by four companies of Lancashire foot and a troop of horse.[40] An unverified report of 20 August, probably taken from contemporary newssheets, related:

> This evening about seven of the clock came to the Council of State one of their messengers from the Lord Lambert with this message, viz. Remember me to my friends of the Council, and tell them the enemy is routed, and as soon as I can I will send the particulars. The messenger said he saw three of the enemy's colours, red, white and blue, and six or seven men killed, and said the engagement was at a stone bridge near Northwich, and after a sharp conflict the enemy fell into disorder, and ran two ways, part towards Chester and part towards Lancashire; they as went towards Chester were pursued, and the Lord Lambert was drawing out part of his forces to send towards them as ran Lancashire ward.[41]

In the meantime, the two companies of foot (possibly the 160 men referred to by Mordaunt) and two troops of horse of Booth's army still holding Northwich were attacked by a detachment consisting of Captain William

37 *Life of Adam Martindale*, p.140.
38 Bod. Lib., MS Clarendon 64, fol. 149r.
39 *Autobiography of Henry Newcome*, p.112.
40 *Another great Victory*; *CWTC*, p.180.
41 *Clarke Papers*, IV, p.46.

Evanson's troop of Colonel Swallow's regiment, and a company of dragoons, 'who advancing up to the bridge and firing upon them, the enemy drew off in good order; but not being able to make their retreat, was routed, and pursued within two or three miles of Manchester'.[42] They were chased by Swallow's triumphant squadrons. Sir George Booth himself seems to have extricated himself quickly from the scene and ridden to the temporary shelter of Chester. The turncoat Gilbert Ireland, with about 100 troopers, made again for Liverpool, whilst others escaped into further parts of Lancashire and Cheshire. Less than 48 hours later a dispatch from Captain Richard Brown of Colonel Hewson's regiment, recounting the next stage of military operations, reached Whitehall. Though brief, and from the perspective of a company commander, it not only provides an impression of what was clearly a fast-moving series of events but includes an early list of some of the prisoners taken:

Colonel Massey of Cheshire
Major Harrison, lately a captain of Colonel Gibson's regiment
Captain Philip Egerton
Major James Schofield
Captain Martland
Captain Smith
Cornet Grosvenor, son of Sir Richard Grosvenor
Captain Cosel
Lieutenant Davies
Ensign Ward
Ensign Longshaw
Lieutenant Seare
Cornet Gill
John Bromley of Wolverhampton, gent.
Captain Stukeley
Captain Davies

Captain Brown further stated that when he left the field, the rebels had suffered 30 dead, although 236 common soldiers, 16 officers, 30 colours and sundry horses had been taken.[43] Casualties – often more numerous during the rout and pursuit phase of early modern battles – were probably minimised by Lambert's appeal for clemency toward the fleeing infantry in particular, and the fact that many of the fugitives who had not fled to Chester were rounded up by local inhabitants, or had handed themselves in voluntarily. Amongst those killed was Gustavus Mackworth, son of Henry Mackworth, baronet of Normanton, Rutland, a relative of the Mackworths of Betton Grange, Shropshire. On 27 November 1659 Lady Dorothy Grey petitioned the Committee for Compounding 'that since the death of her husband, Lord Grey of Groby, she married Gustavus Mackworth, who was engaged with

42 *Another great Victory*; *CWTC*, pp.179–80.
43 *CWTC*, pp.171–2.

Sir George Booth, and slain.'[44] The Cheshire quarter sessions petitions for October 1660 provide a level of uncommon detail into the numbers and nature of the casualties among the ordinary soldiers in Booth's army, each of whom had been recruited locally. Jane Batty, in appealing to the magistrates for financial aid for herself and children, stated that her husband David had 'enlisted as a trained soldier under the command of Captain Leigh for the township of Purleston and in the engagement at Winnington lost his life', whereas another widow, Elizabeth Barrett of Over Tabley, petitioned that her late husband Hugh had entered 'into service for a free parliament upon the undertaking of Sir George Booth, and the command of Captain Shepley, and was in that service slain.'[45]

Among the wounded were John Hind of Little Budworth, who during the First Civil War in the Royalist cause had served under the Colonel Marrow in Cheshire, 'and in the late insurgency in this county was a soldier under the command of Captain John Trevis in the regiment of Sir George Booth, baronet ... [and] was wounded at Winnington Bridge and lay a long time before he was able to do anything towards supporting himself or his wife'. Also wounded was John Hind – 'very poor man' – of the same township, while Humphrey Bristow (by profession a webber) testified that having enlisted in Captain John Leech's company for the township of Newton-juxta-Chester, he 'was dangerously wounded with a brace of bullets in the right shoulder. Of which this wound was under the surgeon's hands from August 1659 till September 1660'. Likewise, there was Henry Sherwood of Brereton, 'who went for a soldier for that township, returned home, being shot through the body at the aforesaid fight' and was still suffering from his wounds over a year after the battle.[46]

The Parliamentarian losses were slight. In his first dispatch to the Speaker Lambert wrote, 'And though I cannot say your victory was great in respect of prisoners or men slain, yet I judge it a total rout, or which by the providence of God may be improved to so much. I cannot hear that we have above one man slain outright, and not above three dangerously wounded.' Moreover, in his 'letter to a friend in London', his surgeon reported, 'I cannot give you particulars, divers are killed. I do not know or hear of any we have had killed, and but a few wounded, and I hope none mortally; I was with them and dressed some few.'[47] According to contemporary accounts, losses among the government forces were reckoned at one killed and three 'dangerously wounded', although it is likely that there were some minor injuries. The rebel horse, described by Lambert as 'a gallant body', was estimated by him to be 1,700–1,800 in number. Yet although Sir George Booth's entire army was said to have been about 4,000, the Parliamentarian commander declared that 'in our view, [there] never appeared above two thousand', although he may only have been talking about the forces that appeared at Winnington Bridge, there having been the '700 of their best foot' which Mordaunt claimed to have

44 *CCC*, V, p.3254.

45 CRO, QJF/88/3/43; 88/3/46.

46 CRO, QJF/88/4/23; 88/4/24; 88/4/32; 88/4/62; 88/4/49.

47 *Lord Lambert's Letter*; *Another great Victory*.

been left behind in Chester. This would compute to a figure of roughly 1,500 foot under Booth's command being present at the battle. In allocating credit for the victory, Lambert particularly emphasised the conduct of Lieutenant Colonel John Duckenfield, 'who showed himself a worthy servant this day to you and his country'. Such accomplishment, though comprehensive, was also partly opportune, for later in the day Lambert received a message from Colonel Croxton, brought by a soldier who swam the Dee, reporting that Chester Castle was without victuals and was unlikely to hold out any longer.[48]

Yet as events would turn out, the rebel troops in the city were hardly in a position to seize the fortification, let alone defend it against Lambert's combined forces. In seeking to rationalise the nature and scale of the defeat of Sir George Booth's army, Martindale later wrote:

> It must be less than a miracle if raw undisciplined men (as the greater part were), though with some good soldiers mixed among them, not well formed into an army, not sufficiently furnished with arms and ammunition, should be able to stand before Lambert's men, who were veteran soldiers, well-disciplined, excellently appointed and bravely commanded, flushed with victories and resolved to keep up their trade. God seemed to frown upon them, the weather being so very foul, in the midst of summer, that many were thereby discouraged from going to their musters, and those that came were scarce able to stand upon the ground, much less to exercise with firearms. This much hindered their men into order. Having missed the taking of Chester Castle, they had no place to hide their heads in safety; for how was it possible for them to defend that part of the walls that was near the castle from an enemy's army, the defenders being obnoxious to the cannon and muskets of the said castle? This army (if I may call it one) was like Mahomet's angelical cocks, made up of fire and snow; for many, both of the commanders and soldiers, were not only different, but contrary in their principles … some were zealous for the restoring of the king in pursuance of their covenant, which excluded the prelates; and some were resolved that they would have both or neither. Mr Henry Bridgeman told another minister and me at Dunham, that he forsook them at Manchester because he perceived that some of the grandees were cordial for the king but not for the Church.[49]

Following their victory at Winnington Bridge, Major General Lambert and his senior officers established their temporary headquarters in Northwich. One immediate necessity was the guarding of 200 recently taken prisoners of war, who were consigned to the town's parish church of St Helen, Witton. Among them were the former Parliamentarian soldier, Colonel William Massey, and Jeremiah Harrison, brother of Dr Peter Harrison, Presbyterian minister of Cheadle, who was described in post-rebellion depositions as 'major to Colonel George Booth' (probably his foot regiment).[50] Lambert's most pressing objectives were: the relief of the castle and garrison at Chester, which necessarily meant seizing control of Chester from the insurgents and

48 *Lord Lambert's Letter.*

49 *Life of Adam Martindale*, p.136.

50 Earwaker, *East Cheshire*, I, p.230.

Battlefield formations from Joshua Sprigg, *Anglia Rediviva* (1645). (Author's collection)

militia companies within the walls of the city; to rendezvous with the Irish Brigade, and thereby apprehending and nullifying the threat of Sir Thomas Myddelton and his remaining adherents in North Wales; to bring to heel the governor of Liverpool, Colonel Gilbert Ireland, who had declared for the rebellion and was now fleeing thence with a body of cavalry and 'some notable persons', and to return the castle and port into government hands; to neutralise all insurgent activity in Lancashire and the North West; and to apprehend Sir George Booth and those of his remaining conspirators who had not been taken in battle. This formidable programme would be resolved with the same vigour that Lambert and his troops had exercised thus far.

Lambert's immediate course of action in suppressing further insurgent activity was to divide his forces. Colonel Richard Ashfield, with four companies of foot (two of which were mounted as dragoons), and Lieutenant Colonel Duckenfield, with part of Hewson's regiment, together with a suitable number of troops of cavalry, were sent into Lancashire to connect with Colonel Lilburne, in order to help guard against any further trouble either in Lancashire or the western border of Yorkshire. Orders were conveyed to Colonel Zankey and the Irish brigade (currently quartered in North Wales) to proceed to Shrewsbury 'and to expect further orders there in prosecution of the reducement of Chester'.[51] Lambert himself, with the main body of his forces, would the following day advance towards Chester, although not before dispatching his first full account of the campaign to Speaker. Typically, the Major General concluded his report by appealing to the Council of State to alleviate the material wants of his troops: 'I shall here take the boldness to

51 *Lord Lambert's Letter*; *CWTC*, pp.168–71; Mahler, *History of Chirk*, p.190.

represent to you the great necessity of the soldiers by want of pay, we being to issue that small portion we had after the rate of 6d. a day, and already well-nigh spent, so as shoes, stockings, and other necessaries in their long and dirty marches cannot be provided for.'

An important account of the aftermath of the victory won by Lambert's army at Winnington Bridge and the ensuing military operations in the North West and North Wales is contained in a letter from the French ambassador to Cardinal Mazarin, written on 25 August 1659:

> The mere appearance of the troops put Booth's party to the rout, without any loss except of 30 dead, and 200 or 300 prisoners. Lambert, taking advantage of their terror, marches for Chester, where most of the fugitives have retired, but all the chief officers and soldiers abandoning it in the night, next day he found the gates open, and entered with some of his troops, but without suffering any disorder, according to his promise to the inhabitants. Liverpool, being thus left at liberty, sent word that it had always held for Parliament, and that even Colonel Ireland, who commanded there, had declared for the same interest, although he had taken a commission under Booth. Some other small castles, where garrisons had been placed, were reduced without fighting. Only Myddelton remains in arms; he retired to his castle with some troops, without other hope than to obtain a capitulation. If Booth had taken this course, and held Chester, he had avoided the disgrace into which he has fallen … Major General Egerton, one of the other chiefs, and the Earl of Derby, have also been taken, besides many others of quality. By their depositions it does not seem that their party was as strong as reported, never having exceeded 3,000 or 4,000 men. Still by avoiding a fight, this body might have kept up the war some time, and given heart to the disaffected in the provinces to take arms, *but this needed a chief more experienced than Sir George Booth.*[52]

With the remainder of his forces, Major General John Lambert reached Chester the day following Booth's defeat at Winnington Bridge. Confusion prevailed among the civic authorities and rebel troops in the city owing to the appearance of Sir George and some of the leading fugitives, who attempted to persuade them to prepare for a siege. Sir Thomas Myddelton and his party, having been pursued into Lancashire, had recrossed the Mersey via the ferry at Runcorn the previous night. In the company of Lord Kilmorey he passed rapidly across the scene towards Chirk Castle, which had been put into a defensive state under the charge of his son and heir, Thomas. Sir Thomas Myddelton's subsequent whereabouts remained uncertain, but in the knowledge that he was proclaimed traitor he quickly made his departure. According to the editor of the letters of John Mordaunt, both Myddelton and Mordaunt were sheltered in London by the Royalist John Robinson, president of the Honourable Artillery Company and MP for the city, before making their escape to the Continent.[53] On 11 September 1659 a reward was offered by the Council of State for Myddelton's capture, along with information

52 *CSPD 1659–60*, p.147. Author's italics added.
53 *LM*, p. 184, note 2.

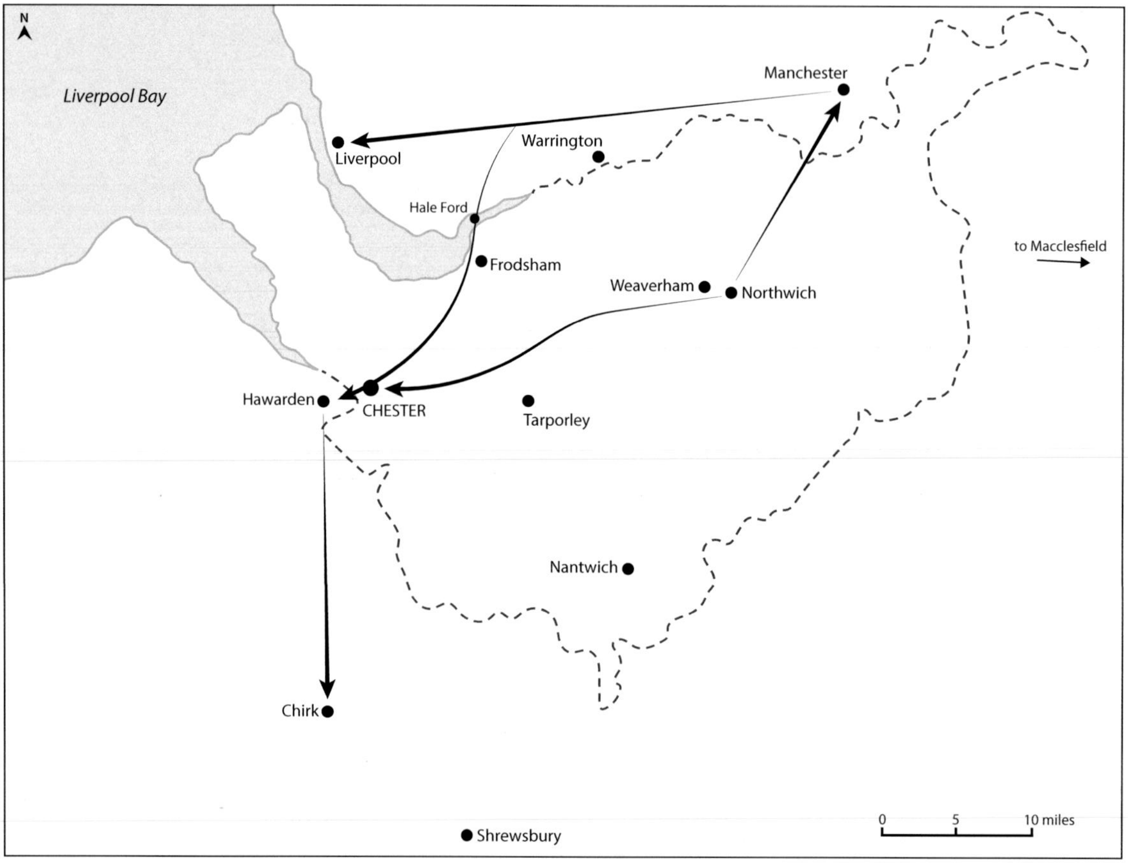

Map 5 Pursuit and final operations, 19–24 August 1659.

about Colonel Robert Werden and William Croft. Sir Thomas was eventually taken and ordered to stand trial with Sir George Booth.

As Major General Lambert approached Chester with upwards of 1,000 troops from his brigade on 20 August, he was met by two envoys from the city who had been instructed by the authorities to offer some terms of surrender, fearing that the city might become prey to looting by his soldiers. As Lambert reported to Parliament:

> Having heard what they had to say, I called together divers of the officers, and acquainted them therewith, who advised me to this answer: that if they would set open their gates on the morrow by ten of the clock, submitting themselves wholly to the Parliament, and receive in such forces as should be appointed, I would engage that no soldier by violence should take anything from them. And lastly, that I would attend for their answer till eight of the clock the next morning, without any further action.[54]

That evening, Booth's men, comprehending their desperate situation, especially as the citizens refused any further aid, and with the officers of the various companies instructing them to make the best they could of the

54 *Second Letter from the Lord Lambert*; *Clarke Papers*, IV, p.38; *CCSP*, IV, p.309.

situation, left the city in small parties. Forsaking Chester and ultimately his own cause, Sir George Booth fled out of the Northgate (in the opposite direction to Lambert's approach) with a few adherents. An eyewitness noted that almost to the last, at least a portion of the Chester trained band remained defiant, perhaps being all too aware of the fate that was about to befall them:

> Thereupon 20 August, tidings being brought the army under Sir George Booth was routed. The said mayor and recorder, being in the Pentice, caused the common bell to toll, which raised most of the city in their arms, my Lord Lambert was approaching near the city, they commanded the Eastgate to be made up with stones and which was accordingly done. Also the two city companies were drawn upon the walls and did hang out their flags in defiance of the Parliament, and there remained upon the watch till Saturday at night 20 August.[55]

The next morning, 'about ten of the clock, finding the gates open', Lambert, who behaved with great restraint in his hour of victory, marched in at the head of a regiment of foot and two troops of horse, with the city quiet and his own soldiers under strict control. That night Richard Dermott confirmed to the Navy Commissioners (presumably via dispatches from the Protectorate ships lying off the Dee estuary):

> The dispute [at Winnington Bridge] was short and sharp; it is reported the foot are all slain, but our horse had the pursuit of the enemy's horse to Chester gates. The town seeing they fled, did not stand, but run away, bid them be gone or submit, or else they would let in the Parliament party, whereupon the enemy stole all away in the night, and the town went to General Lambert, and submitted themselves to his mercy.[56]

A more substantial account was written by the governor of Shrewsbury – who had been something of a linchpin along the Welsh borders in the provision of up-to-date intelligence to the Council of State, both in the weeks leading up to Booth's rebellion and throughout events – reported from the Shropshire town at 10:00 p.m. on 21 August:

> No sooner was the post gone hence yesterday, but a party of my troop returned from my Lord Lambert, who went to convey him some money from this town, and were present in the fight about Northwich, and gave me assurance that my lord had dispatched away an express to your Honours, with an account of that affair, to which I humbly refer your Honours. Just now, the messenger that I sent your letter by, directed to Colonel Croxton this day fortnight, returned back, who came forth of Chester last night at ten of the clock; and before he left the city, Sir Thomas Myddelton, the Lord Kilmorey, with other gentlemen, with five colours of horse, made no small haste from Chirk Castle to Chester. The foot that were in the town mutinied, threw open the gates, tore their colours, and Sir George Booth fled out of the Northgate; they only kept a slight guard at the gates, being

55 TNA, SP23/263, fol. 110r.
56 *CSPD 1659–60*, p.133.

> drawn from the other guards in confusion, and left them in the castle to their own liberty. He assures me, when he came from thence, the enemy were resolved to shift for themselves. I held it my duty to hasten this account. I have sent the horse forth this garrison, since yesterday noon, who are not yet returned. By the letter I received from my Lord Lambert this day, for covert to one, which I dispatched from him to Colonel Zankey, I was given to know, that he divided his army, and intended to march one part towards Chester, the other for Warrington. Just now at writing, a boy of this town, now fled home, confessed he was under one Captain Shenton, who dismissed his company last night at Chester, and bade them shift for themselves. I crave your favour for my rude lines.[57]

No sooner had Lambert taken the surrender of Chester from the city authorities did another deputation reach him, this time from an inhabitant of Liverpool. One Brown, on news of Booth's defeat, claimed that he had gathered together some of the 'well affected' and taken some prisoners. He informed Lambert that the garrison and town certainly had been loyal, and that the governor, Colonel Ireland, had informed members of this deputation beforehand that he meant to stand by Parliament but had now openly declared for the government. There seems little reason to disbelieve this. Major General Lambert had previously sent Sergeant Major Hoare with three companies of foot and three troops of horse to take Liverpool. Having done so with no serious resistance, Hoare carried out his instructions and left a garrison there, before leading the remainder of his forces to strengthen the troops in Lancashire. Lambert also sent a summons of surrender to Hawarden Castle, while Colonel Biscoe was ordered to march to the fortress at Chirk in command of an advance party of three troops of horse and four companies of foot. Here, those who had so far evaded capture awaited the arrival of the army in strength (which would also include troops from the Irish Brigade under Colonel Jerome Zankey, now advancing from Beaumaris).[58] The pace of events was relentless. This is reflected in the postscript of *Another great Victory*:

> The Lord Lambert hath secured Chester, and is in pursuit of them with a considerable party of horse and dragoons towards North Wales. The hearts of the enemy begin to melt like water within them, and Liverpool offers to surrender. The rest are in a languishing condition and know not where to take sanctuary; there being no means left unassailed, to prevent their embarking beyond the seas. Thus, may we see the Lord eminently continuing his wonted hand of mercy, toward them that fear him, and so apparently blasting the traitorous undertakings of adversaries, in every corner of the country.

During the next few days considerable numbers of the Cheshire, Lancashire and Welsh gentry who had participated in the uprising surrendered in droves. Colonel Birch, the military commander in Manchester wrote that he had no prisons to contain them all, although it did not matter because they

57 *CWTC*, pp.175–6.

58 *Ibid.*, p.158.

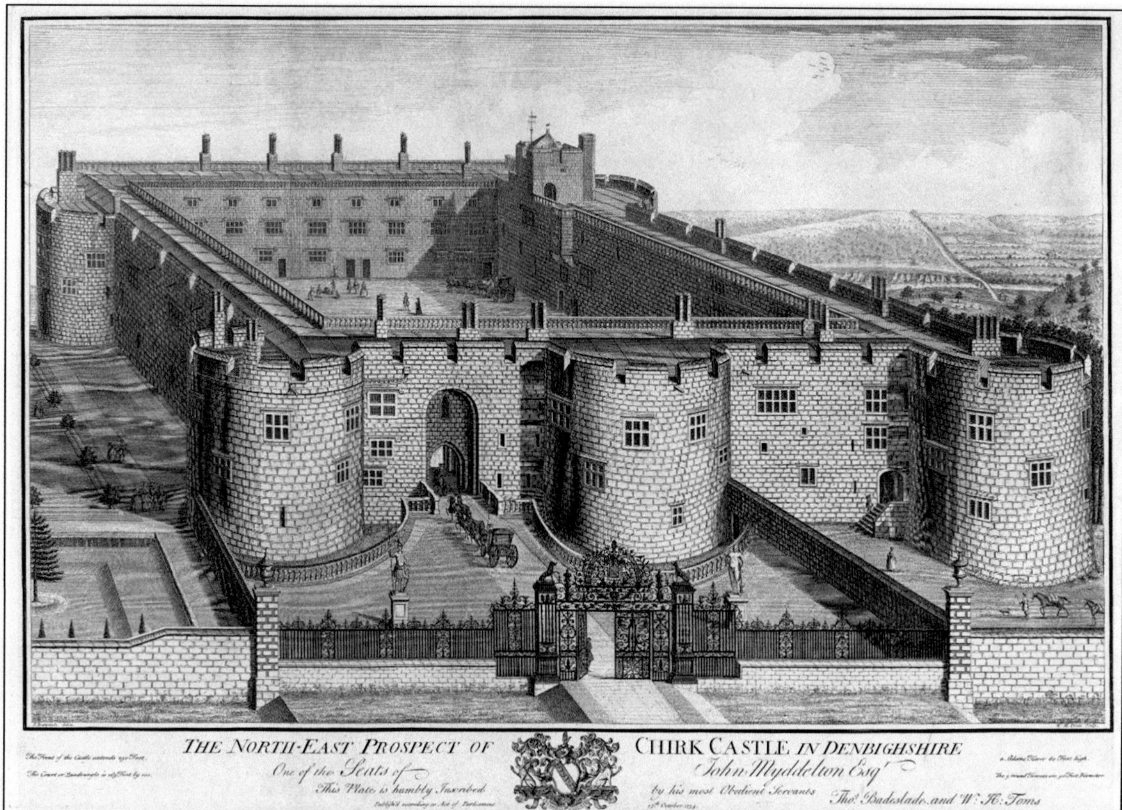

Northeast prospect of Chirk Castle, 1736. (The National Library of Wales. Public Domain)

would not escape, 'they not knowing whither to go'.[59] By 22 August 1659 most of Cheshire and the wider region was under governmental control, while the number of rebel prisoners had risen to 400 'persons of quality'. On 25 August, the Earl of Derby, disguised as a servant, was recognised and captured at Shrewsbury. The Council of State ordered to see that John Roden, who apprehended Derby and his man be given £10 and that the sum figure be granted 'to the man who swam the river at Chester and gave intelligence to Major General Lambert of the state of Chester Castle'.[60] Writing from Chester the following day Lambert provided the government with a list of prisoners, which was read in the Commons on 27 August. Further gentlemen handed themselves in during the ensuing days – on 3 September Colonel Richard Holland, Colonel Henry Brooke and his uncle, Sergeant Major Peter Brooke surrendered to Colonel Birch, presumably in Lancashire.[61]

Lambert reached Chirk on 24 August. There ensued a brief mortar bombardment, which destroyed the Guard and Bell Towers with the eastern curtain wall, and with water in short supply, the garrison surrendered. Sir Thomas Myddelton having escaped, his son and the remaining officers accepted Lambert's offer that they might retire from England within two

59 Bod. Lib., MS Tanner 51, fol. 117r.

60 Whitelocke, *Memoirs*, IV, p. 683; *CSPV*, p.62.

61 *CSPD 1659–60*, p.170.

months, if in that time they had failed to obtain mercy from Parliament.[62] Following the surrender of Chirk Lambert sent a comprehensive report from his headquarters there to the Speaker:

> I now give you the account of the surrender of Chirk Castle, the last remains of this rebellion, which was this day delivered to us upon the terms enclosed. There is now no visible enemy appearing in these parts, and yet I humbly conceive, there rests much to be done for the settling and securing thereof from future trouble. The spirit which led to this undertaking being rather discouraged and disappointed at present, than acquiescing the Providence of God appearing against them; and though I esteem it altogether unnecessary for any to advise you therein, yet I judge it my duty to inform you, that divers great cities and towns in these parts are disaffected to the Parliament, and some of them have been the chief abettors in this late insurrection, and yet still remain as they were, under the same governors and opportunities of raising new troubles, and divers persons who though secretly yet actively have helped in this war still continue with arms in their hands, and begin to smooth their faces and tongues as if they intended nothing but a compliance with your service. Besides a number of others who as neuters would have been ready to appear against you, if the enemy (by obtaining the least success) had given them hopes of prevailing. The knowledge whereof I thought fit to lay before you and submit to your prudence to direct therein for the peace of these nations, as God shall direct you. I think it likewise my duty to acquaint you with the great cheerfulness which has been expressed by your forces, as well as militia as army; for the suppressing the enemy, which was very evident even when danger threatened most. Humbly desiring each due encouragement be given them, as you shall see fit the militia hath been without pay for these three years last past, except what has been lately advanced to them upon account, and now most of them ready to return to their own country, without pay for the present service, or anything in view for their future encouragement I have already taken the boldness to assure them that it will be your care to make due provision for them. There was about 150 men in this place, great store of provisions both for man and horse for many months, one little piece of brass ordnance and a competent quantity of ammunition. The goods and provisions I have already ordered to be converted to the soldiers' use, and at the desire of divers well-affected in this country (it being also the opinion of several of the chief officers of the army) offer that this castle may be demolished, that it may no longer be an occasion of trouble and inconvenience to this country as it often hath been.[63]

The surrender document, included with Lambert's report, as might be expected in the circumstances, was completely unbending. Here it is reproduced in full:

> Articles of Agreement made by and between Colonel Jerome Sankey, Colonel Daniel Axtell, Major Richard Creed and Captain John Hatfield, commissioners

62 *Mercurius Politicus*, 24 August–1 September 1659.

63 Mahler, *History of Chirk Castle*, pp.191–2 (printed in full); [Anonymous], *A Memoir of Chirk Castle from Original Manuscripts* (Chester: Hugh Roberts, 1859), pp.22–3 (partial text).

> appointed by the Lord Lambert, commander-in-chief of the Parliament's forces in these parts, and Colonel Robert Broughton, Colonel Richard Lloyd, Robert Grosvenor, esquire, and Captain Richard Dutton, commissioners appointed by Thomas Myddelton, esquire, governor of Chirk Castle:
>
> Its agreed that Thomas Myddelton, esquire, shall the 24th instant day of August, by 10 of the clock, in the morning, deliver up the Castle of Chirk all arms, ammunition, horses, store of provisions, and what else there is in the castle, without embezzlement, into the hands of the Lord Lambert, or whom his Lordship shall appoint to receive the same, for the use of the Parliament.
>
> That it is agreed by both parties aforesaid, that the governor, Thomas Myddelton, esquire and his commissioners aforesaid, and commanders, shall deliver themselves prisoners to the said Lord Lambert; and upon good security given by them respectively, as his lordship shall approve of, have liberty for two months, commencing from the day of the date of these concessions, to make their application to the Parliament for their money; and such of them as shall not obtain the Parliament's favours to continue within their dominions and territories, shall have liberty to go beyond the seas, they acting nothing in the Interim prejudicial to the present authority, provided, nevertheless, that it is not intended that Lieutenant colonel Edward Broughton shall have the Liberty upon security granted to the rest of the officers aforesaid, until the Lord Lambert's pleasure be further known.[64]

Two days later, the Council of State in London ordered that the castle be demolished and made untenable, although ultimately only one wall was ruined.[65] On 27 August, having approved the surrender of the Chirk garrison, Parliament authorised Lambert to:

> seize and secure, or cause to be seized and secured all the arms and ammunition in the several counties of Lancashire, Cheshire, Derbyshire, and parts adjacent, of all such persons as have not assisted to suppress the rebellion raised in those parts; and that the same be preserved, and safely kept, for the advantage and benefit of the State. And that the said Major General Lambert do give an account to the Parliament, or Council of State, of the said arms and ammunition; and in whose hands or custody they were taken.[66]

In gratitude for their actions, it was ordered that Sergeant Major Richard Creed of Lambert's own regiment of horse and Lieutenant Colonel John Duckenfield of Hewson's foot should have £500 between them. The sum of £100 was also given to Captain Lieutenant Spilman of the Major General's own troop. As for Lambert himself, the Council of State conferred on him £1,000 to purchase a jewel 'as a mark of the favour of Parliament for his signal service', but he used it

64 *CJ*, VII, p.769; HMC, *Thirteenth Report, App. I*, p.684; [Anonymous], *Memoir of Chirk Castle*, p.23.

65 *CSPD 1659–60*, p.150.

66 *CJ*, VII, pp.769–70; *CSPD 1659–60*, p.154.

to pay his soldiers for whom he had frequently requested money and supplies.[67] Eventually Lambert's brigade received its arrears in pay, for on 20 August, the day after their victory at Winnington Bridge, Parliament had ordered the Army Committee to issue warrants to the treasurers at war to dispatch £14,000 by wagon to Chester, 'or wherever else Lambert shall appoint, there to be issued by his warrant for such persons as he thinks suitable to receive a month's pay, whether of the horse, foot, and dragoons raised by the militia commissioners, or of the standing army, and issue it on musters or attestation of two or more commissioned officers of each troop; also for payment of contingent charges'.[68] The local militia was also to receive pay. Hawarden Castle, having previously surrendered to the victorious Lambert, all resistance came to an end after a relatively brief, yet dynamic campaign.

By now Sir George Booth, who had quit Chester with a small company during the night of 20 August 1659, had fallen into government hands. He was discovered three days later by the astute innkeeper of the *Red Lion* in Newport Pagnell, who suspected that a Mrs Dorothy – who had taken a room for the night – was more than she appeared to be. A request for a razor seemingly aroused suspicion, causing his host and his friends (now suitably armed) to detain Sir George and turn him over to the authorities.[69] Booth was transferred under guard to the Tower and there interrogated by Sir Arthur Hesilrige and Sir Henry Vane, with 'a sufficient guard to be by him kept close prisoner for high treason, in levying war against the Parliament and Commonwealth'.[70] The next day the Council of State ordered the sum of £40 to be paid to enterprising innkeeper as a reward, with a further £60 'for distribution amongst those who brought him up'. Moreover, although one Tippin, Sir George Booth's servant, was apprehended by the authorities, the three cases of pistols and three or four swords, belonging to an associate, Thomas Gotten, and seized by soldiers according to Lambert's direction, were restored to him.[71] Somewhat triumphantly, but with a hint of relief at the passing of the emergency, on 5 September Colonel Bamfield, a member of the Council of State, reassured the English ambassador in Brussels, 'All the risings are suppressed, most of the chief officers taken prisoners, the rest fled. Sir George Booth is in the Tower, Major General Egerton, Sir William Neale, and others coming up. The country people took more prisoners than the soldiers. There is now such a fine settlement here as this is likely to remain a Commonwealth.'[72]

---

67 *CJ*, VII, pp.769; *CSPD 1659–60*, pp.132, 134, 137, 145, 147, 154, 162–3; *Second, and a Third Letter from the Lord Lambert*.

68 *CSPD 1659–60*, pp.126, 129.

69 *A True Narrative of the Manner of the taking of Sir George Booth on Tuesday Night last, at Newport Pagnell, being disguised in woman's apparel, with his speech Mr John Gibbs, minister of the town, upon the entering of his chamber. Likewise, the Parliament's resolve touching the said Sir George; and the order for committing of him a close prisoner to the Tower of London for high treason, on Wednesday in the evening; and to be kept from having the use of pen, ink or paper. Also, his examination in the Tower, by Sir Henry Vane, and Sir Arthur Haselrige, according to order of Parliament* (London: Thomas Richardson, 1659), Carte, *Letters*, IV, p.47; *CWTC*, pp.182–4.

70 *CWTC*, p.185.

71 *CSPD 1659–60*, pp.141–2.

72 *Ibid.*, p.148.

8

Aftermath

For several frenzied months following the Battle of Winnington Bridge, the recapture of Chester and the failure of the revolt in North Wales, the county of Cheshire itself remained in turmoil. Although some fierce moves were made to punish the leaders, early expectations of severe reprisals were prevented by the disagreements that erupted between the Rump and the army about any form of settled government, which led ultimately to Lambert's expulsion of the Parliament. Paradoxically, although Sir George Booth's rebellion was a failure, it accomplished much more than any military victory could have done. Triumphantly, on 22 August 1659 Sir Arthur Hesilrige wrote, 'Their designs were universal through the nation, but by the blessing of God were frustrated immediately they broke out, and now our prisons are full.'[1] Such optimism, however, was misdirected. From the Army's perspective, its victory over the insurrectionaries was important in a military sense, but it also provided a much-needed boost to morale. As with the campaigns culminating at Worcester eight years before, the soldiers believed that they had earned the right to put pressure on Parliament, having 'been again saved by the Lord, and have had a late view of his appearance as of old'. They also informed the Rump that 'The Lord hath once more appeared to own You and Your Army'.[2]

Lambert emerged from the Cheshire campaign with enhanced prestige, but he was somewhat resentful of Parliament's rejection of Lieutenant General Fleetwood's proposal to restore his substantive title of major general. It may have evoked the Rump's earlier refusal to make him lord deputy of Ireland. On 16 September 1659 the senior officers who had served in the expedition under Lambert – Colonels Mitchell and Zankey, Lieutenant Colonel Duckenfield and Sergeant Major Creed – met at Derby, where they drew up a set of proposals (known as the Derby Petition) which demanded drastic measures against the Royalists and their sympathisers, and the immediate appointment of four generals for the government of the army (and in doing so, verbalising its anger at the failure of Parliament to prosecute the demands

1 *CSPD 1659–60*, p.135.

2 *The Humble Representation and Petition of the General Council of the Officers of the Armies of England, Scotland, and Ireland* (1659), p.3.

of the petition of 13 May).[3] The Petition has been described as 'the spark which started the conflagration that destroyed the Commonwealth', and 'brought greater focus on the clash between Lambert and Hesilrige as the personification of the Army–Parliament split'.[4] Lambert returned to London on 20 September, while his brigade, 'a little flushed' with their recent victory, followed within a few days. He and his senior officers, including Fleetwood and Disbrowe, held daily meetings at Wallingford House, and there seemed no reason to doubt that the Derby Petition or another similar manifesto would be championed by the army throughout England. Whether, however, it would be equally acceptable to the rest of the army remained unclear.

On 22 September the Commons, which had decided that there would be no change to the command structure of the army and that Fleetwood should have authority over it, received the petition by Hesilrige, who thus exacerbated the tension between army and Parliament. Baker noted, 'this put the House into a jealousy of Lambert; to whom, in their private discourses, they attributed the whole contrivance', whereas the Venetian Resident observed that 'the chief object of the army was to raise Lambert to the post of generalissimo and then by degrees to that enjoyed by Oliver'.[5] On 12 October John positioned his infantry regiments around Parliament, thus effectively preventing the Speaker and MPs from attending. Hewson's regiment, which had been commended for its actions in suppressing the Booth rebellion, played a key role. Lieutenant Colonel Duckenfield stopped the Speaker's coach and 'demanded whither he was going', while his soldiers informed Lenthall, when he professed to be their legitimate commander, that 'they knew no such thing; that if he had marched before them over Warrington Bridge, they should have known him'.[6] However, when Lambert and his officers presented a second petition to Parliament, he and eight other colonels were cashiered.[7]

Sir George Booth and the leading conspirators in the Cheshire insurrection remained in the Tower of London until February 1660, but the Rump had no thirst for blood and all the prisoners were ultimately released without being brought to trial. Instead, the government intended that the estates, real and personal, of the leaders, and all others who since 7 May 1659 who had been in arms or plotted against the Commonwealth should be sequestered. The county of Cheshire got off lightly, not least because the leading Parliamentarians in the county, Sir William Brereton and the ardent republican John Bradshaw, pleaded with the Rump Parliament for clemency.[8] In the meantime, various prisoners, captured at Winnington Bridge and during the subsequent operations, were incarcerated in Chester Castle. The situation report sent by Colonel Thomas Croxton to Bradshaw in Westminster on 12 September 1659 mentioned that he had sent Colonel Brooke and Mr

3 *Clarke Papers*, IV, pp.57–8; Baker, *Chronicle*, pp.676–7.
4 Davies, *Restoration*, p.147; Farr, *Lambert*, p.195.
5 Baker, *Chronicle*, p.711; *CSPV*, p.74.
6 Carte, *Letters*, II, pp.247, 266; Ludlow, *Memoirs*, II, pp.138–40.
7 *CJ*, VII, pp.784–96; *Clarke Papers*, IV, pp.56–63; Ludlow, *Memoirs*, II, p.118.
8 *Life of Adam Martindale*, pp.140–1.

Coke as prisoners to London, whilst Jeremiah Harrison of Sir George Booth's own foot regiment had been apprehended in Lancashire and was being 'brought to Stone to meet the rest of the prisoners there'. Croxton also had intelligence that Colonel Mainwaring and Lord Brereton had both supported Booth in the plot, adding, 'A day of thanksgiving was kept on Thursday last in the great church at Chester, but few of the city joined with them'.[9] Other gentlemen who managed to evade capture or direct implication included Colonel John Booth, Lieutenant Colonel John Brooke, Colonel John Daniell and Colonel Robert Werden.[10]

William Lenthall, Speaker of the House of Commons. (National Portrait Gallery. Public Domain)

Croxton's update of events to Sir Henry Vane, president of the Council of State (penned on 23 September) continued, 'Yesterday sent up Colonel Nathaniel Booth, but Colonel John Booth and Captain Weaver are not yet taken. Weaver burnt his papers after the fight at Northwich. Colonel Nathaniel Booth (never in arms before this insurrection and therefore more-free from suspicion), has been employed by Sir George Booth as a messenger to London'. On 3 October 1659 Croxton provided further reports of all prisoners taken so far, and details of their release from his custody.[11]

On 24 August – as Lambert's troops were bringing the last of the insurgents to heel in North Wales – Parliament established a commission composed of four Cheshire committeemen charged with the task of investigating the recent uprising.[12] Three days later, the Commons passed a special Act for Sequestrations to deal with those involved in the Booth uprising, while on 1 September the joint Cheshire and Chester committee, headed by Lieutenant Colonel Gilbert Gerard, took charge of dealings with local insurrectionaries.[13] Moreover, on 3 September the Council of State issued a series of instructions to the committees for sequestration for the counties immediately affected by the insurrection, and named members for them. In most instances very little was achieved, and the county committees found their authority somewhat imprecise and asked for their instructions to be amended. The dismissal of Parliament on 13 October 1659 appears to have ended or delayed proceedings in many locations.

The instructions to the county committees for sequestration for Cheshire, Lancashire, Shropshire and the counties of North Wales declared:

9 *CCSP*, IV, p.368.
10 CRO, QJF/88/3/150/2.
11 *Ibid.*, pp.382–3, 398.
12 BL, MS Harley 1929, fol. 22r.
13 *A&O*, II, p.1347; BL, MS Harley 1929, fol. 22r.

1. You are to sequester the estates, real and personal, of Sir George Booth, Sir Thomas Myddelton, Randolph Egerton, and Robert Werden.
2. To discover any others who, since 7 May 1659, on behalf of Charles Stuart or any other, have been in arms or raised forces against Parliament, or plotted or consented thereto, or concealed the same; or who have adhered to Booth, Myddelton, &c., or who have, since 30 January 1649 promoted the pretended title of Charles Stuart to be king, or have corresponded with him, or lent arms, horses, or money to him or his party.
3. On such discoveries, you are to bring charges against the persons, and summon them before you, secure their estates, and stop payment of their rents, and certify to us the value of the estate, names of the tenants, and answers of the delinquent.
4. When any defend themselves, you are to take examinations and cross examinations on oath, and send them to us.
5. You are to keep perfect registers of all your proceedings, that there may be duplicates when required.
6. You are to divide yourselves, sit in convenient places in the county, and appoint your own agents and officers, qualified as in the Militia Act.
7. You are to see that all grain belonging to delinquents' estates be carefully inned [brought in], and secured for the State, as well as that already gathered.
8. You are to sequester all who were taken in actual arms, and are now prisoners of war, and return their names to us.[14]

Surviving documents illustrate that despite being hindered by inadequate, and at times rather broad instructions, the Cheshire sequestration committee carried out its duties in a conscientious and effective manner.[15] Nevertheless, Gerard – the leading prosecutor in Cheshire – wrote to the commissioners for sequestrations in London from Chester on 3 September:

> In the absence of the governor, I opened your packet to him, myself, and others, and found a commission with two Acts of Parliament and instructions for sequestering delinquents in this county and city. As none of the other commissioners are within twelve miles of the town, I will go to the governor, and shall be ready to join him and the rest. Your commission is for the city and county of Chester, but your instructions are for sequestering delinquents' estates in Cheshire, not naming Chester, which is a distinct county. Pray let the commission and instructions run parallel. Also appoint your faithful, suffering servant, Thomas Robinson, as our clerk, and we will appoint the rest of our agents.

On 13 September 1659 Parliament responded:

> Commissioners for Sequestrations to the County Committee for Chester. We send you a supplemental instruction. It is true we only named four persons to be sequestered and ordered charges against others, but that does not prevent

14 *CCC*, I, p.746.

15 TNA, SP23/246, fol. 54r.; BL, MS Harley 1929, fol. 22r.; *CCC*, I, pp.745–8.

> proceedings against those who acknowledge delinquency within the Act. The engagement being so notorious, they will hardly put themselves to the expense of a trial, but the charge should be made on oath, and they should have liberty to defend themselves. The estates of those who acted by force must be seized; but upon appeal, we will distinguish between them and volunteers. You can appoint your clerk and agent, and state what you think should be allowed them. The charge of gathering delinquents' crops and tithes must be deducted from the profits of their estates, and the allowance to wives and children will be made when desired. The personal estate of the four named is to be sold by the candle for ready money, and after due posting up and appraisement in presence of some of the commissioners; but if they themselves will pay the sum appraised, the goods are to be sold to them without posting.

Gilbert Gerard of Crewood Hall was foremost among those determined to bring the rebels in Cheshire and Chester to justice. Described as an 'Anabaptist fanatic', he had been one of the most religiously radical officers in the Parliamentarian army commanded by Brereton. Gerard's military career included service as captain and lieutenant colonel in Colonel John Leigh's regiment of foot, captain of dragoons and governor of Northwich.[16] He was a highly capable officer and talented administrator, who throughout the 1650s acted as an energetic magistrate, and remained loyal to the Commonwealth and Protectorate. The suppression of Booth's rebellion reveals Gilbert as vigorous, ruthless and completely loyal to what remained of the Commonwealth. On 24 August 1659 the Chester antiquary Randle Holme III noted, 'The commissioners to examine out who were in this rising begun to sit and in the Pentice, viz.: Colonel Gerard, Mr Berkit, Mr Bruen, Stanley of Alderley, when many were daily called before them and many sent to prison'.[17] At the Restoration numerous complaints that Gerard and his assistants had exceeded their authority were made to the Justices, ironically in the main, by former insurgents, who had been returned to the 'county establishment' and no doubt anxious to distance themselves from their former actions.[18] On 14 May 1660, for example, the militia committee of Cheshire reported Gerard to be 'a person of dangerous principles and these parts a ringleader of the fanatic party'.[19] Moreover, on 6 September the magistrates and former enemies of Gilbert's – Peter Leycester, Philip Egerton, Henry Brooke and Thomas Marbury – informed the keeper of the gaol at Chester Castle that he 'is a very dangerous and disaffected person to his Majesty, his person and government'.[20]

Gerard and his colleagues were convinced that many leading gentlemen from the county had been involved in the rising but had avoided capture or direct implication. The petitions among the post-Restoration quarter

16 TNA, SP28/152/4, unfol; SP28/208, fols 33v.–4r.; *BLB*, I, 385, note 8; Morrill, *Cheshire*, pp.81, 311, 325–6.

17 BL, MS Harley 1929, fol. 22v.

18 CRO, QJF/88/3/149/1–3; 88/3/150–2; 88/4/65.

19 CRO, QJF/88/3/151.

20 CRO, QJF/88/3/152.

sessions material show that he was especially keen to collect evidence against Marbury. Thus, Peter Drinkwater of Grappenhall gave evidence that following his own capture at Winnington Bridge he was brought to Chester Castle, and put before Gerard:

> who asked this informant where Mr Thomas Marbury, esquire, was, who answered for anything he knew at home, then the said Mr Gerard gave this informant and other fellow prisoners, most cruel words as calling them rebels, traitors and bloodsuckers, and committed this informant to the Castle Guard, and when this informant was brought before him to be examined touching the intention of the council of war and whether commissions were granted, and other questions, the said Mr Gerard called to the marshal and told him he thought he had been more a soldier than let prisoners come before him with gloves, coats and spurs on, and that he ordered every soldier, whether officer or other, to pay the marshal a day's pay according to their commands they had ridden with Sir George Booth at the rising. This informant further says that the sequestrators commanded by their warrant this informant to appear before them at Knutsford, to be examined on behalf of the late Lord Kilmorey, Thomas Woodham, esquire, and John Brooke, esquire, and that the said Mr Gerard and one Makin, his fellow, instead of demanding (after oath taken) on the part and behalf of those gentlemen, told him this informant, he knew all the gentlemen in Cheshire or officers as party with Sir George Booth, and named to him most or all of the gentry of Cheshire, and the yeomanry, and many of Lancashire and other parts where this informant knew not, but did not examine this informant a word on the said gentleman's behalf.[21]

The methods employed by the Cheshire commissioners are hinted at in the petitions of suspects, or those onto which pressure was placed to inform on others. At Great Budworth in September 1660 Thomas Mason, husbandman of Dutton, claimed before the justices Sir Peter Leycester, Sir Phillip Egerton, Henry Brooke and Thomas Marbury that after the failure of the Booth rebellion 'Mr Gerard told him he was an impudent rogue for not confessing he was sent by my Lady Kilmorey to Sir George Booth, who denied but that he went voluntarily.' Gerard apparently informed Mason that 'he should be forthwith hanged without mercy', and forced to 'pay 4s. down on the nail to the soldiers, the redcoats, and said it should be something for them and commanded soldiers to commit him to prison where 6s. was taken out of his pocket besides 2s. 6d. to the marshal and all his charges, and 4s. 6d. more to the marshal'. Similarly, Thomas Roe of Stretton described that as constable he had received a warrant 'to bring all concerned at Northwich with Sir George Booth to Chester, and going to make a return thereof Lieutenant Colonel Gerard bade him pursue all such with hue and cry, and if they overwent him to shoot them, and if they took any house, to fire that house on their heads'.[22]

As for the city of Chester, its leaders – given their track record of disobedience towards the government – would now feel the full weight of the

21 CRO, QJF/88/3/150/2.

22 CRO, QJF/88/3/47. For similar complaints, see also the petitions of Thomas Partington of Onston, William Hynd of Ince and John Maddock of Halton (CRO, QJF/88/3/149/1–2).

State's actions against them. Two petitions issued from the city in the name of the 'well-affected citizens of Chester' were addressed to 'the Parliament of the Commonwealth of England'. The first implored:

> That being divers of the aldermen and common councilmen of the city by their complying with the rising party under Sir George Booth have rendered themselves incapable of bearing any office therein, request that for the immediate future with the consent of Parliament, the city may be governed by a fewer number of aldermen and common councilmen by such persons as are mentioned in this annexed list, being all men approved faithfulness to the Commonwealth.[23]

It was duly proposed that the Bench should contain of 15 members and that the Common Council be composed of 18 rather than its existing 40. The second petition, submitted on 17 September in the name of the 'well-affected', it was proposed that until the city's Assembly was restored to its previous size the military governor should be given special powers to deal with the existing crisis.[24] Two days later, on 19 September, Parliament sequestered Recorder John Ratcliffe and dissolved Chester's corporation charter. The separate administrative jurisdiction of County Palatine was also ended, while the city's mayor, Gerard Jones, and the two sheriffs were heavily probed about their part in recent events and dismissed from their positions. In beginning its investigation into the conduct of the city leaders, both leading up to and during the Booth rising, on 22 September 1659 the commissioners for sequestrations in London informed the county committee for Cheshire:

> We have received such information about the persons in the enclosed list that you are to seize and secure their estates, and exhibit a charge against them to this effect:
>
> That on 9 August 1659, they sat in an assembly held in the 'Inner Pentice', Chester, when it was agreed that three companies of foot soldiers should be raised. That the monthly assessment should be disposed of by order of the mayor. That a watch should be kept at the Pentice by the mayor, and what was done by him and the justices of peace, in defence of the city, was approved. That they also had some secret conferences with Colonel John Booth about opening the city gates to Sir George Booth, and on news of the insurrection at Derby, bonfires were made up and down the city, with 'God save the king' in the Close.[25]

Subsequently, the mayor, recorder and several aldermen were charged with having held secret meetings with Colonel John Booth, uncle of Sir George Booth junior, for the delivery of Chester. The evidence submitted by a number of witnesses shows clearly that there had been collusion between various anti-Cromwellian aldermen and Booth, and that Ratcliffe was not wholly responsible for the insurrection as some alleged, although his own testimony

23 BL, MS Harley 1929, fols 10r.–11v.

24 *Ibid.*, fols 26v.–27v.

25 *CCC*, I, p.748.

was viewed with suspicion by the government authorities.[26] Robert Moulson, the crier, related that he:

> by his place by his place and office did usually keep the keys of the city gates, and upon Monday night the first day of August last, Mr Heywood and one of the sheriffs of the city of Chester, who was then the captain of the watch, did take the keys from this examinant, and this deponent saith that these persons upon the watch were armed with muskets and halberds, and that Captain Witter and Mr Street were upon the watch the Tuesday morning after this examinant was called out of his bed by a soldier, being upon the watch to come to open the city gates, whereupon this examinant came to the Pentice of the said city, and then Mr Heywood and the rest of the watch with him did command this examinant to open the city gates, which he did accordingly, being at the Newgate then to the Eastgate, then to the Northgate, then to the Watergate, than to the bridge, and before this examinant had opened the last gate Sir George Booth and his confederates were entered the city and a high shout was made in the city. And after which examinant brought the keys to the captain of the watch, who commanded him the examinant to keep the keys till night.[27]

Numerous witnesses recalled that on the morning of 2 August Sir George met with the mayor, recorder and several aldermen in the Pentice. There Booth made a speech declaring the grounds upon which he had taken up arms, which became the substance of his *Declaration*, which Crier Moulson was ordered to proclaim at the High Cross in the centre of Chester, and barely yards from the Pentice, later that morning.[28] The other main evidence for collusion and rebellion on the part of Chester's authorities was that during the days leading up to the rising, three companies of militia were mobilised in opposition to Colonel Croxton's military garrison and supposedly 'in defence of the city'. Even so, the procedures taken by Parliament and the committee in Cheshire during September 1659 proved ineffective because no mechanism existed for implementing them. By the end of the year relations between the government in Westminster and Chester had broken down, and in the following months none of the proposals for a modified Assembly were adhered to. Although the citizens endured military rule, with the imposition of regular searches and full quarter, the city of Chester was restored to its old position by the Long Parliament in March 1660.[29] In the first week of May the aldermen submitted the city's petition of 'laudation and congratulations' to Charles II upon his restoration.[30]

Repercussions and the search for fugitives continued elsewhere, none more so than in North Wales. In late September the previous year, barely weeks after the surrender of Chirk Castle to Lambert's forces, Thomas Myddelton, son of Sir Thomas, had petitioned Parliament, 'humbly placing himself at the mercy of the house' for his apparently unintentional involvement 'in

26 SP23/263, fol. 107r.; *CCC*, I, p.751.
27 SP23/263, fol. 112r.; *CCC*, I, p.751.
28 SP23/263, fols 115r.–117r.; *CCC*, I, p.752.
29 BL, MS Harley 2125, fol. 162r.; CRO, ZA/F/37c/4.
30 *CSPD 1660–61*, p.4.

the rash undertaking', and begging that he and his father might be admitted to the composition. This, with similar entreaties from their associates, Lieutenant Colonel Robert Broughton, Richard Lloyd, Lieutenant Colonel John Dolben, Captain Richard Dutton, John Edwards, Thomas Brereton, William Brereton, Fulk Lloyd, Richard Myddelton, Charles and Timothy Myddelton (the other younger sons of Sir Thomas), John Edwards senior and Edmund Mainwaring, were read in the Commons on 5 October 1659.[31] Support for the Booth rebellion among the local Anglican gentry and former Royalists had been extensive from North Wales. On 6 February 1660 the Council of State issued a directive to the commissioners for sequestration in the region, including a list of insurgents who had already been apprehended or remained under suspicion:

> The Council being informed that several persons lately secured in Denbigh and Flint for adhering to Sir George Booth in his late insurrection, a list of whose names you shall here enclosed receive, and now at liberty and permitted to go at large whither they please. And being very sensible of what dangers such their liberty and enlargement may at this time especially, be to the public peace and safety of this Commonwealth have thought fit for the obviating the mischiefs which might ensue by occasion thereof to require, and hereby they do require and authorise you to command the said several persons into custody into such safe holds and places there they may be best secured from complotting or acting anything to the disturbance of the Commonwealth. Herein you are desired not to fail and to return an account of your proceedings to the Council with what convenient speed you may.[32]
>
> The list of names in the precedent letter:
> Colonel Lloyd of Llwyn-y-Maen
> Major Bevis Lloyd of Llanrhaeadr
> Major Richard Broughton of Iscoed
> Captain William Broughton of Marchwiel
> Captain Nanney Lloyd of the Roft
> Captain Ellis Sutton of Gwersillt
> Captain John Edwards of Stanstey
> Quartermaster Elias Preston of Wrexham
> Quartermaster Berkley of Brumbo
> Lieutenant Edward Jones of Wrexham
> Ensign Richard Ellice of Wrexham
> Major John Edwards of Christioned
> Captain John Trevor of Trevor
> Captain John Hughes of Bronbuckle
> John Salusbury of Bach-y-Craig, esquire
> Hugh Meredith of Pentre Bach, gentleman

31 *CCSP*, IV, p.394; *CJ*, VII, p.791. For details of the compounding of the possessions of lesser Welsh participants, including Hugh Pennant of Plas Ucha, Flintshire, in September 1659, see *CPCC*, V, pp.3246–54.

32 TNA, SP25/59, fols 36r.–7v.

Captain John Roden of Isycoed
Lieutenant Thomas Williams of Isycoed
Roger Williams of Isycoed, gentleman
Captain Matthews of Mold
Captain Thomas Baker of Wrexham
Captain William Edwards of Richall
William Phillips of Guernhayled, gentleman
Randle Edwards of Isycoed, gentleman
John Edwards of Isycoed, gentleman
John Conwy of Llanrhaeadr, gentleman
Robert Lloyd of Chirk, gentleman
Richard Wynne of Llanfair, gentleman
Captain Dennis Llong of Mold
Captain William Lloyd of Llanynys
Captain John Whitley of Shotton

In addition to these, Captain Robert Davies of Gwysaney and his son Mutton surrendered at Winnington Bridge on 19 August 1659. Norman Tucker assumed that 'doubtless they were the Captain Davies and Lieutenant Davies' mentioned in Lambert's list, but Mutton had received a commission from Colonel Whitely on 9 August 1659 'by virtue of his commission from the king as colonel of a regiment of horse appointing him captain therein'.[33] Robert's father Thomas was a professional soldier, having been commissioned captain by the States General of the United Netherlands in 1624, of a company of 115 men in the regiment of Robert Devereux, third Earl of Essex, and in 1627 he participated in the unsuccessful expedition to La Rochelle.[34] Thomas also acted as the Royalist constable of Hawarden Castle in 1643, but died in 1655. Robert Davies, his son, was involved in the insurgency in Wales in June 1658, and set at liberty from Chester Castle by the Parliamentary governor.[35]

The same official, Colonel Croxton, granted parole to 'Mutton Davies, prisoner in Chester' on 28 January 1660 following the intervention of Sir William Brereton, MP for Cheshire:

> to go to Woodhey [near Nantwich, the home of Davies's wife] in the said county upon his parole for the space of one month and render himself prisoner to me again at Chester or sooner if he be required, and in the meantime not to act anything prejudicial to this present government and the Commonwealth: Given under my hand at the castle of Chester the 28th day of January 1659–60.[36]

One of the most active searchers in North Wales was Captain Roger Sontley of Bron Deg, near Wrexham. During the First Civil War he and his kinsman, Robert Sontley of Sontley, were adherents of Sir Thomas Myddelton. Roger

33 Tucker, 'Richard Wynne', p.61; HMC, *Thirteenth Report, App. I*, p.687.
34 FRO, D/GW/B/14; Norman Tucker, 'Volunteers in the Thirty Years' War', *JNLW*, 16 (1969), pp.61–76.
35 FRO, D/GW/B/1020/10.
36 FRO, D/GW/B/1020/9.

John Speed's map of Denbighshire, 1610.

served as a troop commander in Myddelton's cavalry regiment, and was probably sent with Captain John Jones by him to raise recruits in south-east Wales in 1644.[37] By 1648 Sontley was an experienced and trusted officer, who vigorously participated in Parliamentarian military operations in North Wales. For a period in 1653 he was captain of 'the Welsh troop' in Colonel Thomas Harrison's regiment of horse, which had been led by Colonel Jones before he went to Ireland in early 1651. During the Interregnum Roger was a member of the Committee for the Propagation of the Gospel in Wales, a group of politicians and clergy charged with improving the quality of the Church in the principality. His role in suppressing the Booth uprising earned him a lengthy spell of imprisonment after the Restoration.[38] John Manley was another experienced army officer and loyal servant of the Republic in Denbighshire. The third son of Cornelius Manley of Erbistock, Cheshire, his elder brothers were both Royalists. Surviving pay warrants from 1643 to 1645 place him in Sir Thomas Myddelton's service, whilst during the 1650s he acted on government business, rising to the rank of captain.[39]

37 TNA, SP28/346/1, fol. 11r.; SP28/139/20, fols 210r.–28r.

38 Firth and Davies, *Regimental History*, I, pp.185–6, 190; Tucker, *Denbighshire Officers*, pp.129–30.

39 TNA, SP28/346/1, unfol.; *CSPD 1651–2*, p.555; *CSPD 1659–60*, p.159; Tucker, *Denbighshire Officers*, p.69.

Among the suspects in 1659–60 were Edward Vaughan of Llwydiarth, sheriff of Denbighshire and MP for Montgomeryshire. As a Parliamentarian, in 1644 he had led the Montgomeryshire Accounts Committee, but was one of the Members arrested at Pride's Purge. Although released, Vaughan was kept under house arrest until February 1649. He was subsequently harassed by the Rump Parliament, both for his continued refusal to surrender Llwydiarth, and alleged embezzlement of money allocated to pay his garrison's arrears at their disbandment in 1647.[40] His loyalty to the state came under scrutiny again in March 1651, when along with Sir Thomas Myddelton and Sir Hugh Owen, Vaughan was identified by spies at the exiled Stuart court as ready to undertake an armed rising for Charles II.[41] As the events of 1659 began to unfold, he was quickly targeted by members of the Denbighshire committee. On 3 August he was 'violently seized by a company of soldiers under Captains Sontley and Manley, rudely handled, and with two servants and horses, carried prisoner to Shrewsbury'.[42] Moreover, from Shrewsbury Castle Vaughan claimed to have been completely ignorant of the late rebellion and had always been loyal to government. As A.H. Dodd puts it, 'Vaughan's neighbours, however, were not as readily convinced as the higher authorities by his protestation that he had been 'utterly ignorant' of the plot.'[43] Among others suspected were John Wynne of Melai, Jeffries of Acton, Eubule Thelwall and John Edisbury a previous steward to Sir Thomas Myddelton.[44] In the main, repercussions against them were swift.

The steps taken by local commissioners and military officers to apprehend Richard Wynne of Gwydir and others, indicate the determination and methodology of their actions, which included offers from Captain Roger Sontley in particular, of generous treatment for those who surrendered. Arguably the government could afford to be generous, or at least pragmatic, given the political dissatisfaction of a large portion of the North-Welsh gentry. On 10 May 1659 Wynne's associate in London, William Glynne, reminded him of the potential dangers of supporting a rebellion, by stating, 'When a kingdom is tossed in a blanket, happy are they who are out of it. The commonweal is turned into a commonwealth'.[45] Whether Richard was at Wrexham when his brother-in-law, Myddelton, declared Charles as king at Wrexham, is uncertain, but he did flee into North Wales soon after the fighting in Cheshire. As Tucker asserts, even though direct evidence of Wynne's actions is thin on the ground, his participation in the rising is strongly inferred by letters written by his kinsman, William Dolben, now among the Wynne of Gwydir papers in the National Library of Wales. On 28 February 1660, during Richard's incarceration in London, Dolben informed his wife that like other delinquents, her husband had 'only attempted the redemption of the nation'. In another, this time to Wynne himself, he reminded him that

40 *CSPD 1645–7*, pp.230–1, 441, 461, 491; *CCAM*, 995–7; Underdown, *Pride's Purge*, pp.152, 168, 195.

41 *Thurloe*, I, p.749.

42 *CSPD 1659–60*, p.159.

43 A.H. Dodd, *Studies in Stuart Wales* (Cardiff: University of Wales Press, 1952), p.167.

44 *Ibid.*, p.174.

45 NLW, 9065E/2188.

Llwydiarth, Anglesey, John Ingleby, 1794. (National Library of Wales. Public Domain)

'The soldiers they say claim a property in that they take in the field, but if any other person that bought him not of a soldier have him, you may have him again.'[46] Even so, his activities were enough to convince the authorities of his complicity in the uprising. Richard Wynne was soon taken, however, and temporarily imprisoned in Caernarfon Castle.

On 3 September, nine days after the capitulation of Chirk Castle, two of Captain Sontley's men were spotted in the area of Pentrefoelas, near Betwys-y-Coed, making enquiries about the fugitive Richard Wynne and others. Sontley, with his colleagues, Captains Edward Taylor, William Wynne and Thomas Ball, had been commissioned to raise men for two troops of militia horse at the beginning of the insurgency.[47] The following day a neighbour, Robert Price of Giler, apprised Richard's mother, Lady Grace Wynne of the situation:

> Madam, John Evans the trumpeter, and another trooper was here yesterday being sent purposely by Captain Sontley, to summon and require my neighbour Mr Ellice Price, my son and others to appear, and submit themselves to Captain Sontley. He gives them a week's time to come in, and bring in their horses and arms, promising to use them civilly, and show them all favour that shall lie in his power in the future if they submit and come in unto him. I understand by the troopers and by another friend that came yesterday from Wrexham that several gentlemen, as namely: a son of Mr Salusbury of Bach-y-Craig, Mr Puleston of Emrull; Captain Chambers and other have submitted already and that they are civilly treated. I hope to understand more of their proceedings at Bromfield ere

46 NLW, 9065E/2222–3.

47 FRO, D/G/3275/80; D/G/3276/17–30; *CSPD 1659–60*, p.99; *A&O*, I, 979, 1097; II, 343, 46, 313, 482, 679, 1086, 1335.

> long. The two men that were here did only enquire where Mr Richard Wynne was, and I answered them the truth, that I did not know where he was, but that I did believe that he was not at or near home. Sir George Booth for certain was taken at Newport Pagnell. No other certain news all being quiet in Yorkshire and all other places, as they say… Lieutenant Colonel Edward Broughton is sent prisoner to Chester; it is feared that he shall lose his life upon account of having broken a former parole.[48]

On 14 September Price wrote again to Lady Wynne, advising her:

> Your son's present condition hath run constantly in my mind, and I have much studied how, and by what means his estate might be saved from rigour and narrow searching of the sequestrators whom I fear are very strict, especially towards some persons; therefore Madam … its is not only requisite but very necessary that Colonel Madryn [Thomas Madryn, Parliamentary governor of Caernarfon] be made his friend, at least that he be engaged not to appear, or be against him, for it is easy to do mischief.[49]

Besides, his associate, Ellice Price, had returned from Wrexham, having made his peace with the authorities, employing the somewhat dubious excuse that he had merely called upon Sir Thomas Myddelton at Chirk on business and had been caught up in the rebellion. In the meantime, Richard Wynne had requested his kinsman, Colonel Hugh Wynne of Bodysgallen, to mediate on his behalf. This, and an apparent bribe from Lady Wynne, seems to have worked, for on 30 September 1659 the governor issued a parole for Richard:

> Whereas Richard Wynne of Gwydir in the county of Denbigh, esquire, is now a prisoner here and hath made his request has made his request that he might have his liberty to pass hence to the place of his habitation, and there to remain for the space of eight and twenty days. And that I am ordered to grant him his parole for the time aforesaid; and that after the time expired, he is to return here and render himself prisoner. These are therefore to desire all officers and soldiers, and others whom it may or shall concern to permit and suffer the said Richard Wynne, esquire, together with his servants, to travel hence to the place of his habitation at Gwydir aforesaid, and there to remain during the said time about his lawful occasions without let, trouble or molestation, he acting nothing prejudicial to the Commonwealth of England.[50]

Wynne's parole was renewed during the winter of 1659–60, and although on 3 February 1660 General Monck entered London, he was still a prisoner three weeks later, by then, removed to the Tower.[51] By August, however, he succeeded his father as fourth baronet and subsequently entered into the Cavalier Parliament of Charles II. During the shifting changes of fortune

48 NLW, 9065E/2193.

49 NLW, 9065E/2195.

50 NLW, 9065E/2198–9, 2201.

51 NLW, 9065E/2203; 2222–23.

and localised politics brought about by the Restoration, on 5 September 1665 Sir Richard and other deputy lieutenants of Caernarfonshire were instructed by the Earl of Carbery, lord president of Wales, to look to raising the militia and the imprisonment of suspicious persons. Caught up in this was one of Wynne's former adversaries, Captain Roger Sontley, now himself a prisoner in Denbigh Castle. On 2 November 1665 he solicited Sir Richard 'to answer for his peaceable behaviour, in order that I may regain my liberty. I have long since taken the oaths of allegiance and supremacy, and conformed himself to the government of the Church, as appears by my certificates'.[52] Wynne subsequently arranged his release.

Sir John Owen (1600–66). (The National Library of Wales, Public Domain)

Probably one of the most experienced leaders of the 1659 uprising was the Royalist commander, Sir John Owen of Clenennau. A soldier of Continental experience, he was sheriff of Caernarfonshire and Merioneth during the 1630s, and next year, and when the Civil War broke out in 1642 Owen joined the commission of array for Caernarfonshire, was commissioned by Charles I to raise a regiment of foot from the three counties of Gwynedd, and acted as governor of Conwy. In February 1645 he was appointed sergeant major general of foot under Lord Byron (governor of Chester) to assist the operations of Prince Maurice, and took an active part in the fighting in North Wales and the Chester area.

Although he took the Covenant in 1647 Sir John returned to Royalist service the following year. He spent much of the following decade avoiding sequestration and involvement in plots against the government, although he continued to associate himself with exiled Royalists.[53] Items among the Clenennau letters and papers reveal his activities during the events of 1659. On 14 May one of Owen's contacts, David Hanmer, reported to him, 'there is here information given … that you hold correspondence with several eminent cavaliers and that you are to head an army in South Wales very shortly against Parliament'. Moreover, on 12 July Sir John received a personal appeal from James, Duke of York, from Brussels:

> Having understood by divers of your friends in these parts that you have preserved a constant duty and affection to His Majesty's person and his most just cause, and seeing that in all likelihood the season draws near for action and resolution, wherein by God's help and His Majesty's approbation I am resolved to have my

52 NLW, 9067E/2437; 2446.

53 Tucker, *Royalist Major General*, pp.11–12; A.H. Dodd, 'Owen, Sir John (1600–1666), Royalist commander', *DWB*.

> part in it, I thought fit to advertise you of it that you may be in readiness with your friends.[54]

Sometime after his capture, a charge of delinquency was made against Owen by the commissioners for sequestration for North Wales, that he, 'Lately known by the name of Sir John Owen [had since 7 May 1659] raised war against the Parliament and Commonwealth, and was actually in arms with Sir George Booth and Sir Thomas Myddelton in Chester, and was in the fight in or near Northwich at or about the nineteenth of August.' On 8 November the sequestration committee for Denbighshire and Merioneth outlined the rights of the accused and that security should be taken against him. Moreover, an undated letter addressed to the commissioners for Denbighshire and Flintshire, and signed by Colonel Thomas Madryn, Cornet Richard Edwards, Cornet Jeffrey Parry and Thomas Michael, assured them that they had received securities from Sir John and provided the details of their interrogation of various witnesses into Owen's conduct. Going by the names of these witnesses, they were local men. The document infers that Sir John was charged with raising troops against the government, taking up a command with the leaders of the rebellion, and being present in command of troops in battle at Winnington Bridge. In his defence, Owen claimed that he had merely been present in Chester on personal affairs at the time of its seizure by Booth and his adherents, that he had expressed his disapproval of the events, but was captured in the city, having been forced involuntarily to join the insurgents.[55]

However, in December 1659 sequestration proceedings against him were snowballed upon the intervention of his brother, Colonel William Owen. A statement signed by Thomas Ellis, Owen Lewis, Robert Owen, Hugh Evans and Owen Humphrey, contended that following receipt of a letter from the Commissioners of Haberdashers Hall, and likewise upon the desire of William Owen, 'we the commissioners subscribed do agree to leave the personal and real estate of Sir John Owen, secured and registered as it now remains until further orders from the honourable commissioners aforesaid'.[56] Ultimately, however, on 3 February 1660 General George Monck, who, having been summoned from Scotland to save the Rump, marched into London at the head of the only disciplined force remaining in the country. Under the restored Lambert, the army's increasing unpopularity with the civilian population and the failure of its own leaders to provide any acceptable form of government was brought sharply into focus, as Monck won enormous popularity by insisting that it restore its excluded members and dissolve itself. Under him the 'secluded' MPs were readmitted on 21 February 1660, thus restoring the Long Parliament, originally called by Charles I in November 1640. The Convention Parliament, which assembled on 25 April 1660, was almost entirely made up of Presbyterians or Royalists

54 NLW, Clenennau letters and papers, 691–2.

55 NLW, Clenennau letters and papers, App. II/34/1–3.

56 NLW, Clenennau letters and papers, App. II/34/5.

too young or too cautious to have fought in the Civil Wars. It seemed certain that the King would be recalled.

Monck's arrival also led to the release of all the leaders of the Booth rebellion who had been confined in the Tower. When on 10 March 1660 a new militia commission for was allotted for Cheshire, all except one of the 15 named in it (eight former Parliamentarians and seven Royalists) had supported Sir George in August the previous year.[57] When the Convention Parliament assembled on 25 April 1660, among its members were Sir George Booth and Thomas Mainwaring, two erstwhile moderate Cheshire Presbyterians, whose paths had deviated in the 1650s. The Convention, endorsing a 'free parliament' – one owing neither allegiance to the Commonwealth nor to the monarchy, and that the government of the country should be by 'king, lords and commons' – would fail to demand limitations on royal powers of the type which had been debated between Parliament and Charles I in the 1640s. The pressure to accomplish a speedy settlement was too great, and on 29 May King Charles II returned to London.

57 CRO, ZCR/63/2/696, fol. 149v.; *CJ*, VII, p.869.

Appendix I

Documents of Sir George Booth

A Declaration of Sir George Booth, at the General Rendezvous on Tuesday last, near the City of Chester, with the number other Horse & Foot, their advance to the City, & the joyning of Col. Ireland with their Army. Also, the securing of the Castle, the Governor's Resolution, and the mounting of the strong Walls, Bulworks & Towers, etc.(London: G. Horton, 1659); *CWTC*, pp.164–7.

Sir George Booth, formerly a member of parliament, and knight of the shire for Lancashire, being very much dissatisfied in judgment touching the present transactions and affairs, invited the gentry in those parts to several meetings, declaring his resolutions for a free parliament, and a single person. And to that end, proposed several particulars tending thereunto, amongst which, the putting of themselves into a posture of defence was one, which took high with the malcontented party, and proved very effectual, divers sparks appearing in this great flame. Insomuch, that in few days they became numerous, many hundreds coming into them with their arms. The gentry of Cheshire, as well as those in Lancashire, carried on this design with abundance of secrecy, as well as policy, and after a considerable time spent in private listings and buying of arms, the word was given for a general rendezvous, the place appointed at Rowton Heath within three miles of Chester, and the time prefixed was on Tuesday last. Which day they accordingly met, being above 3,000 horse and foot, well mounted and armed, with drums beating, colours flying and trumpets sounding. After they were all drawn up in the heath, Colonel Brooke and Colonel Ireland divided the horse and foot into several bodies, placing them in sundry warlike figures and postures. After which, they were united and brought into one entire body, where Sir George made a speech to them, showing the grounds and reasons of their present engagement and undertakings, and withal (by several specious pretences) declared for a free parliament; publishing a declaration for the same end and purpose, and several invitations for all those that way affected to join with them, they holding a correspondence with those of the same party in the city of Chester, who it is said, and frequently discoursed, set upon the city gates, and gave them admittance. Whereupon the cavalry being exasperated, and growing mighty prevalent, Colonel Croxton, the governor betook himself to the castle, and secured the mounts, bulwarks and batteries, mounting the parliament's colours and ensigns upon the battlements, being resolved to maintain and defend the same, according to the trust reposed in him. And not to violate his fidelity, upon the menacing threats and summons of any party whatsoever, Darius junior like, accounting nothing more sacred than faithfully to keep, and perform all his leagues, covenants, and promises; and may fitly be ranked with that renowned soldier and noble captain of Caesar (Pontius Centurio) who being taken by Scipio, Pompey's father-in-law, had his life offered with an honourable place in Pompey's army, if he would surrender, and leave Caesar, and serve heroic Pompey. But he stoutly answered Scipio, that though he thanked him kindly for his kind offer, yet that he would not accept of life upon such unequal conditions, choosing rather to die, than to falsify his faith to Caesar. Many of the citizens of Chester seem to embrace neutrality and decline both parties. But the major part affect new changes and are very instrumental to promote the present designs and insurrections, which daily increase in those parts, but the timely care of the council in sending several parties of horse and foot into those parts, may probably put no small stop to their great career. Besides, Colonel Lilburn and Colonel West are united in Lancashire, and expect more forces from London very suddenly, from whence four regiments of horse and foot are said to march. And on Friday last several red coats were drawn forth of each company, both in the Tower and elsewhere, were mounted for dragoons upon the horse brought in and seized of in divers stables. This design was laid and contrived in most counties in England, their policy (as supposed) being to draw the soldiery from the city, that so the citizens might be involved in insurrections. But the militia of London being settled in the hands of prudent commanders, there is little fear of any opposition, considering their great vigilancy in public duty and the great care of the parliament, in agreeing with the Council of State, that the several militia troops and companies, that by order from the council have been raised in several counties, cities and towns, shall be paid equal with the army for such time as they shall be employed, out of the assessments. And that the Committee of the Army do grant their warrant to the treasurers of the army for their payment accordingly. By which means, the designs of many are frustrated and the public peace preserved, so that the present affairs of such counties where this first rising or Insurrection began in England is in a good posture and need not (bar an invasion from abroad or internal divisions amongst them at home). The chief actors and conspirators being taken in most parts of England, except Cheshire, where some have been also taken going towards Beeston Castle. Divers others being apprehended in adjacent parts, several papers have been seized, wherein is declared the justness of their cause, in taking up of arms, and their resolution to vindicate and maintain the freedom of parliaments, against all violence whatsoever, and the known laws, liberty and property of the good people of this nation. But it is observable, that although they pretend for a free parliament, and a single person, law, liberty and freedom, yet it hath and is arranged by the most desperate persons and spirits of division, as papists, jesuits and others. But the three principal commanders designed for the three quarters of England are said to be Sir Marmaduke Langdale's son for Cheshire, Lancashire, Cumberland, Northumberland, Westmorland, Yorkshire, Lincoln, Derby, Nottingham, Stafford, Warwick, Northampton. The second, is Major General Massey, who is said to be designed commander-in-chief of the counties of Gloucester, Hereford, Wiltshire, Salop, Somerset, Devon, Cornwall, Worcester, Berkshire, Buckingham and the rest of the western parts. And the third is, the Lord Byron, for the southern parts, that is to say, Kent, Surrey, Sussex, Middlesex, Essex, Hertford, &c. and divers other places. But the design being discovered, their actions are diverted, and all possible means used for apprehending of the chief ringleaders. As touching the retaking of Colonel Massey, it appears dubious, notwithstanding the great care taken therein, but true it is, that Lieutenant Colonel Armstrong was surprised near Shrewsbury, going towards Chester, and divers others. But the number of prisoners daily brought in are so many, that to give a particular list of their names and designs would be too voluminous.

The Declaration of the Lords, Gentlemen, and Citizens, Freeholders and Yeoman, in this once happy Nation, 1 August 1659. Baker, *Chronicle*, p.671.

Since it hath pleased Almighty God to suffer the spirit of the division to continue in this distracted nation, and to leave us without any settled foundation of religion, liberty and propriety, the legislative power usurped, at pleasure, and condemned; the army raised at first for our defence abused, and misled into unwarrantable actions by the cunning and ambition of some of the superior officers; no face of government appearing either in any single person, or a body of men in council lawfully constituted, to whom the grievances of the people may with any probability of success be properly addressed. Therefore we being conscious of our duty, and sensible of our own and the nation's ruin if these distractions continue, or issue in a more fixed oppression by some settlement inconsistent with the laws, peace and interest of these nations, have taken arms in defence of ourselves and all others who will partake with us in the vindication and maintenance of the freedom of parliaments against all violence whatsoever, of the known laws, liberty and property of the good people of this nation, who at present groan under illegal, arbitrary, and unsupportable taxes and payments unknown to our ancestors. This being our duty to God and to Man, and our only design, we cannot despair of the blessing of Him who gives victory; nor of the cheerful concurrence of all good people, nor of the undeceived part of the army, whose arrears and increase of future pay, and advancement of high command, we shall by all means procure, suffering no imposition of force an any man's conscience; and, to do this we doubt not but all honest Englishmen will say Amen, Amen.

A Letter from Sir George Booth to a friend of his shewing the reasons of his present engagement in defence of his country's liberties, &c., 2 August 1659 (London: 1659); *CWTC*, pp.185–7.

Sir,

I think myself, and the gentlemen, and others you know to be now engaged with me, have no hopes, by new troubles, to better our present condition. With thankfulness we may say it, God hath made our lot larger than our desires in that kind, and we suppose by that blessing put an obligation upon us, as we are considerable members of our country, to have more sober and courageous thoughts in time of extremity than other men have. And though the indifferency that lies upon other men's spirits might flat ours; yet we cannot think, but if it were represented to them, how the present power doth oblige us to put out our right eyes when they require us to acknowledge them as a parliament, and lay upon us such heavy and grievous burdens, and such deceitful ones as a year's tax in three months, besides the many other impositions for Excise &c. and by raising among us a militia, they cut off our right hand by subjecting us under the meanest and fanatic spirits of the nation, under pretence of protection, their spirits would be warmed into the same zeal that ours are kindled with. Now consider what it is we ask, and consider whether it be not the same thing we have asserted with our lives and fortunes, a free parliament. And what a slavery it is to our understanding, that these men that now call themselves a parliament, should declare it an act of illegality and violence in the late aspiring General Cromwell, to dissolve their body in [16]53 and not to make it the like in the garbling the whole body of the parliament from 400 to 40 in 1648. What is this but to act what they condemn in others. Why do they associate themselves to the present army, or indeed to the present commanders-in-chief, and keep out their numerous and fellow members: if committing violence upon a parliament be so notorious a crime? And how do they teach the soldiers boldly to do that, which themselves practice, and make them instruments of? What is this but under another shape to act the condemned acts of usurpation and tyranny in their old general? What is this but to necessitate men to complain? And upon complaint to be invaded by their power, so to raise (if the English spirits be not dissolved into baseness and aptitude for slavery) a civil war; and to endeavour to water their own root with the blood of many thousands of their countrymen, or to gape after those confiscations, which by a victory. upon presumption of the unity of their army they hope to gain over all those that dare with danger assert their liberties (which presumption yet may fail them); for the soldier hath and may declare himself no mercenary, but an English freeman; which indeed though it be now contrary to his actions, may return to his thoughts again. And what will be the issue of all this? Must a mean and schismatical party depress the nobility, and understanding Commons, the land must waste itself, and foreigners or others must take the advantage of all? I dare say, I profess for myself, and the greatest part with me, have no aspect, but this singly, that we be not possessed as waste ground is, only by the title of occupancy, or that the next that gets into the saddle, ride us. Let the nation freely choose their representatives, and they as freely sit without awe, or force of soldiery, and whatever, in such an assembly, is determined; shall be by us freely and cheerfully submitted unto. If this satisfy you, I am glad of it; for you are my noble friend. I use it not as an artifice either to engage you, or make other counties follow our example, which if they do not, let their posterity judge of their action and ours; for we are born for our country, and our country, our religion, and our lives are in danger; and we will not be unconcerned. But we are faithful and peaceful in the land, and if they in authority will decline hostility, and agree of a means to admit the old members of both houses, or to call a new free parliament let him be, and he only is truly a traitor that resolves not his judgement, and obedience into their determinations.

Chester, 2 August 1659.
Your humble servant,
George Booth.

A True Narrative of the Manner of the taking of Sir George Booth on Tuesday Night last, at Newport Pagnell, being disguised in woman's apparel, with his speech Mr John Gibbs, minister of the town, upon the entering of his chamber. Likewise, the Parliament's resolve touching the said Sir George; and the order for committing of him a close prisoner to the Tower of London for high treason, on Wednesday in the evening; and to be kept from having the use of pen, ink or paper. Also, his examination in the Tower, by Sir Henry Vane, and Sir Arthur Haselrige, according to order of Parliament (London: Thomas Richardson, 1659); *Carte*, IV, p.47; *CWTC*, pp.182–4.

On Tuesday night about seven of the clock, came to Newport Pagnell two gentlemen, and took up a room for some gentlemen and gentlewomen (as they said) that were coming upon the road; the innkeeper showed them one room after another, but none pleased them, till at last, one room that was within another they accepted of, being one of the [most] inferior lodgings as was in the house: at last, came one man more, and one in woman's habit; the innkeeper being in the yard, offered the civility of helping the supposed gentlewoman down, but she refused, and leapt off from the horse, and went from him. At last, the innkeeper made up to her and the gentlemen, and asked, if they did not belong to a company that already were in his house? They denied it; but at the last, the servants leading them out of one room into another, one of the gentlemen that were there before, took acquaintance of the gentleman that came with the supposed gentlewoman: Sir, said he, I have seen you before now, it is like you have said the other, at last they proved to be acquainted, and the two rooms that they had bespoke, and taken up, they were invited to; as also to take part of their supper, which was two joints of meat. Whilst supper was making ready, they sent for a barber, and the three men were all trimmed by him, and one of them taking a razor out of the case, and asked the barber what he would take for it: he answered, that he could not sell one out of his case, because it would mis-sort his other instruments, but saith he, 'have one at home, what will you have for it?', replied the gentleman, 'half a crown', said the barber. So he bid him bring it, together with a wash bowl. Now, supper is ready, some of the maid servants came to offer their services to the supposed gentlewoman, who was all this while in the inner room, and refused to be helped in any manner, as to have her hoods, scarfs, or safe-guard, put off, but lay upon the bed. One of them called her Mrs Dorothy and asked if she could eat any supper. After supper they retired themselves into the inner room, having called for water, pipes, wine, chamber pot, and other necessaries; they shut the doors to them, and set a screen before the door of the inner room, that went to a back pair of stairs. The inn keeper perceiving all this, did suppose that then they were shaving the supposed gentlewoman, Mrs Dorothy, as it appeared afterwards. Upon this he went to a kinsman of his, an apothecary in the Town, and consulted what to do. Immediately they got two constables together, and told them that he had suspicious persons in his house. One of them he was confident by several circumstances, that he and his servants observed was a man woman's apparel. The constables got together thirteen or fourteen persons well-armed, sword, and pistols, and set a guard upon the back stairs of five men, and they went up and demanded the to open the door. They attempted to escape at the back stairs, but being prevented by the guard placed there, they called for quarter. The apothecary afore mentioned came up to Mrs Dorothy, and set a pistol to her breast; she called for quarter. He demanded whether she was a woman or a man. She answered, if that he would spare her life, she would tell him. Speak the truth, said he, and I will. Thereupon she said, she was a man. As you are a gentleman tell me the truth. I am, said be, that unfortunate gentleman, Sir George Booth. At which saying it did much amaze the guard that secured him, being all townsmen; but they disarmed them, and secured them, and one of the constables went to raise the town, got them ready, and brought two of them to St Albans that night, and sent other two to Aylesbury by another party. On the way Sir George did discourse very freely, and ingenuously did acknowledge he was misled and deluded by the gentry, who promised him to aid him. He is now in custody in the Tower of London, and one of his servants in the serjeant at arms' hands; the other two are coming up from Aylesbury.

Report of the capture of Sir George Booth, probably from contemporary newssheets. Clarke Papers, IV, pp.47–8.

25 August 1659. Yesterday Sir George Booth was taken in women's apparel at Newport Pagnell, where alighting from behind a servant and off a pillion without a cloth at the Red Lion (the only well affected inn there), the master of the house taking him off and finding him ponderous, his steps very long, desiring a private and inward chamber, was jealous that he was a man in women's apparel; and sending two maid servants to attend him they found he was called by the name of Mrs Dorothy, and they inviting her into another chamber for the convenience of her sex, she refused, but rather chose to repose herself upon a bed in the same room, where one of the maids espied her foot to be something big and her shoe to be broad toed, came down and told her master that she believed Mrs Dorothy was a man in woman's apparel, which confirming his own former jealousy, sent the maids up again to make some further discovery; and coming in they found the men looking about the room for holes or crevices, and placing a screen (which they had out of the next chamber) before those in the door to prevent any inspection into the chamber. After a more plentiful supper then such seeming ordinary guests usually have, a barber was required, who shaving two of the men, one of them bought a razor and a wash ball off him. The master of the inn sending for ten well-affected neighbours, told them the grounds of his jealousies, who arming themselves, about one in the morning break open Mrs Dorothy's chamber door, who running her breast against one of the men's pistols cried for quarter. They demanded what she was; she said a gentlewoman travelling out of Derbyshire toward London. They replied she was no woman but a man and demanded his name. Then he told them there was the providence of God seen in his discovery, and therefore he would not conceal his name, but confessed it was Sir George Booth, at which they were more astonished than he was before affrighted. They procured a gentleman's suit of clothes for him in that town, bought him a new hat and a new pair of boots, and sent him away presently with a guard. The House committed him to the Tower close prisoner, and not to have benefit of pen, in ink, or paper, and appointed Sir Henry Vane, Sir Arthur Hesilrige, and Major Salway to examine him. This day he denied the proclaiming of Charles Stuart by his order, or holding any correspondence with him, but confessed he met frequently with Mr Mordaunt, his agent, when he was last in London. This day the House ordered that the said committee should further examine him as they saw occasion.

Appendix II

Documents of Major General John Lambert

The Lord Lambert's Letter to the Right Honorable the Speaker of the Parliament, concerning the Victory which it hath pleased God to give the Forces of this Commonwealth over the Rebels under Sir George Booth in Cheshire. Read in Parliament, Monday, 22 August, to which is added a List of the Officers which are Prisoners, with the number of Soldiers and Colours taken, according to the Relation made by Captain Brown who was present in the Fight (London: Thomas Newcombe, 1659); *CWTC*, pp.168–71; Mahler, *History of Chirk*, p.190.

The Lord Lambert's Letter to the Right Honorable the Speaker of the Parliament.

> Sir,
> I have given the Council of State an account of our several proceedings, since the time that by their commands we left London, and having had nothing which I thought worthy your knowledge, I have refrained hitherto from giving you that trouble, but now think it my duty to acquaint you how the good Hand of Providence hath lately appeared in an engagement betwixt your forces and the enemy. Upon the Lord's day last, the two regiments of foot which marched from London, with the horse under the command of Colonel Swallow and Major Creed (being in all nineteen troops) united at Drayton in the county of Salop. But by reason of the weak condition of the garrison of Stafford (the safety whereof I judged very considerable) I sent back the militia troop under the command of Captain Backhouse thither. Also, to the assistance of your friends in Derbyshire the militia troop of that county, and Captain Sabberton's. And with the rest I marched to Nantwich in Cheshire on Monday last, where we stayed two days, till four companies of Colonel Biscoe's regiment, and one troop of my regiment came up to us, and three troops more of Colonel Lilburn's, and two companies of Colonel Ashfield's, were advanced as far as Uttoxeter. Upon Thursday morning, although it proved very unseasonable for rain, yet judging your service required expedition, and finding a great resolution in the soldiery to encounter all difficulties, according to former resolution upon full debate with the superior officers, resting upon the Providence of God, we advanced towards Chester. And

being marched about five miles, we had certain intelligence, that the enemy, with about four or five thousand horse and foot, were marched towards Northwich, which caused us to alter our resolutions, and to march directly toward the forest of Delamere, over which they were to pass; and being arrived thither, we had notice that they were about three miles before us. Your forces marched with that cheerfulness, that had we had day enough, we should in all probability have engaged them before they had reached Northwich, but do what we could, we only gained a view of their rear-guard in the dusk of the evening, and took three or four prisoners. That night they quartered at Northwich, and we at a small village called Weaverham; from whence the next morning we advanced very early towards them, and before we had marched a mile, we discovered them both horse and foot, half a mile on this side of Northwich, drawing amongst the enclosures, where it was impossible for horse to do service, and not without difficulty for the foot to break through. We presently engaged them, and after a short dispute they quitted their grounds, and retreated from hedge to hedge, yet in that order as they suffered very little damage, it being impossible for our horse to fall in amongst them, and at length came to Winnington Bridge, behind which they retreated, without any other loss than that of reputation, and discouragement in meeting with those whom they found of equal courage, but engaged in a better cause. Their next endeavour was to secure that bridge, which they had good reason to hope for, considering the advantages they had both in regard the river was unfordable, the bridge narrow, flanked with a strong ditch on the far end, and a high hill, up which no horse could pass otherwise than along the side in a narrow path. But the forces having their former courage increased by seeing the presence of God with them, fell on as if they had been upon equal terms; and after a short dispute, the enemy having spent two or three good volleys, our men still advancing upon them, they quit their station and gave way, for both horse and foot to march over. Our horse, which hitherto had been useless to us, advanced over the bridge, together with some foot. The horse made towards a party of theirs, which I judged was of their choicest, and came to secure the retreat of their foot; and the foot scrambling up the hill after their retreating colours, our horse charged, but by reason of the narrowness of the way, in small parties. To speak truth, that of the horse was performed on both sides like Englishmen; but ours got the better, and the enemy turned their backs. We had the pursuit of them above a quarter of a mile, where they again made head, but were routed, and thereupon their horse and foot fled on all hands, and our work was only to give them chase. Most of their foot got into enclosures, and escaped, our wearied foot not able to overtake them, nor possible for the horse to get to them. Their horse divided, some towards Chester, and some towards Warrington; we had the pursuit as far as Frodsham and Warrington, where they could proceed no further, the latter being garrisoned with four companies of foot and a troop of horse. The enemy had left this while in Northwich two companies of foot and two troops of horse; which when I understood, I sent the adjutant-general, with Captain Evanson's troop, and a troop of dragoons, who advancing up to the bridge and firing upon them, the enemy drew off in good order, but not being able to make their retreat, was routed and pursued within two or three miles of Manchester. And though I cannot say your victory was great in respect of prisoners or men slain, yet I judge it a total rout, or which by the providence of God may be improved to so much. I cannot hear that we have above one man slain outright, and not above three dangerously wounded. Of the enemy not above 30 slain; of prisoners I have no full account as yet, but I suppose about 300, whereof most horsemen and some field officers of quality. I shall upon better information give you an account thereof. The enemy reported themselves to be above 4,000, but to our view there never appeared above two. The service done by the foot was chiefly performed by Colonel Hewson's regiment. The same day we marched with the foot back to Northwich, whereupon consideration of your affairs we have determined to divide your forces; Colonel Ashfield, with his four companies, Lieutenant colonel Duckenfield (who showed himself a worthy servant this day to you and his country) with part of Colonel Hewson's regiment, and a convenient number of horse, to march for Lancashire, where, if there be any root left for renewing this rebellion, I judge it lies. I have likewise writ to Colonel Lilburne who is with some horse and foot about Wakefield, to unite with them if they see cause. The other part of your forces I intend to march towards Chester, having received this day a message from Colonel Croxton, governor of the castle, by one of his soldiers who swam the river and came to me, that he cannot for want of victuals hold out longer. I have likewise ordered Colonel Jerome Zankey with the Irish Forces, who by common fame I hear is landed at Beaumaris, to advance with all speed towards Shrewsbury and to expect further orders there in prosecution of the reducement of Chester (which if your occasions may not require them elsewhere, I desire you will please to confirm). The enemy left there four companies of foot, a troop of horse, besides what escaped thither from the fight near Northwich, and what that disaffected city will afford in townsmen. I shall here take the boldness to represent to you the great necessity of the soldiers by want of pay, we being to issue that small portion we had after the rate of 6d. a day, and already well-nigh spent, so as shoes, stockings, and other necessaries in their long and dirty marches cannot be provided for. Your former care in this assures me I need say no more, and therefore shall break off this discourse, wherein (maybe) I have mentioned many particulars not worthy your notice, and shall beg of God that he will direct your Counsels to such things, as may be for his glory, and suitable to these great mercies bestowed upon you. Assuring you that what may further concern your service in these parts, shall be diligently performed by

(Sir)
Your most faithful and humble servant,
John Lambert, Northwich, 20 August 1659.

Letter of Captain Robert Brown to the Council of State, 22 August 1659. *CWTC*, pp.171–2.

The foregoing letter was brought by Captain Brown of Colonel Hewson's regiment, who was in the engagement, came from thence on Saturday-noon, and arrived yesternight about midnight, and relates that:

Sir George Booth flying with some horse toward Chester, was pursued by Major Creed within two miles of the city. Another party of them running towards Manchester, were pursued by Colonel Swallow, and Colonel Ireland, with about 100 horse, ran towards Liverpool. He says their horse at first were a gallant body, betwixt 1,700 and 1,800. The officers which were taken prisoners before he came away, he names as follows, viz.:

Colonel Massey of Cheshire
Major Harrison, lately a captain of Colonel Gibson's regiment
Captain Philip Egerton
Major James Schofield
Captain Martland
Captain Smith
Cornet Grosvenor, son of Sir Richard Grosvenor
Captain Cosel
Lieutenant Davies
Ensign Ward
Ensign Longshaw
Lieutenant Seare
Cornet Gill
John Bromley of Wolverhampton, gent.
Captain Stukeley
Captain Davies

That the number of private soldiers taken were 236. About thirty colours, and good store of horse. Their word, he saith, was 'Have at all'. Ours, 'God with us'. This was the account of things, as they stood at the time of his coming away. Our forces being then upon pursuit of the enemy several ways.

A Second, and a Third Letter from the Lord Lambert, dated at Chester, August 21, and read in Parliament, Tuesday, August 23, the one directed to the Speaker of the Parliament; the other, to the Lord President of the Council of State; together with a Letter from Major Edmund Waring, Governor of Shrewsbury, of the same date. Wherein is set forth the Manner of the Surrender of Chester, with the Names of the Principal Persons taken Prisoners, and the state of Affairs concerning the issue of this Rebellion, 21 August 1659 (London: Thomas Newcombe, 1659; *Mercurius Politicus*, 18–25 August 1659); *CWTC*, pp.172–5.

The Lord Lambert's Letter to the Right Honorable the Speaker of the Parliament.

Sir,

Being according to those Resolutions I last acquainted you with, upon our march towards Chester, we were met by two persons from that city, who were instructed to offer some terms of surrender thereof; I suppose upon fear, least the town should become a prey to the soldiers. Having heard what they had to say, I called together divers of the officers, and acquainted them therewith, who advised me to this answer: that if they would set open their gates on the morrow by ten of the clock, submitting themselves wholly to the Parliament, and receive in such forces as should be appointed, I would engage that no soldier by violence should take anything from them. And lastly, that I would attend for their answer till eight of the clock the next morning, without any further action. Whereupon the enemy finding themselves incapable to stand upon their own defence, and the city declining all further assistance, that night in confusion, in small parties, they left the town, and about ten of the clock, finding the gates open, we marched in with our regiment of foot, and two troops of horse. Upon my march thither, I met with two inhabitants from Liverpool, and one Mr Brown who had formerly been in your service, who upon the route of the enemy, got some well affected together, and took divers prisoners of the routed forces, which had fled that way. They inform me that that Town hath continued very faithful to your service, and that the governor appointed by the enemy, did assure them before hand, that he would keep that place for your service, and hath now declared for you. Before I had this information I sent Major Hoare with three companies of foot, of Colonel Hewson's regiment, and three troops of horse to reduce that place, whom I have ordered notwithstanding this, to proceed according to his former instructions, and having secured that place by putting in some of his men to march up to a conjunction with the rest of that regiment in Lancashire, in case they should meet with any opposition there. It is the earnest desire of those persons, that the castle may be demolished, which I humbly conceive may be for your service, and pray your directions therein. I have sent a summons to Harwarden Castle which I hope will be delivered. It is likewise the desire of some of the well-affected in these parts, that the castle may be demolished, which I likewise submit to your consideration. Sir Thomas Myddelton yesterday passed over the ferry at Runcorn, and came to this town, and as I am informed, is gone to Chirk Castle. I have sent thither a summons, and have accompanied it with three troops of horse, and four companies of foot, under the command of Colonel Biscoe and intend (if it please God to give a blessing to your forces gone into Lancashire) to go thither myself tomorrow, I doubt not but the insurrection in these parts will be wholly broken. I have no more at present worthy your knowledge, and therefore shall only on their behalf desire, that the forces may be supplied with some proportion of pay, whereof at this time they stand in great need.

Sir, I shall humbly subscribe
Your most faithful and most humble servant,
John Lambert
Chester, 21 August 1659.

Sir,
The enclosed is a list of some gentlemen and prisoners taken in the fight. The soldiers expressed great zeal in this service; many lost and spoiled their horses, whereof I humbly desire your consideration.

The Lord Lambert's Letter to the Right Honorable the Lord President of the Council of State, 21 August 1659. *CWTC*, p.175.

My Lord,
I take the freedom to refer your Lordships to mine, to the Parliament of the 21st instant, for an account of our proceedings with the city of Chester, which is now possessed by your forces.

I find this City hath shewn itself very malignant, and those few friends you have are in great expectations, that you will put the power of this place as well civil as military, into such hands as may be faithful to you, and a security and protection to them. In which I humbly offer that some effectual course may be speedily taken. If there be any thing in these parts which may require my further service and attendance, I shall desire your speedy commands therein, which shall be most readily observed by

My Lord
Your Lordships most faithful humble servant,
John Lambert.
Chester, 21 August.

Another great Victory obtained by the Lord Lambert against Sir George Booth, on Sunday morning last; with the manner of his taking the city of Chester and throwing open the gates; the taking of 500 prisoners and divers eminent commanders, viz. Major General Egerton, The Lord Kilmorey, Colonel Brooke and Sir William Neal. Also another Desperate Fight at Liverpool, the taking of the town, the beating and pursuing of the enemy towards Wales; and the Escape of Sir George Booth with 200 horse, to Chirk Castle (London: Edward Horton, 1659); *CWTC*, pp.176–81.

Another Great Victory obtained by the Lord Lambert, against the forces of Sir George Booth; and the taking of the City of Chester.

The Parliament having received a letter from the Lord Lambert, giving an account of the defeat and routing of the forces under the command of Sir George Booth, near Northwich in Cheshire, another express likewise came on Tuesday morning, of their taking of the city of Chester; a perfect narrative whereof, together with the dispute and engagement, we shall here impartially communicate, viz.:

The Lord Lambert understanding that Sir George Booth was marching towards him with an intention to fight, drew out his army into battalia on Friday morning last, near Northwich, where the enemy quartered that night; who being discovered, drew out of the town amongst the enclosures, where it was impossible for horse to do service, and not without difficulty for the foot to break through. Nevertheless the Lord Lambert presently drew out a party to engage them, and after a short dispute, and some small skirmishes (but gallant volleys), they quitted their grounds, and retreated from hedge to hedge, yet in that order as they suffered very little damage, it being impossible for our horse to fall in amongst them; and at length drew back to Winnington Bridge, behind which they retreated, without any other loss than that of reputation, and discouragement in meeting with those whom they found of equal courage, but engaged in a better cause. Their next endeavour was to secure the bridge, where they drew up their foot on both sides, and their horse upon a hill behind them; great advantages they had, both in regard the river was unfordable, the bridge narrow, flanked with a strong ditch on the far end, and the hill so high, up which no horse could pass otherwise than along the side in a narrow path. But the van of our foot, which was Colonel Hewson's regiment, advanced up with three troops of horse within half pistol shot, receiving two volleys of shot from the enemy. Upon which we charging, the enemy's foot threw down their arms, quit their station, and fled to their horse, scrambling up the hill after their flying colours. Major Creed pursued with a party of horse; and marching up the hill in pursuance of the enemy, who had rallied some foot on the top of the hill, they fired on him, but he answering their charge, their horse fled. But, to speak truth, they fought gallantly at the first; and, to the fame of both it may be said, the action on the horse was performed on both sides like Englishmen. We had the pursuit of them above a quarter of a mile, where they again made head, but were routed, and thereupon their horse and foot fled on all hands, and our work was only to give them chase. Most of their foot got into enclosures and escaped; our wearied foot not able to overtake them, nor possible for the horse to get to them. During the time of this dispute, the enemy had left in Northwich two companies of foot, and two troops of horse; which when the Lord Lambert heard of, sent the adjutant-general, with Captain Evanson's troop and a troop of dragoons, who advancing up to the bridge and firing upon them, the enemy drew off in good order; but not being able to make their retreat, was routed, and pursued within two or three miles of Manchester. For the number slain and hurt, we shall refer you to the letter hereunto annexed, sent from a surgeon in the army, to his friend in London; a true copy whereof follows:

Sir,

I am now I am now (blessed be God) furnished with news for you: no less than the routing and total defeating of Sir George Booth's army this day. Yesterday we marched from Nantwich (having stayed for some time there to refresh our men, and the coming up of the rest of our foot) intending to march to Tarporley within seven miles of Chester: but understanding by some warrants of theirs, by which they had required provisions to be brought to them that morning for 5,500 foot and horse, that they were for a march, and having certain intelligence they marched towards Northwich, my lord altered his first intentions, and marched after them over the forest of Delamere. And when we were a little entered upon the forest, we discerned their body. It being a fine champion, we made all the haste we could. But they marched off the forest before we could come up, only our scouts fell upon their rear and took some prisoners, but night coming on, hindered any further action. And so we marched into Weaverham and they into Northwich, two miles distant. This morning we drew out as soon as we could see, and gave them a great alarm, and [they] drew into battalia upon Hartford Green, between Weaverham and Northwich towards us, as though they would have fought; but we pressing upon them, their van marched over Winnington Bridge leading to Warrington, thinking to escape us. But we fell on upon their rear and put them to flight. They thought to have kept the bridge, which was of great advantage to them, and disadvantage to us. They having at the end of the bridge, hedges and a bank. Yet after a short dispute, our foot undauntedly marched over the bridge, and put them to rout, up a high hill, where their horse were drawn up, and the hedges lined with foot, from whence also they were quickly beat, and put to a total rout, throwing down arms and colours, and we had the pursuit of them a great way in lanes and enclosures. Their foot are all broke and disbursed. If it had been a champion country, few of them had escaped to carry home news. One party of them fled to Chester, and another to Warrington; the horse are still in the pursuit of them. One is returned from our horse, who brings word, that Major Creed pursued them within five miles of Chester and went still on. Our wearied foot returned here from the pursuit about twelve or one of the clock to quarters. Here are in the Church about 200 prisoners. I cannot give you particulars, divers are killed. I do not know or hear of any we have had killed, and but a few wounded, and I hope none mortally; I was with them and dressed some few. We had a force march upon Thursday, but God carried us through all; and with that courage and alacrity, that I have not seen. Our men went on with such shouts and acclamations, that I think astonished the enemy. The terror of the Lord of Hosts was surely upon them. Communicate this, that God may have the glory. I rest, etc. My Lord marches tomorrow to Chester, and also sends a smart party to Warrington and Manchester.

Appendix III

List of prisoners taken at Winnington Bridge, Chester and elsewhere by government forces during the Booth rebellion. *Mercurius Politicus*, 18–25 August 1659; Ormerod, *History*, I, p.lxvi; *CWTC*, pp.174–5.

Robert Needham, Viscount Kilmorey
Sir Thomas Powell
Major General Randolph Egerton
Major General Robert Broughton
Colonel Gilbert Ireland
Colonel Henry Brooke
Colonel William Massey
Colonel Nathaniel Booth
Sir William Neal
Colonel John Daniell
Colonel Peter Leigh of Bruch
Colonel William Stanley
Lieutenant Colonel Edward Done
Thomas Needham, brother to Lord Kilmorey
Major Jeremiah Harrison
Major William Shepley
Major John Trevis
Captain Thomas Cholmondeley of Vale Royal
Captain Francis Cholmondeley
Captain Phillip Egerton
Peter Rogers
Captain Lathom
Captain Edmund Pesall
Captain Robert Stukeley
Captain Richard Dutton
Captain Shenton
Captain Hewitt
Captain Robert Cotton of Combermere
Charles Cotton, his brother
Captain John Leech of Carden
Lawrence Wright
Thomas Green
Richard Minshull
Thomas Dickinson
Richard Acton
Edward Minshull of Stoke
Thomas Minshull of Erdswick
William Tatton of Wythenshaw
John Wybunbury of Hankelow
Robert Wybunbury his brother

Captain Markland
Major Smith
Captain Thomas Egerton
Captain Mytton Davies
Captain John Bridges
Captain John Coul
Captain John Trevis
Bromley
Thomas Grosvenor, son of Sir Richard
Broughton
Elisha Mainwaring
Spurstow of Spurstow
John Beverley
Lieutenant John Key
Lieutenant John Booth
Lieutenant John Comberbach
Lieutenant Acton
Ensign Henry Hall
Ensign Longshaw
Ensign John Leigh
Henry Trevis
Cornet Gill
William Hinde
Edward Foard
Christopher Sidney
John Johnson
Thomas Powell
Brooke
Thomas Parry
Thomas Annion
Frederick Conway
Charles Hughes
John Edwards
Cotton of Cotton
Aldersley of Spurstow the younger
Knevet of London
Roger Mainwaring of Kermincham
Elcocke of Poole
John Beverley
John Crew
John Trafford
Robert Evans
William Carter
Robert Davies of Gwysaney the elder
Corporal William Walker

[Chester] City officers:
Captain William Wright
Captain Richard Wright
Captain John Witter
Lieutenant John Langley
Lieutenant Richard Bridge
Lieutenant Fearnough
Ensign Thomas Leigh
Ensign Thomas Street
Ensign Burroughs
Mr Cooke, minister of St Bridget's, Chester
Mr Finmore, minister of Runcorn

Bibliography

Manuscript Sources

Aberystwyth, The National Library of Wales
Chirk Castle Estate Records, F7442; Clenennau letters and papers 691–2; Sweeney Hall MSS; MS 9065E (Wynne of Gwydir papers)

Birmingham, City Archives
MS 595611

Chester, Cheshire Archives
DBW/P/J/10; DDX/384; DDX/428; DLT/B3; QJF/88/3–4; ZA/F/37b/10; ZA/F/37c/4; ZA/B/2; ZCR/63/1/30; ZCR/63/2/129; ZCR/63/2/696; ZCR/72; ZF/30/2; ZML/2

Hawarden, Flintshire Record Office
D/GW/B/14; D/GW/B/1020/9; D/GW/B/1020/9–10

London, Dr Williams's Library
MS Modern 12.7 'Parliamentary army officers' colours and standards':
(a) The colours, or standards, and armorial bearings of certain officers in the parliamentary army 1642, drawn by Jonathan Turmile, fols 1r.–117r.

London, The British Library
MSS Add. 11331–3; 18981; 36914; MSS Harley 1929; 1943; 1970; 1999; 2073, 2119; 2125–8; 2137; 2144

London, The National Archives
E121/2/10; E121/5/7/95; SP14/72/94; SP16/513/1; SP23/197/39; SP23/263; SP28/25/29; SP28/25/59; SP28/30/7; SP28/35/5; SP28/36; SP28/78; SP28/87–8; SP28/96; SP28/123/1–2; SP28/124/1; SP28/128/10; SP28/128/13; SP28/129/20; SP28/134/2; SP28/152/4; SP28/152/7; SP28/208; SP28/224/2; SP28/225/4; SP23/246; SP28/263; SP28/346/1; SP28/513/1

Manchester, Chetham's Library
CPP/1–5

Manchester, John Rylands Library (The University of Manchester Library)
EGR1/1–3; EGR3/4/1/2/1–2; JOD/62c; TW/262; TW/282; TW/287; TW/342; TW/1071–3; TW/1431–2

Matlock, Derbyshire Record Office
D1232

Oxford, Bodleian Library
MS Tanner 51; MS Top. Cheshire e. 3; MS Eng. hist. e. 309; MSS Clarendon 63, 64

Preston, Lancashire Archives
Quarter Sessions (QS); QSC Commissions of the Peace

Printed Primary Sources

Contemporary Newsbooks

The Kingdome's Weekly Intelligencer
Mercurius Aulicus
Mercurius Politicus
Perfect Occurrences
The Weekly Intelligencer

Contemporary Tracts and Pamphlets

A Declaration of Sir George Booth, at the General Rendezvous on Tuesday last, near the City of Chester, with the number bother Horse & Foot, their advance to the City, & the joyning of Col. Ireland with their Army. Also, the securing of the Castle, the Governour's Resolution, and the mounting of the strong Walls, Bulworks & Towers, etc. (London: G. Horton, 1659)

A Letter from Sir George Booth to a Friend of his shewing the reasons of his present engagement in defence of his country's liberties, &c. (London: 1659)

A Great Victory by the Blessing of God obtained by the Parliament's forces against the Scots forces, commanded by the Earl of Derby, on the 25 of August 1651, near Wiggon in Lancashire, certified by a letter from Col. Lilburne and two letters from Chester, also a letter from Col. Birche to Mr Speaker (London: 29 August 1651)

An Express from the Knights and Gentlemen now engaged with Sir George Booth; to the City and Citizens of London, and all other Free-men of England [London: s.n., 1659]

Another great Victory obtained by the Lord Lambert against Sir George Booth, on Sunday morning last; with the manner of his taking the city of Chester and throwing open the gates; the taking of 500 prisoners and divers eminent commanders, viz. Major General Egerton, The Lord Kilmorey, Colonel Brooke and Sir William Neal. Also another Desperate Fight at Liverpool , the taking of the town, the beating and pursuing of the enemy towards Wales; and the Escape of Sir George Booth with 200 horse, to Chirk Castle (London: Edward Horton, 1659)

A Second, and a Third Letter from the Lord Lambert, dated at Chester, August 21, and read in Parliament, Tuesday, August 23, the one directed to the Speaker of the Parliament; the other, to the Lord President of the Council of State; together with a Letter from Major Edmund Waring, Governor of Shrewsbury, of the same date. Wherein is set forth the Manner of the Surrender of Chester, with the Names of the Principal Persons taken Prisoners, and the state of Affairs concerning the issue of this Rebellion (London: Thomas Newcombe, 1659)

A True and Full Relation of the late Skirmishes at Warrington, etc., with the present condition and station of our own and the enemies forces, drawn out of severall expresses from Knotsford, Congerton, etc., on the 17th and 18th instant (London: 1659)

A True Narrative of the Manner of the taking of Sir George Booth on Tuesday Night last, at Newport Pagnell, being disguised in woman's apparel, with his speech Mr John Gibbs, minister of the town, upon the entering of his chamber. Likewise, the Parliament's resolve touching the said Sir George; and the order for committing of him a close prisoner to the Tower of London for high treason, on Wednesday in the evening; and to be kept from having the use of pen, ink or paper. Also, his examination in the Tower, by Sir Henry Vane, and Sir Arthur Haselrige, according to order of Parliament (London: Thomas Richardson, 1659)

Declaration of the Officers and Soldiers of the County Palatine of Lancaster (London: 19 May 1648)

The Humble Representation and Petition of the General Council of the Officers of the Armies of England, Scotland, and Ireland (1659)

The Lord Lambert's Letter to the Right Honorable the Speaker of the Parliament, concerning the Victory which it hath pleased God to give the Forces of this Commonwealth over the Rebels under Sir George Booth in Cheshire. Read in Parliament, Monday, 22 August, to which is added a List of the Officers which are Prisoners, with the number of Soldiers and Colours taken, according to the Relation made by Captain Brown who was present in the Fight (London: Thomas Newcombe, 1659)

Two Letters from Colonel Robert Lilburne, the one to the Honourable William Lenthall, Esq., Speaker of the Parliament, the other to his Excellency the Lord General, containing the particulars of the total Rout and Overthrow of the Earl of Derby, and the Forces under his command, in Lancashire, on the 25th August, 1651. By Parliament's forces under the said Colonel Robert Lilburne (London: [30 August 1651])

Books and Edited Collections

Abbott, Wilbur Cortez (ed.), *The Writings and Speeches of Oliver Cromwell*, 4 vols (Oxford: Oxford University Press, 1986–8)

Atkinson, James, *Tracts Relating to the Civil War in Cheshire, 1641–1659* (Manchester: CS, 1909)

Baker, Richard, *A Chronicle of the Kings of England from the time of the Romans' Government unto the death of King James* (London: 1670 edn)

Barber, Richard (ed.), John Aubrey, *Brief Lives* (Woodbridge: Boydell, New edn, 1998)

Barwick, G.F. (abr. & ed.), *The Life of Dr John Barwick, Dean of St Paul's* (London: Robinson & Co., 1903)

Bennett, J.H.E. (trans. & ed.), *The Rolls of the Freemen of the City of Chester*, 2 vols, RSLC, 51, 55 (1906–8)

Birch, Thomas (ed.), *Thurloe State Papers*, 7 vols (London: 1742)

Byron, Lord, 'Account of the Siege of Chester', Rawlinson MS 210 in Bodleian Library, reprinted as 'John Byron's Account of the Siege of Chester 1645–1646', *CS*, 4th series, 6 (1971), pp.1–25

Calendar of State Papers Relating to English Affairs in the Archives of Venice, 32, 1659–1661 (London: HMSO, 1931)

Calendar of the Clarendon State Papers Preserved in the Bodleian Library, 5 vols (Oxford: Clarendon Press, 1869–1916)

Calendar of the State Papers Relating to Ireland, 4 vols London: HMSO, 1900–03)

Carte, Thomas, *A collection of original letters and papers, concerning the affairs of England, from the year 1641 to 1660, found among the Duke of Ormonde's papers*, 2 vols (London: J. and P. Knapton, 1735)

Carte, Thomas, *The Life of James, Duke of Ormond*, 5 vols (Oxford: Oxford University Press, 1851)

Coate, Mary, *The Letter-Book of John Viscount Mordaunt 1658–1660* (London: RHS, 1940)

Dasent, J.R. (ed.), *Acts of the Privy Council of England*, 1626 (London: HMSO, 1938)

Dore, R.N. (ed.), *The Letter Books of Sir William Brereton*, 2 vols, RSLC, 123, 128 (1984, 1990)

Firth, C.H. (ed.), *The Clarke Papers: Selections from the papers of William Clarke, secretary to the Council of the Army, 1647–1649, and to General Monck and the commanders of the army in Scotland, 1651–1660*, 4 vols (London: Longmans, Green & Co., 1891–1901)

Firth, C.H. (ed.), *The Memoirs of Edmund Ludlow, Lieutenant General of the Horse in the army of the Commonwealth of England, 1625–1672*, 2 vols (Oxford: Clarendon Press, 1894)

Firth, C.H. and Rait, R.S. (eds), *Acts and Ordinances of the Interregnum, 1642–1660*, 3 vols (London: HMSO, 1911)

Green, M.A. (ed.), *Calendar of the Proceedings of the Committee for Advance of Money, 1642–1656* (London: HMSO, 1888)

Green, M.A. (ed.), *Calendar of the Proceedings of the Committee for Compounding*, 5 vols (London: HMSO, 1889–92)

Hall, James (ed.), *Memorials of the Civil War in Cheshire and the adjacent counties by Thomas Malbon, of Nantwich, Gent., and Providence improved by Edward Burghall*, LCRS, 19 (1889)

Hawkins, Edward (ed.), Brereton, Sir William, *Travels in Holland, the United Provinces, England, Scotland, and Ireland* (Manchester: CS, 1844)

Hutchinson, Lucy, *Memoirs of the life of Colonel Hutchinson* (London: H.G. Bohn, 1863) *Journals of the House of Commons, 1547–1687*, 9 vols (London, 1742)

Journals of the House of Lords, 1509–1681, 13 vols (London, 1771)

Lee, Matthew H. (ed.), *Diaries and Letters of Philip Henry, MA of Broad Oak, Flintshire, AD 1631–1696* (London: Kegan, Paul, Trench, 1882)

Long, C.E. (ed.), *Diary of the Marches of the Royal Army during the Great Civil War; kept by Richard Symonds*, CS, Old Series, 74 (1859)

Llwyd, Richard, *The poetical works of Richard Lloyd, bard of Snowdon: comprising Beaumaris Bay and other poems: with a portrait and memoir of the author* (London: Wittaker & Co., 1837)

Macray, W. Dunn (ed.), Hyde, Edward, Earl of Clarendon, *The History of the Rebellion and Civil Wars in England*, 6 vols (Oxford: Clarendon Press, 1888)

Myddelton, W.M., *Chirk Castle Accounts, AD 1605–1666*, 2 vols (Privately published: 1908)

Ormerod, George (ed.), *Tracts Relating to Military Proceedings in Lancashire during the Great Civil War* (Manchester: CS, 1844)

Parkinson, R. (ed.), *Life of Adam Martindale* (Manchester: CS, Old Series, 4, 1845)

Parkinson, R. (ed.), *The Autobiography of Henry Newcome* (Manchester: CS, Old Series, 26, 1852)

Pennant, Thomas, *A Tour in Wales*, 2 vols (London: Henry Hughes, 1778)

Razzell, P.E. (ed.), Richard Gough, *The History of Myddle* (Pittsburgh, PA: Caliban Books, new edn, 1979)

Rochefort, Albert Jouvin de, *Description of England and Ireland under the Restoration* (Paris, 1672)
Rushworth, John, *Historical Collections of Private Passages of State*, 8 vols (London: D. Browne, 1722)
Secombe, John, *Memoirs containing a genealogical and historical account of the ancient and honourable house of Stanley* (Liverpool: Sadler, 1741)
Stanning, J.H. (ed.), *The Royalist Composition Papers: being the proceedings of the Committee for Compounding, A.D. 1643–1660, so far as they relate to the County of Lancaster*, 6 vols (Manchester, 1891–1942)
Steele, R.R. (ed.), *Tudor and Stuart Proclamations 1485–1714*, 2 vols (Oxford: Clarendon, 1910)
Stewart-Brown, R. (ed.), *Cheshire Inquisitions Post Mortem: Stuart period, 1608–1660*, 3 vols, Record Society of Lancashire and Cheshire, 84, 86, 91 (1934)
Tibbut, H.G. (ed.), *The Letter Books of Sir Samuel Luke* (London: HMSO, 1963)
Turner, J. Horsfall (ed.), *Memoirs of Captain John Hodgson of Coalley-Hall, near Halifax; Touching his conduct in the Civil Wars, and his troubles after the Restoration* (Brighouse: A.B. Bayes, 1882)
Turner, J. Horsfall (ed.), *The Rev. Oliver Heywood, BA 1630–1702; His Autobiography, Diaries, Anecdote and Event Books*, 3 vols (Brighouse: A.B. Bayes, 1882).
Warburton, Eliot, *Memoirs of Prince Rupert and the Cavaliers*, 3 vols (London: Bentley & Fley, 1849).
Warner, G.F. (ed.), *The Nicholas Papers, correspondence of Sir Edward Nicholas secretary of State*, 4 vols (London: Camden Society, 1892–1920)
Whitelocke, Bulstrode, *Memorials of the English affairs from the beginning of the reign of Charles the First to the happy restoration of King Charles the Second*, 4 vols (Oxford: Oxford University Press, 1853)

Reports of the Historical Manuscripts Commission

Seventh Report (1879).
Tenth Report, Appendix IV (1884–5).
Tenth Report, Appendix VI (1887).
Thirteenth Report, Appendix I (1891).

Secondary Sources

Books and Reports

Abernathy, George R., *The English Presbyterians and the Stuart Restoration, 1648–1663* (Philadelphia: TAPS, 1965)
Anonymous, *A Memoir of Chirk Castle from Original Manuscripts* (Chester: Hugh Roberts, 1859)
Barbour, Hugh, *The Quakers in Puritan England* (New Haven: Yale University Press, 1964)
Barlow, T.W. (ed.), *The Cheshire and Lancashire Historical Collector* (Manchester, 1853)
Barratt, John, *'Better Begging than Fighting': The Royalist Army in Exile in the War against Cromwell 1656–1660* (Solihull: Helion & Co., 2016)
Blackwood, B.G., *The Lancashire Gentry and the Great Rebellion* (Manchester: Manchester University Press, 1986)
Booker, John, *A History of the Ancient Chapel of Birch, in Manchester Parish* (Manchester: CS, 1859)
Braddick, Michael, *Parliamentary Taxation in Seventeenth-Century England: Local Administration and Response* (London: Royal Historical Society, 1994)
Broxap, Ernest (ed.), *The Great Civil War in Lancashire, 1642–1651* (Manchester: Manchester University Press, 1910)
Boynton, Lindsey, *The Elizabethan Militia* (London: Routledge & Kegan Paul, 1967)
Bull, Stephen and Seed, Mike, *Bloody Preston: Battle of Preston, 1648* (Lancaster: Carnegie, 1997)
Capp, Barry, *England's Culture Wars: Puritan Reformation and its Enemies in the Interregnum, 1649–1660* (Oxford: Oxford University Press, 2012)
Capp, Bernard, *Cromwell's Navy: The Fleet and the English Revolution 1648–60* (Oxford: Oxford University Press, 1989)
Clark, Peter and Slack, Paul (eds), *Crisis and Order in English Towns 1500–1700: Essays in Urban History* (London: Routledge, 1972)
Coward, Barry, *The Stanleys, Lords Stanley and Earls of Derby 1385–1672* (Manchester: Manchester University Press, 1983)

Coward, Barry, *The Cromwellian Protectorate* (Manchester: Manchester University Press, 2002)

Dawson, W.H., *Cromwell's Understudy: The Life and Times of General John Lambert* (London: Hodge & Co., 1938)

Davies, Godfrey, *The Restoration of Charles II* (Oxford: Oxford University Press, 1955)

Dodd, A.H., *Studies in Stuart Wales* (Cardiff: University of Wales Press, 1952)

Dore, R.N., *The Civil Wars in Cheshire* (Chester: Cheshire Community Council, 1966)

Durston, Christopher, *Cromwell's Major Generals: Godly Government During the English Revolution*(Manchester: Manchester University Press, 2001)

Earwaker, J. P., *East Cheshire: past and present*, 2 vols (London, 1877–80)

Farr, David, *John Lambert, Parliamentary Soldier and Cromwellian Major General, 1619–1684* (Woodbridge: Boydell, 2003)

Firth, Charles and Davies, Godfrey, *The Regimental History of Cromwell's Army, 2 vols* (Oxford: Clarendon Press, 1991 edn)

Gardiner, S.R., *History of the Commonwealth and Protectorate*, 4 vols (London: Longmans, 1903)

Gaunt, Peter, *A Nation Under Siege: The Civil War in Wales 1642–1648* (London: HMSO, 1991)

Gratton, J.M., *The Parliamentarian and Royalist War Effort in Lancashire 1642–1651* (Manchester: CS, 2010)

Gruber von Arni, Eric, *Justice to the Maimed Soldier: Nursing, Medical Care and Welfare for Sick and Wounded Soldiers and their Families during the English Civil Wars and Interregnum, 1642–1660* (London and New York: Routledge, 2001)

Hall, James, *A History of the Town and Parish of Nantwich, or Wich-Malbank, in the County Palatine of Chester* (Nantwich: Privately published, 1883)

Harris, Tim, *Restoration: Charles II and his Kingdoms* (London: Penguin, 2005)

Helsby, Thomas (ed.), Ormerod, George, *History of the County Palatine and City of Chester*, 3 vols (London: Routledge, 2nd edn, 1874)

Hill, Christopher, *God's Englishman: Oliver Cromwell and the English Revolution* (London: Penguin, new edn, 1990)

Hill, Christopher, *The World Turned Upside Down: Radical Ideas During the English Revolution* (London: Penguin, new edn, 1991)

Hill, P.R. and Watkinson, J.M., *Cromwell Hath the Honour, But…: Major General Lambert's Campaigns in the North, 1648* (London: Frontline, 2012)

Hill, P.R. and Watkinson, J.M., *Major Sanderson's War: The Diary of a Parliamentary Cavalry Officer in the English Civil War* (London: Spellmount, 2008)

Hutton, Ronald, *The Restoration: A Political and Religious History of England and Wales, 1658–1667* (Oxford: Clarendon Press, 1985)

Laurence, Anne, *Parliamentary Army Chaplains, 1642–51* (Woodbridge: RHS, 1990)

Little, Patrick and Smith, David L., *Parliaments and politics during the Cromwellian Protectorate* (Cambridge: Cambridge University Press, 2007)

Littler, Joyce, *Protector of Dunham Massey: Dunham Massey Estate in the 18th Century – A Study of the Management Carried Out by George Booth, 2nd Earl of Warrington* (Altrincham: Joyce Littler Publications, 1993)

Lowe, Norman, *The Lancashire Textile Industry in the Sixteenth Century*, CS, 20, Third Series (Manchester, 1972)

Mahler, Margaret, *A History of Chirk Castle and Chirkland* (London: G. Bell and Sons, 1912)

Matthews, H.C.G. and Harrison, B. (eds), *Oxford Dictionary of National Biography*, 40 vols (Oxford: Oxford University Press, 2004)

Mayers, Ruth, *The Crisis of the Commonwealth* (Woodbridge: Boydell, 2004)

Morrill, J.S., *Cheshire 1630–1660: County Government and Society during the 'English Revolution'* (Oxford: Oxford University Press, 1974)

Morrill, J.S., *Oliver Cromwell and the English Revolution* (London: Longman, 1990)

Morris, Rupert H., *The Siege of Chester 1643–1646* (Chester: G.R. Griffith, 1924)

Newman, Peter, *The Old Service: Royalist Regimental Colonels and the Civil War, 1642–46* (Manchester: Manchester University Press, 1993)

Owen, H. and Blakeway, J.B., *A History of Shrewsbury*, 2 vols (London: Harding, Lepard & Co., 1825)

Palmer, A.N., *A History of the Older Nonconformity of Wrexham and its Neighbourhood* (Wrexham: Woodall, Minshall and Thomas, 1888)

Palmer, Samuel, Edmund Calamy, *The Nonconformist's Memorial*, 3 vols (Liverpool: Button & Son, 1802)

Parry, Edward, *Royal Visits and Progresses to Wales, and the Border Counties* (Chester, 1850)

Phillips, J.R., *Memoirs of the Civil War in Wales and the Marches, 1642–1649*, 2 vols (London: Longmans, 1874)
Reay, Barry, *The Quakers and the English Revolution* (London: Temple Smith, 1985)
Reece, Henry, *The Army in Cromwellian England 1649–1660* (Oxford: Oxford University Press, 2013)
Reese, Peter, *The Life of General George Monck: For King and Cromwell* (Barnsley: Pen & Sword, 2008)
Richardson, R.C., *Puritanism in North-West England: A regional study of the diocese of Chester to 1642* (Manchester: Manchester University Press, 1972)
Roberts, D.H., *Matthew Henry and his Chapel, 1662–1900* (Liverpool: The Liverpool Booksellers Co., 1901)
Roberts, Keith, *Cromwell's War Machine: The New Model Army, 1645–1660* (Barnsley: Pen & Sword, 2005)
Scoble, Andrew R. (trans.), Guizot, François, *Monk: Or the Fall of the Republic and the Restoration of the Monarchy in England in 1660* (London: Henry G. Bohn, 1851)
Shercliffe, W.H. (ed.), *Wythenshawe: A History of the Townships of Northenden, Northen Etchells and Baguley* (Didsbury: E.J. Morten, 1974)
Smith, Geoffrey, *Royalist Agents, Conspirators and Spies: Their Role in the British Civil Wars*, 1640–1660 (London: Routledge, 2010).
Smith, Geoffrey, *The Cavaliers in Exile, 1640–1660* (London: Palgrave, 2003)
Spring, Laurence, *Waller's Army: The Regiments of Sir William Waller's Southern Association* (London: Pike & Shot Society, 2007)
Stone, Brian, *Derbyshire in the Civil War* (Matlock: Scarthin Books, 1992)
Sylvester, Dorothy and Nulty, Geoffrey, *The Historical Atlas of Cheshire* (Chester: Cheshire Community Council, 1958)
Tucker, Norman, *Denbighshire Officers in the Civil War* (Denbigh: 1964)
Tucker, Norman, *North Wales in the Civil War* (Wrexham: Bridge Books, 1992 edn)
Tucker, Norman, *Royalist Major General Sir John Owen* (Conwy: Gwasg Gee, 1963)
Tucker, Norman, *Royalist Officers of North Wales 1642–1660: a Biographical List* (Denbigh: Gwasg Gee, 1961)
Underdown, David, *Pride's Purge: Politics in the Puritan Revolution* (Oxford: Clarendon Press, 1971)
Underdown, David, *Royalist Conspiracy in England 1649–60* (New Haven: Yale University Press, 1960)
Venn, John and J.A., *Alumni Cantabrigienses: a biographical list of all known students, graduates and holders of office at the University of Cambridge, from the earliest times to 1900* (Cambridge: Cambridge University Press, 1922)
Wanklyn, Malcolm, *Reconstructing the New Model Army Volume 1: Regimental Lists April 1645 to May 1649* (Solihull: Helion and Co., 2015)
Wanklyn, Malcolm, *Reconstructing the New Model Army: Volume 2: 1649–1663* (Solihull: Helion and Co., 2015)
Ward, Simon, *Chester: A History* (Bognor Regis: Phillimore, 2009)
Warmington, A.R., *Civil War, Interregnum and Restoration in Gloucestershire, 1640–1672* (Woodbridge: Boydell, 1997)
Webster, William (ed.), Thomas Skinner, *The Life of General Monk, Duke of Albemarle* (London: J. Graves, 1724)
Williams, Richard (ed.), Yorke, Philip, *The Royal Tribes of Wales* (Liverpool: Foulkes, 1887 edn)
Woolrych, A.H., *Britain in Revolution: 1625–60* (Oxford: Oxford University Press, 2002)
Woolrych, A.H., *Commonwealth to Protectorate* (London: Phoenix, 1982)
Woolrych, A.H., *Penruddock's Rising, 1655* (London: The Historical Association, 1955)
Worden, Blair, *The Rump Parliament 1648–53* (Cambridge: Cambridge University Press, rev. edn, 2008)

Articles and Chapters

Alebon, P.H., Davey P.J. and Robinson, D.J., 'The Eastgate, Chester 1972', *JCAS*, 59 (1976), pp.37–49
Anderton, Paul, 'The Booth Uprising in Cheshire, 1659: Another Look at Some of the Evidence', *CH*, 39 (1999–2000), pp.7–14
Auden, J.E., 'Ecclesiastical History of Shropshire during the Civil War, Commonwealth and Restoration' *TSANHS*, 7 (1907), pp.241–310
Auden, J.E., 'Shropshire and the Royalist Conspiracies between the end of the First Civil War and the Restoration, 1648–1660', *TSANHS*, 10 (1910), pp.87–168

Auden, J.E., 'Sir Jerome Zankey (or Sankey), of Balderton Hall, co. Salop, and of Coolmore, co. Tipperary', *TSAS*, 50 (1939–40), pp.171–8

Axon, Ernest, 'The family of Bothe (Booth) and the church in the 15th and 16th centuries', *TLCAS*, 53 (1938), pp.32–82

Blackwood, B.G., 'Agrarian Unrest and the early Lancashire Quakers', *JOFHS*, 51 (1966), pp.72–6

Button, Andrea E., 'Penruddock's Rising, 1655', *Southern History*, 19 (1997), pp.99–111

Calladine, Amy, 'Public Ritual and the Proclamation of Richard Cromwell as Lord Protector in English Towns, September 1658', *HJ*, 61 (2018), pp.53–76

Challinor, P.J., 'Restoration and Exclusion in the County of Cheshire', *BJRL*, 64(1982), pp.360–85

Cole, Alan, 'The Social Origins of the Early Friends', *JOFHS*, 48 (1957), pp.99–117

Cooper, Scott, S., 'Extracts from the Churchwarden's Accounts and Vestry Minutes of St John's Chester', *JCAHS*, New Series, 3 (1890), pp.48–70

Coward, Barry, 'The Experience of the Gentry, 1640–1660', Richardson, R.C. (ed.) *Town and Countryside in the English Revolution* (Manchester: Manchester University Press, 1992), pp.198–223

Craven, Alexander J., 'Ministers of State: The Established Church in Lancashire during the English Revolution, 1642–1660', *NH*, 45 (2008), pp.34–66

Craven, Alexander J., 'The Commonwealth of England and the Governors of Lancashire: 'New Modelised and Cromwellysed'', *NH*, 48 (2011), pp.41–58

Dodd, A.H., 'Flintshire politics in the 17th century', *FHSP*, 14 (1954), pp.22–46

Dodd, A.H., 'The Civil War in East Denbighshire', *TDHS*, 3 (1954), pp.41–89

Dore, R.N., 'The Cheshire Rising of 1659: A Study of Local Origins', *JLCAS*,69 (1959), pp.43–69

Dodd, A.H., 'The Early Life of Sir William Brereton', *TLCAS*, 63 (1953), pp.1–8

Edwards, Peter, 'Turning Ploughshares into Swords: The Arms and Military Equipment Industries in Staffordshire in the First Civil War, 1642–1646', *MH*, 27 (2002), pp.52–79

Farr, David, 'John Hodgson. Soldier, Surgeon, Agitator and Quaker?', *JFHistS*, 58 (1999), pp.220–34

Farr, David, 'The Quakers and the religious Identity of Major General John Lambert', *JFHistS*, 59 (2000), pp.19–39

Firth, C.H., 'Royalist and Cromwellian Armies in Flanders, 1657–1662', *TRHS*, New Sers, 17 (1903), pp.67–119

Foster, G.C.F., 'Civic Government in Chester, 1642–1660', *NH*, 37 (2000), pp.83–103

Gibson, A. Craig, 'Every-Day Life of a Country Gentleman of Cheshire in the Seventeenth Century', *THSLC*, 15 (1862–3), pp.67–92

Gratton, J.M., 'The Earl of Derby's Catholic Army', *THSLC*, 137 (1988), pp.25–54

Gratton, J.M. and Booth, P.H.W., 'Sir George Middleton of Leighton, a Lancashire Penruddock?: documents on preparations for a failed Royalist rising in north Lancashire, 1655', *TLCAS*, 91 (1995), pp.17–33

Greenspan, Nicole, 'Charles II, exile, and the problem of allegiance', *HJ*, 54 (2011), pp.73–103

Hirst, Derek, 'Local Affairs in Seventeenth-Century England', *HJ*, 32 (1989), pp.437–48

Johnson, A.M., 'Politics in Chester during the Civil Wars and the Interregnum', Clark, Peter and Slack, Paul (eds), *Crisis and Order in English Towns 1500–1700: Essays in Urban History* (London: Routledge, 1972), pp.204–36

Johnson, A.M., 'Wales during the Commonwealth and Protectorate', Pennington, Donald and Thomas, Keith (eds), *Puritans and Revolutionaries: Essays in Seventeenth-Century presented to Christopher Hill* (Oxford: Oxford University Press, 1978), pp.233–56

Johnstone, Hilda, 'Two Governors of Shrewsbury during the Great Civil War and Interregnum', *EHR*, 26 (1911), pp.267–77

Jones, J. R., 'Booth's Rising of 1659', *BJRL*, 39 (1957), pp.416–43

Mawdesley, James, 'Presbyterianism, royalism and ministry in 1650s Lancashire: John Lake as minister at Oldham, *c.* 1650–1654', *TLCAS*, 108(2015), pp.136–59

Morrill, J.S., 'Mutiny and Discontent in English Provincial Armies 1645–1647', *P&P*, 56 (1972), pp.49–74

Morrill, J.S., 'Sir William Brereton and England's Wars of Religion', *JBS*, 24 (1985), pp.311–32

Morrill, J.S., 'The English Revolution in British and Irish Context', Braddick, Michael, J. (ed.), *The Oxford Handbook of the English Revolution* (Oxford: Oxford University Press, 2015), pp.568–72

Nunn, Catherine, 'Henry Newcome and his circle: Presbyterianism in South-East Cheshire in the 1650s', *THSLC*, 150 (2003), pp.7–31

Peacey, Jason, 'The Protector Humbled: Richard Cromwell and the Constitution', Patrick Little (ed.), *The Cromwellian Protectorate* (Woodbridge: Boydell, 2007), pp.32–52

Pells, Ismini, 'Reassessing Frontline Medical Practitioners of the British Civil Wars in the Context of the Seventeenth-Century Medical World', *HJ*, 62 (2019), pp.399–425

Peters, Kate, 'The Quakers and the Politics of the Army in the Crisis of 1659', *P&P*, 231 (2016), pp.97–128

Petty, Reginald, 'The Rebellion of Sir George Booth, August, 1659', *JCAS*, 33 (1939), pp.119–37

Phillips, C.B., 'County Committees and Local Government in Cumberland and Westmorland 1642–1660', *NH*, 5 (1973), pp.34–66

Phillips, C.B., 'Landlord-Tenant Relationships 1642–1660', Richardson, R.C. (ed.), *Town and Countryside in the English Revolution* (Manchester, Manchester University Press, 1992), pp.224–50

Pinkney, P.J., 'The Cheshire Election of 1656', *BJRL*, 49 (1967), pp.387–426

Reay, Barry, 'Quaker Opposition to Tithes, 1652–1660', *P&P* (1980), pp.98–120

Reay, Barry, 'The Quakers, 1659 and the Restoration of the Monarchy', *History*, 63 (1978), pp.193–213

Roots, Ivan, 'The tactics of the Commonwealths men in Richard Cromwell's Parliament', Donald Pennington and Keith Thomas (eds), *Puritans and Revolutionaries: Essays in Seventeenth-Century History Presented to Christopher Hill* (Oxford: Clarendon Press, 1978), pp.283–309

Seacome, John, *The Chester Guide or, a Walk Round the Walls, and Through the City* (Chester: John Seacome, 1828)

Smith, David L., 'Politics and Military Rule in Cromwellian Britain', *HJ*, 48 (2005), pp.545–54

Swarbrick, John, 'Dunham Massey Hall', *TLCS*, 42 (1925), pp.53–79

Tucker, Norman, 'Colonel Roger Whitley', *JFHS*, 22 (1966), pp.9–24

Tucker, Norman, 'Richard Wynne and the Booth Rebellion', *TCHS*, 20 (1959), pp.46–64

Tucker, Norman, 'Volunteers in the Thirty Years' War', *JNLW*, 16 (1969), pp.61–76

Vernon, Elliot, 'The Ministry of the Gospel: The Presbyterians during the English Revolution, Durston, Christopher and Maltby, Judith (eds), *Religion in Revolutionary England* (Manchester: Manchester University Press, 2006), pp.115–36

Ward Clavier, Sarah, "Horrid Rebellion and Holie Cheate': Royalist Gentry Responses to Interregnum Government in North East Wales, 1646–1660', *WHR*, 29(2018), pp.51–72

Ward Clavier, Sarah, '"Round-head Knaves": The Ballad of Wrexham and the subversive political culture of Interregnum North-East Wales', *HR*, 91:251 (2017), pp.39–60

Walker, Katharine A., 'The Military Activities of Charlotte De La Tremouille, Countess of Derby, During the Civil War and Interregnum', *NH*, 38 (2001), pp.47–64

Woolrych, A.H., 'The Cromwellian Protectorate: A Military Dictatorship?', *History*, 75 (1990), pp.207–31

Woolrych, A.H, 'The Good Old Cause and the Fall of the Protectorate', *CHJ*, 13 (1957), pp.133–161

Unpublished Theses

Craven, Alexander J., 'Coercion and compromise: Lancashire provincial politics and the creation of the English Republic *c.* 1648–1653', PhD thesis (Manchester, 2004)

Ive, J.G.A., 'The Local Dimensions of Defence: The Standing Army and Militia in Norfolk, Sussex and Essex, 1649–1660', PhD thesis (Cambridge, 1986)

Nightingale, J. Leslie, '1659–1660: A study in the inter-action of political and religious forces in the period between the fall of Richard Cromwell and the restoration of Charles II', PhD thesis (Durham, 1936)